the
SKY is
FALLING
ON OUR
HEADS

the
SKY is
FALLING
ON OUR
HEADS

A Journey to the Bottom of
the Celtic Fringe

Rob Penn

SCEPTRE

Extract from *Trainspotting* by Irvine Welsh
originally published by Minerva.
Reprinted by permission of the Random House Group Limited.

Copyright © 2004 by Rob Penn

First published in Great Britain in 2004 by Hodder and Stoughton
A division of Hodder Headline

The right of Rob Penn to be identified as the Author of the Work
has been asserted by him in accordance with the Copyright,
Designs and Patents Act 1988.

A Sceptre Book

1 3 5 7 9 10 8 6 4 2

A CIP catalogue record for this title is available from the British Library

Hardback ISBN 0 340 82752 1
Trade paperback ISBN 0 340 83398 X

Typeset in 11.75 Sabon MT by Servis Filmsetting Ltd, Manchester

Printed and bound by
Mackays of Chatham Ltd, Chatham, Kent

Hodder and Stoughton
A division of Hodder Headline
338 Euston Road
London NW1 3BH

To Vicks
– she's honey in her hips
and sweet cherry lips

Contents

Prologue: Old Cader   1

1 The Beltane Fire Festival   15

2 The First Strike of Poetry   36

3 A Poem in the Applecross Inn   57

4 Dancin' with Mighty Penglaz   71

5 Manx Kilts and Ceilidhs   106

6 On Brandon's Height   131

7 The Merry Monk of Mayo   154

8 The Lughnacy Games   167

9 All Over the Irish Sea   187

10 Aigh Vie at the Eisteddfod   198

11 Vive Lorient   233

12 Flying at the Fleadh   260

13 Encore Bretagne   281

14 For a Mod Song   301

15 One Last Poem at Lowender Peran   314

16 Samhain   330

Acknowledgements   341

Author's Note   342

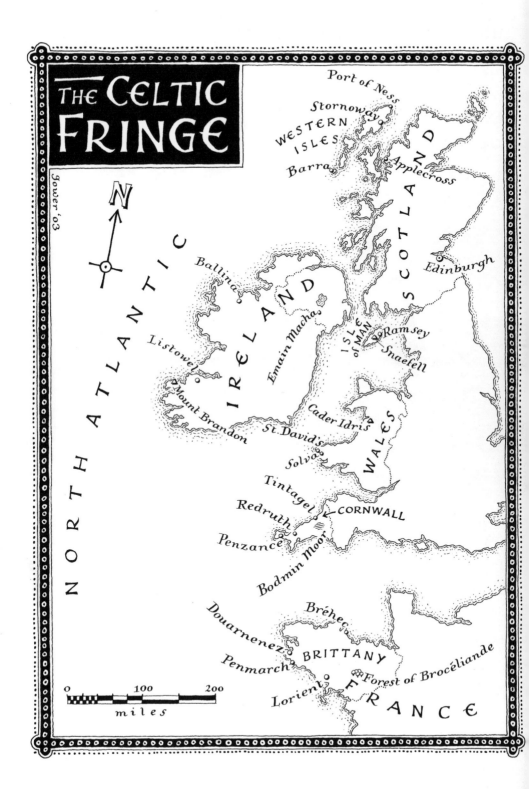

THE CELTIC FRINGE

Gower '03

N

NORTH ATLANTIC

Port of Ness
Stornoway
WESTERN
ISLES
Barra
Applecross

SCOTLAND

Edinburgh

Ballina

IRELAND

Emain Macha

ISLE of MAN
Ramsey
Snaefell

Listowel

Mount Brandon
St. David's
Cader Idris
WALES

Solva

Tintagel
Redruth   CORNWALL
Penzance

Bodmin Moor

Bréhec
Douarnenez   BRITTANY
Penmarch
Forest of Brocéliande
Lorient   FRANCE

0   100   200
miles

Prologue: Old Cader

Good holidays linger in the memory, but bad ones never go away. My family came to mid-Wales in June 1974 when I was seven. We made sandcastles in the rain, we played crazy golf in the rain and we ate ice creams, in the rain. On the day that the heavens decided to demonstrate their full armoury of precipitation, from a mournful drizzle to the sort of thunder squalls that presage the death of honest fishermen, I followed my dad silently up Cader Idris. At 2,930 feet, Cader is no Everest, but with mossy socks sucking at my toes and rivulets of water pouring down my back, it felt like it.

At the top, the cloud lifted long enough for me to check that I still had two hands, though by then they looked like a brace of frozen quail. We rounded the greying trig point where I was totally astonished to make out the shapes of two other people enjoying a Thermos of coffee and biscuits. Then we set off down, still in silence. The whole experience was as uplifting as having a cat vomit in your lap. To the extent that any seven-year-old knowingly can, I made then a lifelong pledge with myself never to tread this path again. Never, that is, until today.

The car park at Minffordd is busy with hikers – that rare breed of people who are comfortable in long johns. One sight of the range of telescopic ski poles makes me aware how rusty my camping skills are. So, I unpack my rucksack again to check my gear: tent, sleeping bag, mat, long johns (for show – I'll never wear them, honestly), matches, stove, pasta, white truffle oil (the hand of my wife), cocoa, whisky and cutlery nicked from the pub.

Confident that I have forgotten something, I repack and tread warily up the steep path beside a stream.

It is a beautiful afternoon. The hills are gleaming. Sunshine warms the hues of the green and yellow slopes and bounces off the granite rocks. As the rucksack bears into my shoulders, I tighten my belt and warm to the task, plodding slowly over the steps that lead out on to the end of a great corrie. When I reach the beje-welled tarn of Llyn Cau, great faces of broken rock tower over me on three sides. Cader Idris has always commanded greater respect and adoration than its height suggests. Darwin wrote of it: 'Old Cader is a grand fellow' and still today it holds a special place in the heart of many experienced mountaineers. This is because, though you are only a few miles and a couple of hours from steak pie and a warm duvet in Dolgellau, it feels like a big mountain. The cliffs and the crag-grit, along with the mist that familiarly curls around the rocky heights, create this aura. I have read that winter climbers occasionally fall here and their bodies are not found for months, which must add a certain tang to the sweet smell of gorse in spring.

Even on this, a perfect day, Cader Idris feels impressive, though unfamiliar. I think I am coming up a different path than the one I trod with my dad, but I wouldn't really know. Then, visibility was around two feet. Today, as I reach the ridge at Craig Lwydn, I can see for fifty miles. Actually, I have no idea how far fifty miles is, but I can see a very long way – the Lleyn Peninsula to the west jutting out into the Irish Sea, Snowdon to the north and rounded hills to the horizon in the east are all clear. It is a tremendous view.

As I reach the last steep, boulder-strewn face that leads to the top, I am still sweating out last night's whisky. The sun is high in the western sky but the easterly wind has a chastening cut to it. At four o'clock, the last of the walkers are on their way down, though I have long since given up with the happy exchanges. One broad-shoul-dered man in blue tights had come skipping past me with his ski poles chinking on the rocks: 'Spank me daily, my friend,' he shouted over the buffeting wind. It dawned on me afterwards that he probably said, 'Spanking day, my friend.' Nonetheless, I thought, you can't be careful enough with nutters like him around. I tracked his descent until he passed out of sight beyond the lake. Whatever he said, I don't fancy sharing a night on the summit with him.

By the time I reach the trig point, the wind is howling across the top of Wales. The bigger gusts sound like 747s coming in to land – a harrowing sound and I make a mental note not to exclaim, 'Whingeing suburban mediocrity!' next time I hear an anti-airport pressure group on the radio. For the first time, it occurs to me that it is going to be very, very cold and I am not entirely prepared. Right now, the beauty of the panorama is enough to take my mind off the impending night of misery and I whisk my tent up and get the stove out. Thankfully, it works. Pasta drizzled with white truffle oil, followed by two tins of pork sausages and beans, make a splendid, if slightly confused, dinner. If Antonio Carluccio worked in a truckers' caff, this would be on the specials menu. I am dreaming up a new TV series – *Changing Kitchens* – when a whopping, buttock-clenching gust tries to take my tent off to Ireland. Clearly, the safest place for me is inside it, so I brew up a mug of cocoa and whisky and retire.

As I am wrestling with my long johns – I swear I'll only wear them this once and never again – my thoughts turn to the night ahead. I have come to Cader Idris not to tune my camping skills, or to expel childhood ghosts, or to re-evaluate my relationship with my dad, though that, I have to admit, does need some work. No, I am here to test the authenticity of an ancient Celtic myth. Cader Idris means 'chair of Idris'. History is not entirely clear on who Idris was but the best guess is that he was Idris ap Gwynddo, Prince of Merioneth, a seventh-century AD Celtic hero, a giant warrior and an astronomer. He won many battles and led his people into a golden age. He probably also broke horses, spoke several languages, seduced loads of women and cooked a mean soufflé, though the annals do not record as much.

The summit of the hill is called Pen y Gadair or 'head of the chair'. Looking down on his seat – a huge north-west-facing glacial cirque, a great scoop out of the mountainside plunging down to another blue lake – I realise what a big fellow our Idris must have been. A rough calculation suggests he was about 1,500 feet tall and a powerful man to boot. His legacy, as recorded in numerous books of Celtic myths as well as in *Brewer's Dictionary of Phrase and Fable*, is this: 'The legend is that anyone who passes the night in this "chair" will be either a poet of the highest inspiration or a madman.' Locals have added a third possible conclusion to a night on this mountain eyrie – death.

Obviously I am vying for the first option. Death and insanity are less than appealing alternatives, but these are the risks that you have to take when you play Celtic roulette. It seems to me that the odds are stacked against a happy ending and a cursory look through the tales from Welsh folklore that bear upon the myth reveals plenty of madmen, a few deaths and not one poet. But this is a risk I am prepared to take. I have a great urge to become a poet and this is the quickest way I know.

Last night, I should have been tucked up in bed early with a cup of cocoa and a prayer book. Certainly, this was my intention when I crossed the threshold of the Wynnstay Arms in Machynlleth for a swift one. But soon enough I got chatting to Seamus, the Irish barman, and the next thing I knew the doors were shut, the curtains drawn, the lights dimmed and I was in the middle of a 'lock-in'. That naughty feeling passed through a crowd of twenty and we suddenly had a party on our hands. Seamus sensed my unease.

'Hev a drop of dee Oirish,' he said, sloshing an unmeasured quantity of Black Bush into a glass. 'S'on de house, now. Yar ar-roit.'

You could stand in a pub in England in a pink bowler hat and gold lamé hot pants for several months before anyone enquired who you were. In Wales, things are very different. Any sort of latent mystique that anonymity carries lasts, at best, a few minutes. So no one except me was surprised when Sarah leant on the bar and, jabbing a thumb towards my chin, shouted across to Seamus: 'Who's this fella then? What's his story?' There was a sense of relief all round. Within the time it took me to drink another quadruple Black Bush, I had met everyone and I was in the midst of a raging debate about the possible outcome of my night on Cader Idris.

No one doubted the authenticity of the myth. It was just a matter of what would befall me. 'You could be a dead poet, and start a society,' Barry said, admiring his pun. 'Ooh, a poet. How romantic,' Evelyn crooned, flicking her four-inch grey quiff and allowing a meaty paw to wander on to my knee. 'All poets are mad,' Nicky declared. 'You must be mad to want to spend the night up there to start with, so it's poetry or death for you, young man,' Gareth chipped in. 'They are all a form of liberation,' the man in the corner whose name I never got added philosophically. By two in the morning, we seemed to have covered all the possible results of the event and everyone was talking about rugby again. Having spent twenty minutes looking for a coat I didn't bring to the pub, I staggered towards the door.

'Ah, we're erl poo-hts anyway,' Seamus declared. 'Be sure ta bring us a poem back. Now, nother drop of de Oirish fore yar go thar, Rob?'

Wrapped in my slim sleeping bag, perched in the awning of my tent, facing the Irish Sea, the fast-fading crimson sky and the twinkling lights of Barmouth, I have time to think through the 'What am I doing here?' thoughts that have been in my head all day. It is fitting since Idris was an astronomer that there is a rare planetary conjunction on this night: an alignment of five planets – Jupiter, Saturn, Mars, Venus and Mercury – that will not occur again for a century. The planets are, I read in a newspaper, visible with the naked eye shortly after sunset. It takes me ten minutes to find them – my teeth are chattering so vigorously I can't focus – but I persist in the belief that I may be marginally improving my chances of finding favour with Idris.

Though I have an appetite for legend, the bottom line is: I do not really believe that I will wake up a poet, mad or dead. Yet, beyond the cynicism required to deal with modern life, I do adhere to the notion that human wisdom can be measured in the respect we show for the unobtainable, the mysterious or simply the different and it is always worth remembering that oral folk tales were often a means for communities to develop common understandings of natural occurrences. Put another way, I believe in fairies, especially if they are bad ones who will waste you if you doubt them. So, I can give a calculated credence to the Celtic myth about Cader Idris, not least because I genuinely need inspiration.

The interesting thing about the legend of Cader Idris is that you dance with death, as it were, to become a poet, not a wizard, a warrior or a king. In a modern analysis, it seems like a dumb gamble – risking your life so you can sit around in pubs with a feckless air, in a beat-up tweed jacket, poncing drinks off strangers and occasionally missing arts grant application dates. But poets, or bards, held a role of fundamental importance in ancient Celtic society, much in the way that teenage pop stars and footballers' wives do today.

Every chieftain had a court poet who wrote precise metres to extol the heroic deeds of the tribe, as well as give moral guidance, mock the enemy and lend wonder to the great mysteries. Poets trained for ten years in the great bardic schools to reach the rank of *filidh* – a title that means both 'seer' and 'poet'. The word derives from the root 'to see' and, to the Celts, vision and poetry went hand in hand. A job advert for a *filidh* might have read: 'Position: exciting opportunity for a poet at the court of Ordovician chieftain; the post arises from the untimely execution of the previous holder. The candidate: educated to *filidh* level; writer of epic poems (to include history, genealogy, anthropomorphism, morale boosting and unlimited praise of the king), good metrical analysis, ability to see beyond the world of convention and into the future, keen interpersonal skills and motivation of warriors, communication with gods a bonus, tax deductible blackthorn stick provided by employer. Serious applicants only.'

I have always fancied that I have the measure of a poet in me. Working as a journalist, there is a continual sense that my tools – words – could be used more precisely and effectively. There is also that restless streak, the 'sensitive soul within' you might call it (before reaching for a bucket), which does not diminish with age. Rather, it grows stronger and more troublesome. But I don't want simply to compose poems: I want to perform them as well. I want to rouse people with the sort of fervour that grips me when I face great imagination and eloquence. A psychiatrist would tell me that I am also dealing with the sense of failure at never fulfilling my teenage ambition to become an actor, whilst my friends tell me it is the early stages of a mid-life crisis. I loved being on stage when I was at school and I have always managed to convince myself I was merely putting off my acting career until I was ready. The terrible truth is, I will never play the Dane. Belting out a poem standing on a driftwood table in a tiny pub in the west of Ireland hardly constitutes 'the boards' I once intended to tread, but I do need to perform something, somewhere, now.

So, whilst it would be nice to be able to turn a rhyme on a whim, or write a sonnet when I am waiting for the bus, these would be peripheral bonuses in the grand scheme of things – I could wake up a visionary. This is my aspiration. I not only want to be a poet, I want to be a poet in the ancient Celtic tradition – a wandering, cadging, strolling storyteller and prophetic bard.

Buried somewhere in this desire is the need to answer a key question about myself: Am I a Celt? I think I am. Though I was actually born in Birmingham to an English dad, my mum is Manx and the Isle of Man – a proud Celtic nation – is the place I call home. Scotland, Ireland, Wales, the Isle of Man, Cornwall and

Brittany, known together as the 'Celtic Fringe', are the glorious lands where the residues of the ancient Celtic people dwell today. Their realm is, quite literally, on the fringe of Europe. They have survived in the hideaways that they were driven into by successive invasions of mainland Britain centuries ago. To explore this question I am going to make a six-month journey through the countries of the Celtic Fringe. This is also my insurance policy. Should Prince Idris turn out to be a phoney, I will follow more conventional methods to find inspiration and let my bardic skills flourish and grow.

In considering my 'Celtic-ness', I cannot ignore the most prevalent and strict definition of a Celt, which is the linguistic one: a 'true' Celt speaks a Celtic language. I don't speak Manx Gaelic and fail by this definition. In fact, the only Manx I can recall nowadays is '*Mora my vrain az gainya sara*' which is how air-hostesses used to welcome passengers on to the flights to the Isle of Man. For all I know, it could mean: 'Drink all the free vodka you can get. The captain's a freak.' I can't even remember the Manx for the female reproductive organs, which I obviously knew when I was a teenager.

But there is much geographical, archaeological and even anthropological evidence that suggests the net is wider than the linguistic one allows. Are the unnameable moods and the inexplicable pulses that I have felt through the years my Celtic roots? When something stirs in my trousers to the skirl of bagpipes, is this my ancestry talking? If so, then my roots can't be denied just because it was unfashionable to speak or learn Manx when I was a kid. So, I may then be a Celt. And if I am only even considering my Celtic roots, then I guess I have started a quest for identity.

Before I can answer the question of my own identity, I have to determine exactly who and what the Celts of today are. We know who the ancient Celts were. They were a race whose brilliance earned them the title 'Fathers of Europe'. A race who had exceptional gifts of craftsmanship and literary talent; who advanced to abstract expression in art centuries before anyone else; who were

8

superstitious, loquacious, hospitable and who dried the brains of their enemies to use as sling shot; who offered human sacrifices; who elevated nature poetry to new realms; a European race who stand alone in being able to ask: 'And what have the Romans ever done for us?'

The Irish, Scots, Manx, Welsh, Bretons and Cornish were largely peripheral to this ancient European civilisation. However, these peoples now dominate the popular understanding of the word 'Celt'. And it is 'now' that I am interested in. How, then, does the relationship between the ancient and modern Celt work? Are there, in reality, two separate categories of Celts: the ancients and the people of the modern-day fringe who occupy the politically created ghettoes on the Atlantic? Have the credentials of the former been passed to the latter? Do my roots lie in a traceable collective consciousness that has witnessed 2,500 years of history, a consciousness that emerges today in the music, speech and imagination of a distinct people? Or have the characteristics of the Fathers of Europe been so diminished by subjugation, cultural infusion and randy Saxons as to be negligible? Are then the people who claim to be Celtic today a self-created, self-nationalised, self-conscious band of fakes? This is what I need to find out. This is at the core of my quest.

Yet, I must not forget this crucial question: Do I want to be a hairy, smelly, fire-breathing, marauding, druid-worshipping Celt anyway? I spent much of my youth denying or at least avoiding the notion that I might be. I fled the Isle of Man before the Celtic renaissance reached the middle of the Irish Sea, before the word 'Celtic' excited the host of romantic images that it does today – gold and music, bards, princes and druids, horsemanship, harps, rocky coasts and wolfskins by the fire. When I was growing up 'Celtic' meant you were bearded and poor; it meant you had an unhappy, injured air and a taste for the drink. No one boasted about it. For me, the very worst thing about being a Celt was looking like one. I was short and fat and ugly with long, black hair. If the Romans had invaded Britain in 1979, I would have been the first man slain. Polite people took one look at me and thought of a naked man running into battle, blaspheming wildly.

'Ooh, you do look like a Celt,' aged Manx relatives used to say on bank holiday picnics. Yeah, and you look like a pig who's swallowed a wasp, but I'm not making a fuss, I used to think. Why couldn't I look like a Viking? – after all they invaded the Isle of Man. I could be six foot and blond with rippling deltoids. I could have keen blue eyes, a lantern jaw and a breathtaking nonchalance amongst beautiful women. I suppose the Viking invaders reached the shores of Man chanting 'rape, pillage and plunder', took a good look at my female ancestors and settled for pillage and plunder. And to be frank, I don't blame them. I have seen Manx girls, a few Bacardi Breezers down, on a Friday night and it's not pretty.

Looking like a Celt was a difficult thing to bear and, naturally, it only got worse when I denied it. Then, some time in the early nineties, the perception of all things Celtic changed. There was a cultural revival. Capital letters with funny whorls and curvaceous jewellery appeared everywhere. People began to play fiddles and started wearing kilts again – all right, they had never stopped, but they were going about it with renewed verve. Dublin, for most of my life a grey city where you had a perpetual hangover, became hip. Long-forgotten pagan festivals were revived. Every cadence of the word 'Celtic' was celebrated. The cash registers began to ring at a whisper of the word. The prototype Celt went from hairy-backed monster with his hand in a barrel of herrings to romantic warrior fit for a romp in the heather, almost overnight. *Highlander*, *Rob Roy* and, oh dear, Mel Gibson in *Braveheart* helped adorn the new image of the Celt: noble, eloquent, fearless and free-spirited, and in the midst of this who would not forgive a little hard drinking and fighting.

It was beyond my comprehension, but I suddenly became appealing simply because I was a Celt. People I had never met invited me to parties and introduced me thus: 'This is Rob I was telling you about. A Manxman . . . very interesting,' and attractive women would tousle their hair.

'A Manxman . . . very interesting'? Come again? I would have been less surprised if they had said: 'This is Rob I was telling you about. A Manxman . . . just keep your hands and feet away from his mouth and you'll be okay.'

A highly eccentric and brilliant history lecturer at university singled me out as one of his favourites, despite the fact that I wasn't clever. An established Welsh poet included me in his intellectual soirées. In Chamonix, where I spent a ski season cleaning fondue pots, I met Pascal from Brittany. He, like all the French, thought the English were skunks, but he treated me like his godson. He showed me how to keep out of trouble in the restaurant. When I ran into him on his day off, we would sit shoulder to shoulder at the zinc counter in Bar des Sports necking rounds of whisky and beer until I fell off my stool. On the way home, we ritually paused to pee into the River Arve from the pedestrian shopping precinct. I have always had a problem with having a freewheeling, porcelain-splattering, shoe-dotting slash when there is someone in the urinal next to me. I think the term is 'bladder-shy'. So when Pascal clamped me with one of his gorilla arms and aimed his penis at the frothing water below, I froze. Dead. Like someone had clamped my urethra. 'Brothers,' Pascal would sigh, luxuriating in the flow. It was like standing next to a farmyard animal at the trough. 'Brothers?' I wondered, rigid like the brass statue of a pioneering climber behind me. We finished with a spirited gob – 'Ah, les Anglais . . . thhoow . . . et les Français . . . thhoow' – before staggering on our way and slipping on the icy cobbles. Pascal insisted we were fellow Celts and we did share a profound camaraderie. Even better than this, his wife Madeleine – the most beautiful woman in the Chamonix valley – became my Celt-sister. To my enduring credibility amongst the poon-hunting, ski bum underclass, Madeleine embraced me daily, in public, like a brother returning from the war. Right then, pressed into the warm clinch of Madeleine's firm breasts, being a Celt was fucking great.

Before I left the Isle of Man, I had always thought of myself as English, with a little Manx twist. Then, along with the 'Hampshire Highlanders' and the 'Plastic Paddies' in Boston, I started to assert my roots. I put my Manxness first. Everywhere I travelled, I went through the rigmarole of explaining where the Isle of Man is. I began to wonder if I was, as people like Pascal told me, part of a distinct social state of 15 million people, distinct that is from the dominant English and French cultural groups.

Thirty years ago, few would have predicted anything but a slow death for Celtic languages and culture. That has all changed and though it is difficult to resist the advance of homogenous culture around the world, the ghettoes of the Atlantic look sound. The languages are being taught in schools again, folk tales are being revived; the kilts and ceilidhs will survive. The Celtic youth of today will be the first generation for centuries to witness their culture unburdened from the threat of extinction. They will also be the first generation that will not be forced by economic necessity to migrate from their homes. This phenomenon has been dubbed the 'New Celtic Age'.

The only way to catch sight of the phenomenon is to dance around it, point towards it, play with it and be open to it. I will spend the summer doing just this, learning to be a poet at the same time. I hope to attend and perform my poetry at a major cultural festival in each of the six countries of the Celtic Fringe. The dates of these festivals mean that I must make an irregular journey, crisscrossing the Irish Sea and the Channel in order to take them all in. Yet the journey, no matter how haphazard, will be the easy part if I do not get the right result out of my night atop old Cader.

Come on, Prince Idris, your greatness, you big fella, you've got to pull this one off for me, I think when I wake before dawn. I have hardly slept. The frost and the wind combined to make the night about as pleasurable as bedding down on the central reservation of a motorway outside Irkutsk.

I can't face lying in my stiff sleeping bag any longer, so I find my pen and notebook and brave the dawn. The ink has frozen in my biro. I do some jigs to warm up. A jig is understating it. I start pogoing around like Joe Strummer singing 'Hateful'. With my hands in my pockets, I leap from rock to rock, bending and arching like a hooked salmon, bellowing, 'Hast thou made me mad, you goat, Idris?'

When the sun comes up, I see that the valleys on each side have been filled with downy cloud, which turns from indigo to orange to white in minutes. The view is one you might use to stir thoughts of the Creation; the sort of vista they encourage you to dream up when you are being stuffed into a flotation tank. It is magical. Trying to capture every ray of warmth, I hastily pack up my kit and head off the top before the spanking hikers are on patrol in the hills again.

By the time I reach the car park, I have still not composed a poem. I haven't even thought of anything to rhyme with Idris. How am I going to fare among real Celtic poets, in front of the Gaelic and Welsh literati in their knotted tweeds and beards? The road is quiet when I drop my rucksack on the verge beside it. For a while I stand over the white lines in the middle, wondering which way to go. North leads to Dolgellau, Scotland, the Celtic Fringe and a summer of bardship. If I am lucky, I could be in Edinburgh in time for 30 April and Beltane – a re-creation of the Celtic fire festival that ends, I have been told, with hundreds of participants bathing naked in the dawn dew on May Day. It would be a fine way to start my journey. South leads to Machynlleth, London, home and another summer in a dull job.

Staring both ways down the empty road, I recall the story of Alexander the Great asking a Celtic envoy which man his people most feared: 'We fear no man,' came the reply. 'We only fear the sky falling on our heads' – a notion no more absurd than expecting a seventh-century prince to imbue me with poetic imagination. 'Mountain master of prophecy, Idris / See my white buns? Now give me a kiss,' I say and, smiling slightly, but not too much, I start walking.

1

The Beltane Fire Festival

'You're looking at me, you banana.' So I am. On the far side of a patch of worn grass I can see Dave waving his phone in the air at me. Official-looking vehicles – police cars, council vans and rubbish trucks – surround him but there is no mistaking Dave for an official. Dressed in a rolled-up Afghan hat and oilskins, he looks like a cross between a Mujahadeen marksman and a cod fisherman. I turn my phone off and wander over. His tobacco-brown lurcher eases towards me, feigns sniffing my scrotum and decides to examine a chip bag instead.

'Dave, thanks for taking the time to see me. You must be a busy man today,' I say, proffering a hand.

'I am, I am. We've got fifteen minutes. Now what can I do you for, man?' he asks, borrowing drug-dealer speak. His accent is . . . well, it is English, which I had not expected. It is not just English, it is the sort of nose-curling, 'neeeeer', I'm not posh, Estuarine English that I was hoping to leave behind in Notting Hill for the summer. Dave is the architect behind Edinburgh's Beltane Fire Festival, the largest re-creation of the ancient Celtic celebration of Beltane anywhere on the planet today, which kicks off in four hours. I had expected him to be a Celt.

'So what's Beltane all about then?' I ask.

Dave looks at me as you might look at a child who has just upended an ice cream on the pavement. He mumbles a disquieted, 'Follow me,' through a liquorice Rizla paper that is clamped between his lips. Then he sets off, rolling a fat cigarette, ordering his dog about and briefing the police chief inspector on the telephone all at the same time.

'What do ya know?' he asks when he stops to fire up his stogie.

'It's a Celtic quarter day?' I suggest. Dave winces. What I do know, I go on to explain, is that the Celtic calendar divided the year into two. The 'lighted half' begins tonight, 30 April to 1 May, and ends with Samhain, the Celtic new year's eve and a celebration of death and renewal, on the night of 31 October when the 'dark half' begins. There are two other quarter days – Lughnasa and Imbolc – which further divide the year neatly into four.

'Right, yeah, I was, like, assuming you knew aw vat stuff,' Dave continues. 'Ver are books abaht it. Should read em.'

I have tried. I have launched into various authoritative texts on the Celtic calendar, Beltane and paganism in ancient Britain, including *The White Goddess* by Robert Graves, supposedly a leading authority, but I have found that reading this literature is like wading through syrup with your feet tied together. My ignorance is, however, embarrassing. Dave and I have a mutual acquaintance who laid it on to him that I am a cutting-edge journalist. What he is clearly wondering now is how he got landed with a monkey only hours before the event that he has worked so hard towards all year kicks off.

'I'll start talkin an if I appen to say enerfing that you *do* know, stop me, right? Beltane Fire Society is fourteen year old. Ov bin in for seven. Ve performance tonight is adapted from a carpull of old folk tales and it's full of the symbolism and significance of the Beltane festival which wus a critical moment in the annual cycle un a big tribal gaverin of the ancient Celts. Right?'

I nod.

'So, ere we go, the May Queen comes out of er winter retreat ere' – we are striding past the giant columns of the Acropolis, Edinburgh's 200-year-old and as yet unfinished Grecian monument – 'the Green Man, symbol of growf, turns up un says "helloow" ut the May Queen. The procession starts. This way!' Dave is already marching off.

'Through the fire arch ere . . . the white women un a blue men are in ur procession. They visit these sites, ere, ere, ere un' – he wheels around on the wet grass, led by his outstretched arm – 'ere – the element sites: air, water, erf un fire, symbols of the year past. The procession builds to an unred un when they get over ere. Pow! The red men un drummers ambush the procession. Don't miss this, man. Best bit. All about fertilit-ee, y'know. Then on fur the dance a life un inta the queen's bower. The Green Man and the May Queen are married. Summer or lighted arf begins. The bon-fire' – Dave points to an enormous towering cone of wood and debris – 'goes off. Chaos un order fused, ying un yang one, all the elements complete, time fur a party. Gor it then, Rob?'

The sky has started to perspire again. You cannot call it rain. It is a mournful drizzle. It is a perfect afternoon to bury a Republican gunman. As we walk back towards the vehicles, Dave indicates vantage points for me to view the action from. 'Vere will be ten fousand people up ere. Beltane's the big one. Wus fur the ancient Celts an is fur us. Samhain is more solemn. This is the one that rocks, yeah? You up for it then?' he says.

We end up back where we started and Dave's phone is ringing again. 'Iz the fuckin' pigs,' he says, looking at the screen on his phone. 'Problem wif the licence. Later, man. Enjoy it.'

Calton Hill rises high enough above the east end of Princes Street and even on this pissy day, I can see Salisbury Crags on Arthur's Seat, and the whole way down Princes Street as far as the castle on the rock that some wit called 'the chip on Scotland's shoulder'. Robert Louis Stevenson thought that this was the best view in Edinburgh, a city with a fair throw of great vantage points. The open patch of land and the gorse lend an element of ruggedness to the hill, which is ill at ease with the monuments on top. There are two Georgian observatories and the half-finished replica of the Parthenon, built after the Napoleonic Wars. They managed to get twelve giant columns up before the cash ran out. It looks a little like the remaining façade of the Temple of Jupiter at Baalbek in the Lebanon, though that was built 1,800 years earlier and is half fallen down, as opposed to half fallen up. I clamber up on to the edifice, thinking how ironic it is that a classical Greek setting should be the stage for a Celtic pagan knees-up, when I am startled by a figure that appears from behind one of the pillars.

'Oh, hi, I didn't see you there,' I say.

'Hi, Geoff, from Milwaukee. Home of the Harley-Davidson.' He carefully uncurls a hand for me to shake.

'Hi, Rob, from the Isle of Man. Home of the . . . er . . . the birch?'

Geoff is dressed in jeans and a biker's leather jacket fastened to his chin. Out of the collar spills a trimmed white beard; two clear green eyes are mounted on the thin strip of bare skin and atop, a Casey Jones cap pulled tight down, the peak unbuttoned. All in all, not a particularly weird rig, but he must be over sixty.

'You involved in this Beltane festival, then?' he asks.

'No, no,' I say and I explain who Dave is and regurgitate some of what I have just been told. All the time Geoff's eyes are boring into me. He has the intensity of looking that suggests that he is either very stupid or very intelligent. Or perhaps his underpants are just too tight. Whatever, it makes me nervous and I am keen to lighten the conversation.

'Are you on holiday, Geoff?'

'No, I am here in Scotland on a mission.'

As if I didn't know already, I have a nutter on my hands, and the party hasn't even begun. 'What kind of mission, Geoff?'

'I am an Asatru pagan. Not a Wicca pagan, no . . . distinct origination history, an Asatru pagan. I work directly with the high gods. I work alone.'

'Oh, good,' I bleat, wringing my hands.

'I have been chosen to make a journey through Scotland. My mission is to bury crystals in sacred places. Places where the long dead are still held in hellish limbo. Culloden Moor, Bannockburn

. . . I will bury crystals and the souls of these dead will be released. I have my instructions.'

I want to say, 'Geoff! Let's just get down right here and cast some runes, brother. Now tell me. What the fuck did they give you in Nam?' But I don't. I just say, 'Umm,' which doesn't really help the conversation forward.

'And are you here on holiday?'

'No, no, I'm . . . Geoff, I have a mission too. And I work alone as well, though I don't have any instructions from the high gods, or indeed the low gods. I am making a journey through the Celtic countries —'

'Really? Which are?' Geoff interrupts me.

'The Highlands and Islands of Scotland, Ireland, the Isle of Man, Wales, Cornwall and Brittany. I know they are not all countries, but this is the easiest way of describing them. So my journey begins right here, tonight, at this Beltane festival.' I have deliberated about this a good deal on my way from Cader Idris to Edinburgh and having talked to Dave, it all fits. It does start here.

'Beltane is the beginning of the lighted half of the year as I am sure you know, and it is also a fertility festival. I am to be a poet. On this night a new creative spirit stirs in the world and I hope to catch a piece of this. The journey will be my stage.'

'Good,' he says emphatically, still staring at me like a Staffordshire bull terrier who thinks I have trousered his tennis ball. Then Geoff unzips his jacket, pulls out a clear plastic, zip-top bag with maybe fifty small, clear crystals. He is for real. He probably does speak directly with the high gods.

'You're packing a lot of crystal there, Geoff,' I say as he rummages among them with his left hand. After a minute, the hand clasps around one and he draws it from the bag.

'This one has got your name on it,' he says, half smiling, and in a cheerier tone. The Agent Orange has temporarily worn off. The bag goes back in his pouch but the one crystal disappears into the deep clasp of his big hand. He holds it there for a few minutes. Is he giving it energy? I wish I had paid more attention to what was going on in the Greenfield at Glastonbury. Or trying to crush it? Geoff stands there in silence between two mighty columns. Geoff wants silence. I want to fill the void with some inanity: 'Man United are doing well,' or 'Have you tried any haggis?' but he flicks me a look that says 'Keep it zipped, shorty.' So I do. Dusk is falling and the yellow lights of Leith are beginning to twinkle beneath us. Eventually, after a long exhalation of breath this big hand opens in front of me. A childish impulse in me wants him to say, 'May the force be with you.' Thankfully, I just about have the wit to realise that he is giving me something that is to him and, perhaps in time to me, not only important but powerful too.

'Take it,' Geoff says. 'You will need it on your journey. Keep it close to you. And beware tonight. There are some strange folk among us.' As I clamber down from the giant steps of the Acropolis, I think, Clearly this is going to be one of those evenings. I need a drink.

It is dark when I walk back on to Calton Hill. The performance has started and there really are 10,000 people up here, maybe more. The May Queen, followed by the epicentre of the performance, is already at the Earth Site halfway round the hill on her journey and the merry crowd surrounding the parade is ten deep. Following Dave's advice I head straight for the Fire Site and find a patch of grass on the hill above it. As I sit down, Gerry, who is sitting a few feet away, introduces himself. He is from South Africa, and he is actually very pleasant. He is backpacking round Europe, but he has stopped to work in Edinburgh for a few months.

'It's a par-tee toon, uh? Beer, buddy?' He hands me a can of McEwan's Export, the ubiquitous premium-strength ale of Scotland. It has a characteristic flavour that my deepest instincts tell me I will taste a second time, when I am bent double in a dank alleyway in the early hours of the wretched morning.

The drumming on the hill – a good African rhythm with djembes and dharbukas and other bits of stretched animal skin that I can't identify – picks up fervour again and the procession is on the move towards us. The performers in front of us make one last effort to move the crowd back, then they dash down to the small fire to light their torches, staffs, chains and wooden wheels in order to greet the procession. There is a huge din now, a cacophony of frenetic drumming and wailing. Half a dozen people are breathing fire, which lights up the awed faces in the front row of the crowd. It is difficult to be sure exactly what the performance contains or means, but the May Queen arrives in her grand procession, escorted by the Green Man, and the fire-breathing and juggling go on furiously around them. When it is part over, I grab Gerry and we dash around the back of the hill to the place where Dave told me the fun really kicks off.

'What are we doing here?' Gerry asks, quite reasonably, as we are standing alone on the grass. Then the procession comes slowly into view. Suddenly, out of the gloom next to us, appear twenty bare-breasted women, painted red from head to toe. They are all in a hysterical lather, cavorting like they are being attacked by a swarm of bees, dancing and wriggling, leaping and prancing. One girl immediately in front of us looks as if she is actually trying to dance her tits off and only when the pair is gathered in a small pile at our feet will she desist from this madness and go home. All of them are wagging their tongues and shrieking like Red Indians at a pale-face scalping session after a dawn raid. This is great. There are loads of nearly naked men painted red too. They are rubbing themselves into a masturbatory frenzy in the mud with any red woman they can grab, and also up against the imperial cannons that decorate the hill. Clearly someone has been snorting Viagra to get in the mood. This is no family show. It is the ambush of the Red Men and their Beastie Drummers.

These painted men and women are the Lords and Ladies of Misrule – key characters in the performance and not just 'some locals having a good time' as Gerry speculates. Dave mentioned them to me, but I had not pictured such a scene of extraordinary bacchanalia and impropriety.

'Feck h-me,' Gerry says. 'Nother beer, buddy?'

'No thanks. I need something stronger,' I reply, rummaging in my pocket for a half bottle of Scotch.

The Red Men are the mischief-makers and this is their big chance to disrupt the procession with lewd behaviour. Tonight, for one night only, they are trying to tempt, seduce and inspire us – the revellers – to forget tomorrow, to carry out acts of foolishness and wantonness, and generally abandon ourselves to the excesses of the night. Dave had said that they do not represent any precise figure from Celtic, or indeed any, mythology. They might be some sort of New Age take on Celtic sexuality. But who cares with all this jigging Bristol-ry.

Into this ribald arena comes the May Queen. She is tall and wearing a pure white gown that reaches the ground, stitched with red budding flowers. Her face is whited out and there is a great V-shaped hat – well, you would hardly call it a hat, it looks more like a piece of public sculpture – towering above her head. She walks with a grace that is amplified by the confusion around her. There is no doubting her historical credentials. The Queen of May, the May Bride, the Maiden, Goddess of Spring, Flower Bride, Queen of the Faeries – she is an anthropomorphic character common to folk customs across Europe. She embodies purity, strength and, crucially for me, the potential for creative growth. She is a key to Beltane and I need to talk to her. I need her blessing for my journey. But not now. Rampaging red breasts would stampede me if I venture into her path at this time. I will wait. The night is still young.

The procession moves on. I have lost Gerry. I head for the May Queen's inner sanctum or 'bower' where the procession finishes up. The crowd are all over the place because it is difficult to know where you are supposed to go next, and all over the place because they have been getting whamoed on strong liquor for several hours now.

I find a place behind the rope at the 'sanctum' and Donnie – I finally meet a Scot, perhaps even a Celt – hands me his one and a half litre bottle of brown, lightly frothing liquid. It is over three-quarters empty.

'What is it?' I enquire innocuously.

'Za fuckun' drink, big mun,' he says, in a tone that suggests I have just questioned the legitimacy of his birth. He looks the easily offended type. I think it was P.G. Wodehouse who said something about how easy he found it to tell the difference between a ray of sunshine and a Scotsman with a grievance. Donnie is eyeballing me and it feels like 'drink or deck' time – a truly Scottish dilemma. Donnie looks like the sort of bloke for whom a little GBH is all part of a good night out. I decide to drink. I take the bottle with both hands, plug it to my lips and invert it. It is rum – four parts, at a guess – to one part warm, fizzy-less, faux-cola. This is not a drink of distinction. It is not a cocktail you would find a delicate-fingered barman with a straw-thin moustache serving up at Harry's Bar in Venice. I hold the liquid in my mouth and taste cheap dark rum, plastic and Donnie's halitosis all in one moment. My epiglottis chooses this instant to mutiny and Scotland's answer to the Bellini comes streaming out of my nose. My eyes water and, unplugging the container from my lips, I gasp for what I briefly imagine to be my terminal breath.

'C-C,' Donnie says, grinning at me, 'Cap'n Morgan and Cola. Knock oot, uh?'

When I am finally upright again and all my passages are clear, Donnie's girlfriend offers me her plastic bottle. I raise my eyebrows inquisitively.

'Vodka Irn-Bru,' she says, 'nooh ice.'

To a great pounding of drums and the rousing skirl of bagpipes, the wailing of tongues and the spilling of people, the Queen of May, still completely composed and walking at her sedate pace, arrives in the verdant bower. The rope and a few lads in green neon jackets prevent us from squeezing in on her. She rests finally in her regal chair, made of branches and leaves entwined in exotic fashion – not the sort of garden furniture you will find at B & Q. I presume that this is the end of the entertainment, but far from it. Just as I am bidding Donnie a less than heartfelt goodbye, there are announcements and the cleared area is squeezed outwards again by the neon waistcoats.

From the bottom of this small arena, a shoeless couple holding hands come skipping past me. And I mean skipping: hopping on the right foot, then on the left and back, all the time hurling their heads back and tossing them gleefully from side to side, like they are in a tampon advert. The bloke – and I suspect from the way he is glancing about that he feels a right plonker doing this – is wearing a cloak-like rectangular piece of cloth round his shoulders, fastened with a brooch. This mantle-type garment is what the ancient Celts called a *brat* and I have never seen one other than on a dummy in a museum. Beneath the cloak he is wearing a long yellow shirt – again, a garment associated with the earliest Irish and Highland Scots and worn until around 1600. This shirt is called a *leni-croich* which means 'saffron shirt' in Gaelic. In sixteenth-century Ireland these garments became a badge of resistance (in the way that the kilt was to be in the Highlands two centuries later) and Henry VIII prohibited the wearing of either of them, in an attempt to subdue the Irish. I have seen some fruity costumes this evening, but this has a badge of authenticity about it. The girl is wearing a floaty number. They both drop on to their knees in front of the May Queen and it dawns on me what is going on. This is a handfasting ceremony, which means one thing: someone is actually taking this evening seriously.

Handfasting is a pagan rite and something that, so far as we know, the ancient Celts practised to mark the taking of a partner. It is the acknowledgement of serious commitment in a relationship, but definitely not comparable to marriage. It might be a precursor to it, a sort of trial run (and not to be confused with the medieval practice of 'trial by ordeal'). In modern terms, it means something like: 'I promise to hand-wash your bras if you will throw out all my trousers with pleats in.' Handfasting was customarily for a year and a day, though I have read that it could be for as little time as the duration of a festival. In many ways, it is a rather sensible arrangement. First, you get to work out just how annoying your partner's foibles are – he leaves floaters in the bowl, she leaves old knickers in his favourite loafers. Of course, anyone under the age of forty today is familiar with this kind of intense warts and all pre-marital experience. But second, and this is where handfasting sets itself apart, it is the recognition that to keep a relationship magical, it must be continually renegotiated. It is not a once-and-for-all settlement, but an arrangement subject to an annual review.

So handfasting is a great idea, though I am not sure that I would wish to make my relationship sacred before a crowd who are spouting warm rum and spittle from their noses. Each to their own. Up they skip to the Queen of May where I imagine their hands are actually tied together with rope and some sort of blessing, which I cannot hear, takes place. The couple then run back down the slope to rapturous cheers. Two more couples, in turn, skip up the damp grass. I know this is daft, but the fact that these couples feel it is important to have this rite sanctified by the Queen of May redoubles my intention to have her bless my own journey.

With all the skipping over, that really is the end of the organised part of the night and the huge crowd breaks up, everyone heading off in search of their own oblivion. A swarm of bodies swells into the queen's arbour and I decide to seek her attendance later. I want to find one of the handfasting couples, but they have melted into the crowd and the night. It is said that their hands must remain tied together with rope until the union has been consummated, so who knows where they might have gone.

The bonfire, or rather the Beltane Fire, has been lit. It is a great sight. Flames thirty feet high curl into the sky. Around the base of the fire is a ring of bright orange faces, dotted with hundreds of brilliant eyes of a heavily drugged global youth. There is a great noise of spitting and crackling and roaring. It is only 1 a.m. but there are already casualties: prostrate bodies on the cold, muddy earth; a fight; the happy, happy sound of a young girl re-tasting a can of McEwan's Export.

Outside the Portaloos, I meet Graziano, who is from Italy. I offer him my Scotch and he hands me a joint. 'Iz skunk-ah. Very spetzial. From Hamsterdam,' he enthuses.

'Are you having a good time?' I ask.

'Good time? Har you joking? Ah bin dancing with ah naked woman for arf hen hour. Her big red bombas going haround and haround, waving hat me, like I dreaming. Ah say, "Ah muster taster this one and then ha muster taster that one," and she say, "Okay. Taster mah bombas!" Iz lak fucking Christmas. This is ah faan-tastic party.'

It is about 2 a.m. when I decide I need a breather from the action on top of Calton Hill and I head down towards the nightclub and the rave. It is an indication of the excess and insanity of the Beltane Fire Festival that a rave offers a chance of repose. There is also, I have been told, some poetry reading going on in the nightclub and I am anxious to catch it. I drift down the path to the foot of Calton Hill in the flow of carousers. At the door there is a queue, but I mention Dave's name and the bouncer lets me straight in. They do not even charge me, probably because they are so surprised to see someone who is straight. Despite the pints, the Scotch and the skunk, I am functioning as normal, at least normal for Beltane.

The club is on three floors. The top two are thumping to the sound of techno. They are like dance floors in any club, save, of course, for the bare-breasted, red-painted women who are still trying to gyrate their udders off. It is pleasing that they have not chosen to re-robe themselves for the club. They are still actively encouraging the crowd to abandon themselves.

The basement is better lit and the music is quieter. In the corner there is a microphone on a stand, where a few men are huddling. One of them turns towards the mic, and in an explosion of incandescent and unintelligible words, he starts rapping. This is the poetry slam, an open mic session for unknown poets. I get a large Jack Daniel's and listen in. The poets take it in turns. The poems are long and difficult to follow. Words are lost in the 'boom boom' from upstairs and swallowed by the 'thoowak' that the PA system screeches when the poets press too close to the mic. Part of me is thinking, These guys are terrible. But then I am comparing them to the very few poets I have seen perform either live or on TV: Benjamin Zephaniah, Ted Hughes, Linton Kwesi Johnson, Seamus Heaney – some of the greatest poets of my time. So it is ridiculous to compare.

The other part of me – the part that tightens the skin around my balls and leaves my mouth dry – knows that I am going to be doing this very, very soon: reading my own poetry to a largely disinterested crowd of drunks in a noisy bar. It is only a few days since I was up Cader Idris, and though I have not yet even written a poem, I know my moment is coming soon enough. I have a glance round and it appears that I am the only person listening to the poets. I am not sure if this is good news or not. Right now, the thought of standing up in front of a crowd of silent strangers, expectant of hearing one of my poems reach the corners of the pub with words I have not yet even written, fills me with a deep, lasting horror. This is the first time I fully comprehend what I have set out to do. In a quiet moment, the barman leans on the lager taps and says, 'What d'ya reckon, eh?', nodding towards the mic.

'I think they're really, really, really . . . brilliant,' I reply feverishly. 'I'd better have another Jack Daniel's, please.'

One of the Beltane myths says that there is a special potency in the dew on the morning of May Day. Women must wash their face in it, or even better their whole body, to remain fair throughout the year ahead. I am inclined to say that too few women in Scotland have taken advantage of these free cosmetics. For men, washing their hands in the dew will make them good with knots and nets, but they remain as hirsute and hideous as they ever were in the coming year, which seems a bit tough on the ladies. Being good with knots and nets is not very useful to a modern Celt who works as a journalist, but I think you have to work these things through metaphorically, so I am back on top of Calton Hill at around 4.30 a.m. lying on the grass wiping the palms of my hands in the dew thinking, Knots of words, the dew may help me untangle knots of words, when a fellow in distressingly tight jeans humps down on the grass next to me.

'Ar yavin foon?' he asks in a thick Brummie accent.

'Just having some time out,' I reply.

'Yow luk comfay thhere.' It is a lisping Brummie accent. He is smashed.

'I am wiping my hands in the dew of May Day morn. It is sup-posed to make men good at untying knots.'

'Ow, can oi rub th-ow?' He is gay. I know this not because I have deduced the signs – a tubby torso in a tight T-shirt showing off white biceps, the John Inman voice, the lustrous eyes. No, I know this because he puts his hand on my lap. And it is not a 'Cheer up, old chap' type hand on lap. It is a 'fancy a blow-job' type hand on lap. His fingers are curled round the top of my thigh. This is a breathtakingly unsubtle pass, but I guess he thinks it is late and he has got to move fast to get a result out of the night.

'I don't even know your name,' I say, slightly diluted by the excess of the whole evening, picking his paw off my leg.

'Truman.'

'Look, Truman, I'm not gay. I'm no good to you. Sorry.'

'Ow, well,' he says resignedly, as if I am not the first to deprive him of a moment of pleasure on this night. 'Moind if I loi ere and rub the dew unyway?'

I am still thrown by how international this festival is. I had half expected a small gathering of bearded Scots and a set of bagpipes, but I have met Italians, South Africans, Australians, Germans, Spanish and Truman, a big beefy bandit from Birmingham in the heart of England. How un-Celtic is that? Not that he is a veritable John Bull. Jeannette Bull, maybe.

Why should the specious re-creation of a centuries-old Celtic festival draw party-people from across the globe? The answers are probably as numerous as the nationalities: Edinburgh's reputation as a festival capital, the success of previous Beltane Fire Festivals, the advance of New Age paganism, but at heart of it is, I feel, the increasing popularity of all things Celtic.

'Why are you here, Truman?' I ask.

'Ooh, oi luvit, loike, un oi live up ear in Edinburgh. Oive bin cumin for yeez. It's an important noit ya now.' He is propped up on one elbow now, like a Roman senator. 'A noit uf fertility, uf sexual release, atchuwely. Ya naw, usbands un woives, in the owl days, cud thek off the weddin rings and go shag sumbudy else. Just un this wun noight a year. It's loike if you wuz not gay, then mehbeh this wun noight yow could be and . . .'

'Forget it. I am not going to sleep with you.' With this, I try to raise my torso off the grass, but I have been lying down for so long that the cold has worked through my body and things happen slowly. I have barely got my shoulder blades up and he is on me, wrestling for a grip on my raincoat, trying to plant his swollen lips on mine.

'What the . . . get off,' I shout, throwing him off sideways. This time I am off the ground like a Chinese gymnast. 'Enough!'

'Awright, awright. Suhray.'

It is, I suppose, one of those nights – a crazy, spinning, mad kind of night. It is the night where the phrase to 'go a-maying' comes from, a night of abandonment. History and folk tales are full of stories of wild sexual antics at Beltane. The carnal Red Men obviously got to Truman, just as they were supposed to. It must be a great night for a poet to be born. I must now attend to this. I turn towards the bonfire.

'I must go and find the May Queen,' I say, walking off.

'What? Thez anuther wun about?' Truman says, lying back down in the dew and starting to laugh.

The purplish-grey, uneasy light is growing. The new day, May Day, the first dawn of the lighted half of the year, is finally shouldering its way into the remains of the wild and heady night. Despite all I have drunk, I am alert to the excitement of this new beginning. This really is the start of my journey and a new phase of my life. This is the first day in the existence of Ned Clague.

Ned Clague? This is the bardic name I have chosen and it is going to take some getting used to. It is pronounced 'Clegg'. There are sure to be some cock-ups when I catch my tongue on this little Celtic twister. 'Hi, I'm Red Ned. Gob to meet you.' 'Good afternoon, I'm Nerod Pig.' 'Well, hello there, my name's Ned Smeg.'

So why take a bardic name in the first place? Well, the name Rob Penn hardly smacks of great Celtic lineage in the way that, say, Aonghas Macneacail or Seán Ó Curraoin or Dewi Cwmtwrch or Mab Stenek Veur do. Am I right? So there is an element of artifice in the adoption – in recognition, I suppose, of how much is in a name. If you meet a Tuareg chief in the Sahara, you want him to be called Mustafa Al Mustafa, and not, say, Lionel Blair. When you are trekking over the high passes of the Karakoram, your guide, a venerated village elder and scion of a great guiding family, ought to be called Ishmael Mohammed Khan and not Billy Goat-Fucker. I can go on, but I have made the point. Clague is a venerable Manx name. I could go with Gelling, my mother's family name and equally venerable, but I prefer the clashing consonants of Clague. It leaves the tongue clattering around the mouth in a good way. Rob would do for a Christian name. Robert is, of course, an honest Scottish name. In Manx, it is Robart. Other Manx Christian names I could slip into, as it were, are Jamys, Iliam and Doolish, but Ned goes better with Clague. Ned Clague.

The idea that poets have bardic names is quite prevalent in

Celtic countries. It is a centuries-old tradition that is still practised today. Throughout Wales, up in the Hebrides and to a lesser extent in Ireland, poets and sometimes writers of prose as well have adopted or have had conferred upon them bardic names or pseudonyms under which their works may be published, and which may be the most widely known name they are associated with. Furthermore, a bardic name may be a poetic interpretation of someone's real name. As such, it can be a prayer, a meditation or a spell. Such a rune can be used to enlighten or confound those to whom it is spoken. 'Writing a ceremonial name for yourself,' I read in an article about poetry in Wales, 'is a wonderful way to celebrate who you are now, who you have been, who you hope to become.' I don't think I want to go down that route somehow. If I devised a name that was also a spell, I would only be setting myself up for a fall. So Ned Clague it is. And with a bardic name decided on, I start to thread my way back across the hill to find the May Queen for the naming ceremony.

I can now make out the rows of sandstone houses way below us in Leith, leading out to the Firth of Forth. Closer by, the Georgian order of Edinburgh's New Town is there for all to see and it strikes me how illicit what we are doing up here must seem to most of the citizens of Edinburgh. Down there is a city hung up on decorum, while up here we are hung over from sex and alcohol, drugs, dancing and drumming. The New Town is no façade. Behind those rows of grand doors and fanlight windows are tight-lipped women in big underpants serving breakfast to rigid men reading ironed newspapers. Order! Edinburgh is all about order and the Beltane Fire Festival is all about disorder. It is no wonder that Dave was having hassles with the police. Someone told me that Christians come up here to reconsecrate the hill on 2 May, so egregious and profane do they find the acts of the Beltane procession to be. They have a point.

The light reveals a scene of carnage atop the hill. Bottles and bodies, cans, plastic bags, butts, roaches, jackets, branches, hats and fag packets – the detritus is scattered everywhere. The gathering around the big fire has reduced from several thousand to a hundred. This deposit of people includes white Rastas, Australian surfers, jaw-grinding scallies in expensive mountaineering coats, posh students, the last of the Mohicans, pretty Spanish girls, pikies with mullets and me. This is the intriguing but now familiar residue that you find at raves and festivals all over the world in these strange times. This muddle of humanity is huddled close about the fire, now a low smouldering pile in the middle of which stands a towering kilted Scot who is toasting his bollocks on the embers.

Beltane was, for the ancient Celts, a livestock festival. They celebrated it when the hawthorn flowered, which meant that the cattle could be driven from the pens up to the summer pastures on the hill where they would remain until Samhain. At Beltane, great fires were lit (Beltane is probably derived from *bealttainn* which means 'bright fire') and the cattle were passed between them. The ancient Celts also customarily leapt the Beltane fire themselves. For fertility – well, hardly – for bravado or to impress the opposite sex or for kicks? Who knows? But they did it, or so the stories go.

We know a great deal about Beltane customs because many of them are alive today. In the Isle of Man, where the festival is called Sheen do Boaldyn, twigs from rowan trees are still hung above doorways. Beltane was celebrated all over the Highlands with great fire festivals until at least the end of the nineteenth century, and within living memory people have gathered on hill tops. At the Cloutie Well, outside Inverness, people still do gather, for a celebration which is unbroken.

I wait for the lad who thinks he is Rob Roy to finish toasting his chestnuts. Then I follow him into the heart of the fire, hoping that the soles of my new boots will not melt. You would need a human catapult to leap this fire, so I reckon walking through will suffice. Most of the brethren at the fireside look as if they are down from their trips. The drugs are over. The hollow, empty faces tell me as much. It is the prefrontal lobotomy crew. If I start leaping around, kicking up the embers now, there would be some heavy paranoia and a few charred faces before anyone knew what was going on. Also, if I take a tumble in the fire pit, it is unlikely anyone will notice. They will assume that the blood-curdling screams and the smell of blackened flesh are just flashbacks of scenes we all witnessed earlier on. So, I edge my way through carefully. I cannot feel the heat through my feet, but my very sensible trekking trousers do go crisp like Melba toast.

There are only a few bodies around the May Queen's throne, in the heart of her bower, when I walk up. They have had their fair share of the party since the performance finished. There are plenty of empty bottles around them and a few on the go too. People are standing, lying and sitting in a semicircle, on the end of which is the queen. Her headdress is off, the white face-paint has smeared, the hem of her long skirt is sullied and she is wearing a pair of Doc Marten boots, which are swinging beneath the bench she is perched on. She has lost . . . how can I put this? She has lost some of her majesty. The regal air that hung about her earlier has all gone. She looks like any old party slapper now. Oh, well. A blessing is a blessing, I guess.

I dip my head in an over-theatrical bow to get her attention. Her eyes wander either side of my face – she is seeing double – and then they gradually zone in on mine. She is not beautiful, or pretty, but she is quite sexy, for a queen. Imagine Queen Elizabeth after a couple of pills and half a bottle of brandy. Quite sexy in that 'I'll still be cutting rug when you are asleep like a little dormouse under the table' way.

That she is neither pretty nor beautiful is, it strikes me now, entirely appropriate. In folk tradition, the May Queen was supposed to be the best-looking bird in the village. However, the women themselves usually chose her. Thus, in a nutshell, she never was the best-looking bird in the village. She was probably not even close. She may have had a great character, been a real team player, told wicked jokes, been in possession of a list of personal attributes that would make Nobel Prize winners look like bit-part players in the progress of humanity but she was never, ever, no way the best-looking girl in the village, not if she was chosen by the women. The Barbie look-alike with long legs, big tits and 'hold on tight' pigtails never got a vote. And you may be certain that, in every village throughout the Celtic lands, in every year for the last two and a half millennia, when the Beltane festival began and the May Queen, the symbol of creativity, the light of summer and the source of new life, was carried in amidst the people of the village, all the single lads' faces screwed up in the same grimace of disbelief and as one, across the pan-Celtic world, they exclaimed: 'They chose her? That's pathetic.'

Our eyes eventually meet. I have mentally rehearsed what I am going to say at this moment a hundred times. In spite of the Scotch and the skunk, the 'CC', the Jack Daniel's and the rest of it, I am nearly sober again. Against the odds, it starts according to plan.

'I am a poet. My bardic name is Ned Clague. I am making a journey through all the countries of the Celts, to gather inspiration from the land and from the ancients. I have come here—'

'Aww, moiht,' she bursts in, 'youz a poet?' Suddenly the plan is scrambled.

'You're Australian?'

'Aw, yeah.'

Oh, no. I had in mind a May Queen who looked like Cate Blanchett as the luminous elf queen, Galadriel in *The Lord of the Rings*; a queen who spoke like an Irish princess with a voice delicate enough to change the colour of a flower's petals and powerful enough to alter the direction of the wind. As it is, she sounds like a brickie from the western suburbs of Sydney. This throws me, but I struggle on.

'Er . . . right . . . anyway. I am a poet and I am making a journey through the countries of the Celtic Fringe to gather inspiration for my poems and to find my tongue. My journey begins here. You are the Queen of May, the symbol and the source of creativity. Will you stir my imagination by sharing the power of the creativity you possess?'

'Woodah slug-a vodka hilp? Nah, just jokin, moiht,' she says, picking up the bottle that is wedged between her legs. 'Okay. I am the May Queen' – she gathers her shoulders up to regain some measure of formality – 'I bless your journey.' Then she takes a big pull on the vodka as I bow and back away. Feeling as if I have just walked off the set of the *Neighbours* Christmas party, I wander across the hill and down into the damp Edinburgh streets, glancing occasionally over my shoulder to check that Truman is not following.

2

The First Strike of Poetry

The story of the Celts is rooted in language. The simplest definition of a Celt today is someone who speaks a Celtic language. There are six of them: Scottish Gaelic, Irish Gaelic, Manx Gaelic, Welsh, Cornish and Breton. They fall neatly into two language groups known as Brythonic or P-Celtic (Welsh, Cornish and Breton) and Goidelic or Q-Celtic (Scottish, Irish and Manx Gaelic). The terms Celtic and Gaelic are often confused, though they mean different things: the Gaelic languages form one of the two groups of the Celtic languages. Within each group, there is enough common vocabulary and grammar for speakers of the three languages to be mutually intelligible. Thus, a Scottish Gaelic speaker from the Isle of Lewis can talk about playing the fiddle with an Irish speaker from the Iveragh Peninsula and a Welsh speaker from Anglesey can discuss worrying young sheep with a Breton speaker from the Pays Bigouden – but only just, mind. The languages are different, but a pint or two of stout usually helps, with the comprehension that is, not with shagging sheep.

However, put a Scottish Gaelic speaker and a Breton speaker together and no amount of stout will help. They will not understand a word the other person is saying. You could throw in a goatherd from Nuristan and a horse-trader from the Turkmen steppe and the level of comprehension will not go down. There is speculation that the Brythonic and Goidelic languages were once mutually intelligible, or even one, but this is way, way back in pre-history and whilst no one really knows, fewer still care. What is more noteworthy about the Celtic languages is how different they are from English, much more so than other European languages. They share no vocabulary (save for what the Celtic languages have borrowed for modern usage) and the syntax is dissimilar.

Across the world today, languages die at the alarming rate of twenty-five a year, or one every fortnight. Of course, languages have been dying throughout history, but there is no doubt that the problem is more acute in modern times. Ask anyone who knows a thing or two about linguistics and they will tell you that new languages tend to be adopted when they offer better access to goods, wealth, status, entertainment, ritual and security – all the things we strive for – than the languages that are abandoned to make way for them. Throughout the Celtic Fringe, English has offered this 'better access' for between 100 and 700 years, depending on where you are. The point I am making is that it is remarkable that these languages have survived at all. That they have is illustrative of one truly Celtic trait: pig-headed resilience. As one Welshman who I have known for years put it to me, 'See, if the English hadn't banged on about the Welsh language so much, I reckon we would have just forgotten it by ourselves. But the clever men from London just did, so we never let it go.' That they have survived is a cause for celebration. All languages, Celtic or otherwise, are extraordinary human creations. They are as marvellous as any of mankind's literary, musical, artistic or architectural achievements. To lose any language is a tragedy.

Okay, so the Celtic languages have not survived well. The last indigenous speakers of Cornish and Manx died, respectively, in 1777 and 1974. At the beginning of the twentieth century, 75 per cent of the population of Brittany spoke Breton. By the mid-1990s it was 15 per cent. The story of Irish is similar. Only 80,000 people still speak Scottish Gaelic. In all the Celtic countries, there are plenty of young (and even old) militants who have struggled to get recognition, funding and visibility for their languages. The languages are being taught widely again (even in the Isle of Man, where my brother's nephew and niece go to a Manx-medium nursery) and they are more prevalent in the media. However, swelling numbers of fluent speakers of the Celtic languages have not as yet followed the efforts of the enthusiasts. At best, they have only arrested the decline.

With the single, shining exception of Welsh (roughly 800,000 speakers), all the Celtic languages are perilously close to extinction. So much so that you have to take yourself to the furthest redoubts of the Celtic countries to hear the languages spoken at all, which is why I am standing on the pier in Ullapool waiting for the Stornoway ferry to depart, on a heavenly spring evening.

The Western Isles, or the Outer Hebrides, are – my tourist brochure tells me – 'the heart of Gaeldom on earth'. I am heading there because, after my experiences with the global underground crew at Beltane, I feel the need to mix it up with some authentic Celts. Also, the 125-mile archipelago, referred to by Dr Johnson as the 'rude and remote parts' of Britain, is the northernmost extremity of the Celtic Fringe and a place where nearly everyone speaks Scottish Gaelic, which I am anxious to hear.

I have heard Manx spoken before, of course. I know a few people in the Isle of Man who know enough of the language to show off at dinner parties when there are English, or 'come-overs' as the Manx people call them, present. (My dad, who is English but married to a Manx girl, is a 'brought-over'.) Also, I have been listening to the lovely voice of Doug Faragher on *Abbyr Shen* (*Say That*), the set of Manx tapes that I am using to learn the language. But it is to hear it spoken in the street and on the bus and in the pub that I am making for the Western Isles. Gaelic remains the first language for the majority of the population, and if you believe all you hear, it is on the increase again too.

The tourists have not reached this part of Scotland in their droves in May – 'They usually arrive with the midges,' the ticket collector tells me – and there is a laid-back 'the ferry'll go when we're all ready' air, so I plonk myself down on a bench beside the water with my pint and my bag of chips.

I am trying to work out precisely how I coordinate drinking beer, eating chips and reading with only two hands and one mouth, without pouring beer or chip grease on the expensive hardback book I have just purchased from one of Ullapool's two good bookshops, when two men about my age sit on the other end of the bench. We exchange cursory smiles. They sip their pints and turn to each other.

'*A veil siv ski.*'

'*Hanell ider.*'

'*An deik do dun vu shower?*'

'*Headache. Tammy ski.*'

'*Tammy Wynette.*'

'*Divertsive.*'

To my delight, they are speaking Gaelic. I put my book down and listen in. I can't be sure that I am transliterating this precisely, but the conversation sounds something like this.

'*Sofia abith dith chin me hairyball.*'

'*Tummy tickle jews unt amdaeus rice.*'

'*Iz toil lehman's in. Flook and salak it's in bag.*'

'*Sgadan is buntata ha taraing tinned macaroni.*'

'*Twenty quid.*'

'*Mor le mannach bed and breakfast beyenach.*'

'*Curried goat for tea, grease and fur.*'

'*Tammy darlek. Hi ho silver lining, can you diggy it.*'

The weirdest thing is the obviously English words and phrases that are included – 'tinned macaroni', 'twenty quid' – but a moment later they both drop into English and then back again into Gaelic. They are, of course, fluent in both languages and what seems like a series of English non-sequiturs are merely borrowed words where nothing similar exists in Gaelic (and frankly, it is some relief to learn that 'tinned macaroni' has not found its way into the vernacular). Naturally, I cannot wait long wondering what subject of conversation could bring together 'bed and breakfast', 'tinned macaroni' and 'twenty quid' so I ask. They repair roads on the Isle of Lewis and they are working out expenses. It had to be boring, I suppose.

I tell them that I am learning Manx. They both think that no one speaks it any more so I try a few recently learnt Manx pleasantries on them: '*Kanys ta shoo?*' – 'How are you?', '*Cre ass t'ou?*' – 'Where are you from?', '*Cre'n ennym tort?*' – 'What is your name?' They both understand me perfectly, despite my atrocious pronunciation. I struggle to understand their replies, but they are delighted with the revelation that they may converse with someone from the Isle of Man (I withhold the news that there are only about three people who speak Manx fluently) and so carried away are we with this little Celtic bonding session that we almost miss the ferry.

From the upper aft deck, as we ease towards the mouth of Loch Broom, the view south over An Teallach, a big Munro at 3,484 feet, and the mountains bordering it, is superb. The peaks are snow-capped and tiered with rings that fade earthwards through shades of brown, then purple and green before reaching the forest. The water is still. The air above the perfectly sculpted wake looks like it has been ladled on to the loch, so dense with vitality is it. The low sunlight slants through, illuminating it. I can barely see them but there is a sense that hundreds of thousands of minute pink diamonds are suspended in the air. This is the sort of dazzlingly beautiful light that makes professional photographers go slack-jawed and weak. It is the sort of light that can change the way you think about light for ever.

Before photography was invented, the same dynamic, Atlantic light drew artists. It still does. I met an English painter in the pub ten minutes ago. Artists were the first tourists to the Celtic Fringe. Save for the odd Viking settlement, the history of most of the Celtic Fringe has been one of continuous emigration. Small colonies of artists, attracted by the light and the tranquillity, were the first to buck that trend. The St Ives colony led by Barbara

Hepworth and the Pont Aven school that grew up around Gauguin in southern Brittany are the best known, but there are plenty of other Atlantic retreats populated at one time by artists: Ile de Bréhat, Tory Island off Donegal, even Durness near Cape Wrath.

For the indigenous people the light has always been an inspiration not to paint or to sculpt, but to write poems. It is almost impossible to overestimate the importance of poetry to the Celts. I read somewhere that today Wales has more practising poets or bards per capita than any other country in the world. It often seems to me that half the Irishmen I meet are poets. A pamphlet I am reading about the Western Isles says: 'It sometimes appears as if every village has its own bard.' That may be tourist-speak these days, but only half a century ago they certainly did. These are not well-known, or even published, poets. They are farmers, fishermen, labourers and bus drivers who happen to turn a poem or two when they have the urge. These 'village bards' represent the last living vestiges of the Celtic past of western Europe. They are the quotidian manifestation of an oral tradition that reaches, unbroken, back to the time of the ancient Celts.

The Roman scribes first noted the eloquence of the Celtic bards and the tradition was most probably old then. We do know roughly when the earliest mythical tales of Welsh and Irish literature were originally written down, but we do not know how many centuries earlier the bards first started proclaiming them. These ancient bards related histories and genealogies, they commemorated events and spread news, they promoted the 'twilight state' of the Celtic psyche in a sort of shamanic role (they were closely related to druids in social status) by promoting mystery, they were messengers from the 'otherworld'. The diverse roles and high status accorded to bards remained until the late Middle Ages. It is no surprise then that the Romans, Angles, Saxons, Normans and ultimately the English were ever conscious of the power that bards had in the Celtic domains. In 1366 the Statute of Kilkenny attempted to restrict the movement of travelling bards in areas of Ireland under English control. When the rebellion of Owain Glyndwr broke out in Wales in 1404, the English immediately banned poetry. In sixteenth-century Wales peripatetic poets were proscribed as 'vagrants, legally whippable, stockable or deprivable of their ears'.

The term 'bard' is much borrowed and often used, but today it is most readily associated with the traditional practice of poets in remote Celtic communities like the Western Isles. Over the ages, though, it has embraced the makers of all kinds of song and poetry, from Cacophonix, the irrepressible and egregious bard in the Asterix books, through the praise-poets of the Heroic Celtic Age before Christ and the saint poets of the medieval period, to the courtly poets of the Middle Ages.

Even today, poets in the Highlands, Ireland and Wales are still accorded slightly special status. Many of them are aware of being heirs of a great tradition, though I can't say that I feel all that history pulsing too keenly through me as yet. However – and this is one thing in my favour – being a poet in these Celtic domains is nothing unusual. All I need to do, then, is write a poem. This is proving more difficult than I had imagined. I cannot even remember the last poem I wrote. I am sure there were a few verses of self-conscious verbal manure scribbled in the back of rough books when I was a spotty adolescent under the influence of the Smiths, but I do not recall them. There may even be a puerile tribute to Ian Curtis, the lead singer of Joy Division who topped himself, engraved with a compass on a bus shelter somewhere. But, again, it has gone from memory. Which means that the last verifiable poem composed by this veritable bard is scratched on the top right-hand corner of the desk in the middle of the back row of classroom 5A and it reads, in tribute to my then geography teacher: 'Oh, Mrs Leech as / A lovely pair a peechas.'

It is not what you would call a strong portfolio. To increase my output of poetic works, I have come to the Port of Ness, a small harbour at the northernmost point of the Isle of Lewis. It is the physical extremity of my journey. The whole of the Celtic Fringe is below me, extending hundreds of miles to Pointe de Penmarch in south-west Brittany. There is a glorious and deserted sandy beach, licked by white-topped breakers which I have just happily walked the length of, admiring the interlinked semicircles of deposited ocean foam. I am now sitting on the snaking concrete breakwater, which forms a small harbour away from the growling Atlantic, watching the waves fill and drain the rock pools. It is another beautiful day, though the cold wind – the residue of a storm that passed over three days ago – carries its own warning. I instinctively know that Ness is the sort of place where you would struggle to light a cigarette on 363 days in any given year.

I get my notebook out and stare for a while at the blank page. Then I stare at the rocks. Then I stare at the blank page again. Where to begin? Medieval and even earlier Welsh and Irish poetry was heavily standardised, or subject to 'strict metre'. The technicalities of these verse forms – syllable patterns, the quality of vowels in rhymes, alliteration, classes of consonants – are immensely complex and take years of dedicated study to master. I started reading about Irish Gaelic medieval poetry and almost immediately came up against this phrase: 'trochaic tetrameter catalectic'. I am serious. To write strict metre Irish poetry, you need to know what a 'trochaic tetrameter catalectic' is. It is a phrase that describes the metrical analysis of a verse form and it is not, as I initially supposed, the missing piece of machinery Flash Gordon needs to launch his spacecraft and get away from planet Zogatron, nor is it, as I later wondered, a surgical throat operation.

Medieval Celtic verse forms are perhaps not for me. There are plenty of other fixed forms of poetry – ballades, villanelles, rondels, rondeaux, rondeaux redoublés, Sicilian octaves – but I am not sure if I have got time for any of them either. I think I am probably better off cowarding away in modernism, the home of 'open form', 'free verse' or 'he hasn't got a bloody clue'-type poetry. There still needs to be some sense of structure, metre, idiom and rhythm, but no tetrameters are required.

Allen Ginsberg said, on writing poetry, 'First thought, best thought,' which led in his case to some pretty dreadful poems. But he is right. I just have to begin. My pen is poised.

> The sea rushes the rocks . . .

I have a line.

> The sea rushes the rocks
> And in the wash there are words.

Two lines. We are off.

> I can see a pair of socks
> And a dozen floating turds.

Pathetic. Try again.

> The sea rushes the rocks
> And in the wash there are words
> The whirling foam she mocks
> Twisting messages downwards.

Well, it's a verse, just. It is not going to bag me a Nobel Prize for literature. On, on.

> To the west the Atlantic
> The sea that defines us
> Howling its song, anti-romantic
> Strafing palisades, smashed to sand.

Anti-romantic song? What on earth does that mean? That verse is awful, but if I axe it now, I am back with just the one verse and I can't quite face that. The second verse stays.

A couple of German sightseers clamber over the breakwater on to the beach behind me. They shout 'Hello' and watch me for a

44

minute. I wonder if they are thinking, Ah, ze young Celtic poet at vurk. It is unlikely. They are probably saying, 'Look zeh-ah. Ze willage dunce. Ze interbreeding on ze irelands means zear are many willage dunces.'

> Cughtagh, deep-throated sea beast
> From the cave he delivers his sermons
> Instead of your seaweed feast
> Why don't you eat the Germans?

Yet more wasted time. I can't use that. Cughtagh is a sea-monster from Celtic mythology, which gets me thinking about the fantastic pantheon of Celtic deities.

> Mannanan, son of Lir
> Your cloak of grey cold
> In the drowning wind, your voice we hear
> In the fisherman's face, your story is told

> The sea swirls on the rocks
> Is this the tongue of the sea?
> The ocean retreats through seaweed locks
> So let's all go and have a cup a tea.

Concentrate, I implore myself.

> The ocean retreats through seaweed locks
> How is it written? What do you tell me?

That will do. I scribble 'Port of Ness' at the top of the page as a title. It is an appalling poem and the whole experience has left me in a foul mood. It is the sort of poem that you would find on the lid of a box of 'Celtic Cornucopia – Chocolates from the Mists of Time'. In truth, it is probably not even good enough for that.

The light is thinning as I start walking back along the road towards Stornoway. It is a good fifteen miles, so I stick my thumb out and the first car stops. I open the passenger door and immediately cheer up. The chaotic contents and the driver of the vehicle are straight out of rural Ireland, but, as I am beginning to appreciate, these Hebrideans are rather like the Irish. It is an estate car, probably once a Peugeot but it has long since lost all forms of identification. There is only one seat, the driver's seat. The rear row has gone altogether and the passenger seat is a *Blue Peter* arrangement – a piece of wood, some foam and loads of gaffer tape. The driver is dressed in a tweed jacket, grey suit trousers and wellies. He has one long eyebrow, kind eyes and bristles sprouting and blooming from every orifice on his face save for his mouth where there is a Dickensian arrangement of teeth. I am eager to go anywhere this old boy is going, but I say, 'I am heading for Stornoway.'

'What luck,' he exclaims. 'Sooh ham I.' The words come out very slowly. He deliberates over the consonants like a Scandinavian student of English, and the sentence finishes on the up, like that of a nursery school teacher. For the greater part of the population of the Western Isles, English is the second language, learnt at school. It is spoken in this purposeful, almost tortured way, as if the summer sun has yet failed to thaw out these people's winter-frozen jaws. 'English on crutches' is how one Highlander described it to me. I jump in and the backboard of my seat collapses.

'Nice day, izun tit?' he asks.

'Beautiful.'

'Oooooohm, it is.' Then he starts singing, in Gaelic. We are still sitting by the side of the road some minutes after he has finished, in silence.

'Shall we go then?' I hesitantly offer, and he raises his long eyebrow at me as if this is the most insightful and intelligent thing anyone has ever said to him. The exhaust-less car thunders to life and we set off down the middle of the road.

The northern part of Lewis is dominated by blanket bog. It is a featureless, tired and ugly landscape, dotted with habitations hardly raised higher than the stacks of peat beside them. The soil is very poor quality – acid and bad drainage – and geology has been equally unkind: there are few worthwhile mineral resources and Lewissian gneiss makes poor building stone, nor is it much good for making tools.

The old boy is a crofter from Ness, though you might call him a farmer since he has a few acres – somewhat more than the small-holding usually associated with a croft. He is, quite likely, the latest incumbent of twenty generations of his family who have tilled the thin layer of topsoil and run a few sheep on the very same piece of land. His name is Uisdean, which is Gaelic for 'Hugh'. It is pronounced a bit like 'Euston' and is a popular name in the Hebrides. No doubt it will be popular amongst models and rock stars one day.

'Ant weir aihr you frome?' Uisdean asks, after we have done where I spent the day, what I did there, where I am staying, why I am staying there, where I am going, what I am going to do there and what is the colour of the underpants I am wearing today. Questions, questions, questions. The Celts just can't help them-selves.

'I am from the Isle of Man,' I say, and he sort of half guffaws, half chokes, slumping forward over the steering wheel as he does so, sending the car careering towards the ditch.

I know this guffaw cum choke. I have witnessed it occasionally through my life and regularly in the last few days. Something tells me that I will observe it frequently over the next six months. It is a convulsive reaction to the news that I am from the Isle of Man, when my plain accent has hitherto indicated that I come from England. This spontaneous emission of air from the body, the instinctive relaxing of the shoulders and the broadening of the smile that follows, is the extraordinary physical expression of this exact sentiment: 'Well, blow me. So you're from the Isle of Man and there was I thinking all along that you were just another arse-hole from England.'

It could hardly be a sentiment that I condone. After all, my dad is English. I am half English. But, along with death, taxes and the sun shining when you are revising for exams, one of the sure things in life is that two Celts from disparate regions will be brought together in a joyous union when one of them takes a dig at the English. I could tell Uisdean that I am from Birmingham, where I was actually born, or from London where I have lived for ten years. But I am eager to measure and understand this anti-Englishness and to do so I have to be on the inside when they are talking about them.

I must, then, play my Manx card at all times, even if it means nearly dying in a car crash in a boggy ditch halfway across Lewis. It is ridiculous, superficial and childish to like and dislike people on account of where they are from, but that is the way the world goes round. It is impossible to resist. What is alarming is that each time I say I am from the Isle of Man, prompting this impulsive moment of glee from someone, I feel that I grow a little bit more Celtic and, correspondingly, a little bit less English.

As we approach Stornoway, Uisdean asks me where I want to be dropped off.

'Anywhere near the harbour,' I say.

'Fine. I am goh-hing too the hoose-pital to see my wife, so I will drohper you at this roundabout-eh.' With one more triumphant eyebrow vault, we are parted.

Poetry stalks the soul of the Celts. I know this from what I have read, but the truth is that I have been doing an emu on facing up to this unsettling reality. How, oh how, am I going to convince these people that I am a poet when I have one poem to my name which has all the literary credibility of a train timetable? I am at a Saturday night ceilidh (the word 'ceilidh' seems to be spelled in many different ways and I have settled on the most familiar Scottish spelling) in the Royal British Legion club in Stornoway when the enormity of my task slaps me in the face like a wet side

48

of cod. It would be easier to convince a gaggle of west London yuppies in frameless glasses, or even the judges of the Orange poetry prize, of my bardic virtue than it will be to gain the respect of a bunch of Hebridean fishermen and farmers.

I am talking and drinking with Calum. He is a welder from Lewis, forced away to work on the oil fields in Holland. He has returned for a few days to help his brother cut peats in the May sunshine. There is a band playing – an accordionist, a drummer and a guitarist with a great voice – and the 'Malt of the Week' costs £1 a dram. I bring up the subject of poetry and Calum is profoundly knowledgeable about it. We touch on Burns and Tennyson, and the great bards of these islands and how important the spoken word still is to these people. Calum tells me that poetry alone avoided the stagnation and provincialism that was strangling Celtic culture thirty years ago and he insists that it has been at the heart of the late twentieth-century recovery that the Scottish psyche has made. In describing the political and social weight that poetry has in modern Scotland, he quotes Shelley, who wrote that poems were 'unacknowledged legislation'. I add that I am making a journey to find inspiration for my poetry and he frowns.

'Ah would seeh thurt the poo-htree is ether in yee, oohr it is not. Ut comes doon like the rain on you. Thun you write.' Unwittingly, or perhaps not actually, Calum is paraphrasing Keats, who wrote: 'If poetry comes not as naturally as leaves to a tree then it had better not come at all.'

'Do you heave a poo-hm then?' he asks. I baulk. He is suggesting that I take the mic when the band have a break and recite a couple of my poems. Well, I only have one and the thought of delivering that in here makes my buttocks clamp so tight you could pop a bottle top between them. I may only be a week into the 'lighted half' of the year, but some time, some time soon, I have got to take that mic. I am suddenly struggling for air like a drowning man going under for the third and last time.

I mutter something about 'unfinished new material', but I am actually saved by a bagpiper who takes the stage at this moment. Calum spots him and turns to me: 'An instrument foo-hr the oh-pen air, a tha moors. Ut hus been a pleasure talking with a Manxman. Slantje-var.' He throws back his whisky and he is gone. I love the bagpipes, but Calum is right – it is an instrument for the great outdoors. It is no accident that the standard British hearing-impaired sign for Scotland is a pumping of the left elbow – that is, the putting of wind in the bagpipes. This tells us two things. One, that the bagpipes are Scotland's most identifiable icon, and two, that listening to them indoors makes you deaf.

Despite the double setback of having my equanimity rocked and my eardrums exploded, at £1 a 'wee goldie' of malt I struggle not to enjoy myself. A sign above the bar says 'Don't drink and die' – the 'r' and 'v' have been scratched out to create a message that might be more appropriate to this gathering. After Calum has legged it, I stick around and fall in with a few of his mates including Murdo, the portly middle-aged guitarist with the great voice. He was once, Calum had told me, a highly acclaimed Gaelic singer.

'Yes, I have wohn medals at the Mod, the Scaw-tish Gallic festival, and I heave trah-velled to higher-land und Wales und even to the mighty Lorient festival in Brittany. Haw, great times, but I am happiest here, having a pint and playing with good friends. Un ah hear you air a poo-ht.'

It is an extraordinary thing: I have been a poet for half a day and most of Stornoway seems to know. However, what is more interesting is the mention of the Lorient festival in Brittany, the great Celtic world-gathering where 400,000 people come together to see and hear 4,500 acts over ten turbulent days in early August. It is the biggest inter-Celtic festival by far and if I have an aim, it is that my poetry is in adequate shape for me to take the stage and perform at Lorient. It is three months away, but for all the progress I have made so far, it might as well be three years away.

At midnight, when the joint really is jumping, the shutters on the bar suddenly drop and the PA is switched off. That's it. The party is over. Just like that, because at midnight it is the Sabbath and in Stornoway it is observed.

The Sabbath is the day of worship, the day of rest from work and the one day in the week when you are supposed to keep off the turps. On the Seventh Day there is no running, no singing, no whistling, no humming, no buses, no planes, no boats, no dancing, no household chores. You can, however, read the good book. Note the definite article there. Don't think you can sit around and read *Catch-22* or Roddy Doyle or the *Viz Annual*. No, you may only read *the* good book, the Bible.

The Sabbath falls on the busy little town of Stornoway like a fire blanket on a banana flambé, snuffing out all activities not connected to godliness. To engage in proscribed activities, to tangle with the splintered forms of the radical Free Churches of Scotland and their fundamentalist Calvinism, is to pour petrol on the hell-fire as it rises to burn your bootstraps. So, when Chris, who I had been drinking with earlier, asks me back to his girlfriend's flat for an all-night party, I duck out of the back door of the club and run home to my hostel, feeling the flames of damnation licking my buttocks.

One of the great anomalies of the histories of the Celtic countries is that over half of them − Wales, the Isle of Man, Northern Ireland, Cornwall and most of the Highlands and Islands − embraced radical Protestantism so vigorously between the mid-1600s and the end of the nineteenth century. I guess the key to why they did so lies neatly in the umbrella title of protestant dissent: 'Nonconformity'. The Celts were fed up with the hierarchy of the Anglican Church and they refused to conform any longer. This is illustrative of a wider Celtic distrust of grand institutions.

However, the anomaly lies in how much the Calvinist doctrines that the dissenters preached − particularly the notion of self-denial − were at odds with the culture and much older hedonistic instincts of the Celtic peoples. The disdain that these independent Churches gathered for the traditional community pursuits – music, step dancing, singing, perhaps a little drinking, even poetry, and the centuries-old rituals and festivals that these pursuits manifested themselves in – did a very great deal of damage to Celtic culture. On the island of Skye, an eminent preacher set fire to a pile of fiddles and bagpipes as tall as a house, warning: 'Better is the fire that warms in the day of peace than the fire that consumes in the day of wrath.'

In many places, noticeably in Scotland, the Protestant Church dramatically changed the culture of the Celts. Even today, you can travel up the west coast of Scotland and in areas where Catholicism prevailed nearly everyone plays a musical instrument. The ancient tradition is undented. Elsewhere, the culture that the Fringe countries not only shared but which had survived astonishingly well over so many centuries took a big hit. It is only in the late twentieth century, with the decline of the authority of the Church, that these types of community-based cultural activities are returning so candidly, just as the festivals that celebrate them are being revived.

No less damaging is the fact that Nonconformism secured – for the Welsh, the Hebrideans and, to a lesser extent, the Manx and Cornish – the reputation as a dour, humourless, inhospitable, joy-killing people: a reputation that has survived to a great extent in the English perception of these peoples today, a reputation that is unjustified. If you look at country life in Wales and the Isle of Man before the advance of fundamental Protestantism, you see a people who were as apt to celebrate life as the Irish are today; a people who revelled in the ritual of social gatherings, drank plenty, made great music and ran around the woods in the nuddy, a lot.

The Protestant northern half of the Western Isles is the only place on the Celtic Fringe where Calvinism still reigns, and though it is weakening even here, you would still not streak around the streets of Stornoway on a Sunday morning. As I walk up towards the old people's home on the outskirts of town, fully clothed, I sense the air of reservation and propriety. The streets are dead, save for churchgoers. I spot four ladies in hats in a Morris Minor – a tremendous sight that reminds me of my youth. In fact, the whole feel of Stornoway on Sunday reminds me of Wales and the Isle of Man when I was a kid, which makes sense. They were like this then.

Much like any old people's home, I smell this one before I see it. I have come to visit a gentleman called Kenneth Smith, who is one of the 'village bards' that I have mentioned. He lived all his life in Earshader, a beautiful and remote spot on the west coast of Lewis. He never trained as a poet, and I believe his poems were never published until they were included in a book about the latest (and possibly the last) generation of Hebridean bards, which is where I read them. They are fine poems recording island life, written in the ancient bardic tradition, to be heard in the traditional ceilidh house. He is a man for whom poetry really did come as 'naturally as leaves to a tree' and I have come to pick his brains.

The nurse, who seems a good deal more excited about my visit than Kenneth Smith is, shows me into his bedroom and gees him up a bit. It is time to be frank, so I say, 'I have read some of your poetry. I am a budding poet from the Isle of Man and I am in need of a little advice. How do you do it?'

He looks long and hard at his slippers before he says, 'Och, it jeest comes. There is nooh easier thing in the wurld but tah write poo-htree.' This is encouraging. 'It was in ma people. My granduncle was a poo-ht and I had ma first poo-hm when I left school. The inspiration jus keem. Always be ready with peeper und pen, to respond to the strikes that poo-htree may make in the mind without fear and favour.' This is not so encouraging. As a journalist, I am never without pen and paper, but these 'strikes' just ain't happening. 'Hard, physical work dud help me. It does leave the mind clear. Write abooht that which is close abooht you. The nature, the comings and goings of people, the land, the sea . . .'

His mind wanders off here and his gentle eyes settle dreamily on the rhomboid of brilliant sunlight that the open window throws on the floor. We sit in silence. Great creases run down his face away from his nose. He has the face of a man who has had a hard life, facing the Atlantic. His hands, at toil every day for sixty years, look like museum pieces resting on the edge of the bed. Here is a man whose values and traditions and way of life stretch back generations, through centuries of minimal change to the rude nations of the first ages. If anyone can reasonably claim to share the bloodstock of the ancient Celts, this man can. Here is a real Celt. Watching him and thinking this make me feel, well, very un-Celtic. I do not simultaneously feel profoundly Anglo-Saxon or English. I just feel empty. I have so little in common with this man. To pretend otherwise is madness, and disrespectful. My skin comes alive with electricity, with fear and doubt. He looks up again, and in his eyes there is a fleeting glimpse of youth and clarity, the hint of a smile.

'Enjoy it,' he says. 'Enjoy writing poo-htree. I am having a little stretch now.' And with that he lies down and falls asleep.

Barra is a little gem – a bite-sized island at the southern end of the archipelago. It contains a bit of everything the Western Isles have to offer, all within one day's walk. There is a good-sized hill with an astonishing view over the great watery immenseness that surrounds Barra, some peatland bog busy with meadow pipits, long strands of pure white sand which make you think that your childhood was happy (one of which serves as the airport runway and flight schedules roll with the tides).

Walking through the shingle across the top of a stony cove on the east coast, I scuff my shoe throwing up a stone of exquisite beauty. It is the size of a milk bottle cap, perfectly formed and pearly white with iridescent waves at one end. I turn it over in my hand for a moment. I am about to drop it, to let it disappear back into the crowd, when I remember the crystal zipped up in a pocket of my rucksack. I press the pebble in beside it.

There are also acres of vivid yellow gorse smelling of coconut at this time of year, rhododendrons in fabulous bloom, the last of the daffodils on grassy banks, and areas of machair, the now globally rare habitat where, on this singularly fine day, I hear for the first time in my life the extraordinary call of a corncrake from within a bed of wild irises. I meet a shopkeeper who is wearing a tie. I pass ruined shielings, stone huts where shepherds and cattlemen would have passed the 'lighted half' looking after the animals on the high pasture. I pass local men who look like they are ready for a feed of roasted cormorant, and starving sheepdogs who gnaw feverishly at their kennels in an attempt to get out and devour my calves. All of this I see in one day – that is the joy of Barra.

Having spent a fortnight walking and hitching the length of the Western Isles from Stornoway, across the uniform watery heart of North and South Uist – a hard landscape for a hard people – I have come to appreciate the small things. The Western Isles are Europe's largest archipelago, in length, though not in landmass or population, I suspect. From the air, the islands must look like a giant camouflage jacket, so numerous are the lochs and rivers and inlets. It is a landscape reminiscent of the moon, before it became popular.

At the end of the day, as I stride back into Castlebay, I have sore feet and a terrible thirst. In the first pub I stop in, there is a group of musicians. They are from Ireland, over for a two-gig tour organised by Iomairt Cholm Cille, a cultural society, they explain, set up to build ties between the Gaelic-speaking communities in Ireland and Scotland. Dee is from Dublin and she plays the fiddle. She is fun and gorgeous and she reminds me of my wife, which makes me feel homesick for the first time in the three weeks I have been away.

The musicians are all slightly bemused by the whole trip – not least because they don't usually have the price of a pint in their pockets and this whole excursion is paid for. But they are enjoying speaking Gaelic with the locals. I pitch in with some Manx Gaelic, which throws them a bit. Sean is from Donegal and he tells me that his accent is most easily understood here in the Western Isles. They play a few of their songs – they are great musicians – and they invite me to come along tomorrow night and read a poem. I explain that my ferry leaves in a couple of hours, so I can't. But I do actually think about rearranging my ferry and staying. I have a new poem and I reckon it is halfway decent. I think I am ready to perform.

3

A Poem in the Applecross Inn

There is some dispute over where the Highlands of Scotland begin and the Lowlands end. Some say the dividing line runs from Stonehaven through Aberfoyle to Helensburgh on the west coast. Others insist the border starts at Loch Fyne and ends at Forres, via the Drumochter Pass. For returning Highlanders, it is the Corran Ferry that marks home. But in my opinion, this is a debate you need not involve yourself in. It is enough to know that it is a different place. Your time is better spent getting far, far into the Highlands because it is one of the most beautiful places on this planet.

It is the sheer pulchritude of the scenery and the remoteness that always draw me back. It is a remoteness that has changed little in the last 2,000 years. Calgacus, the Highland warrior chieftain, roused his men on the eve of a battle with the Romans in AD 83 with these words: 'We, the most distant dwellers upon earth, the last of the free, have been shielded until today by our very remoteness and by the obscurity in which it has shrouded our name.' It is this remoteness that has protected and maintained Celtic culture, including the languages, over the centuries. It is also the same remoteness that, in this age, draws clouds of heavily booted, neon-jacketed, hard-walking wilderness seekers to the Applecross Peninsula on the west coast, a remote part of the remotest parts. On an edgy day, in soft shoes and a cheap cagoule, I choose to join them.

The sign at the beginning of the track where I leave the road says: 'You are entering remote, sparsely populated, potentially dangerous mountain country. Please ensure that you are adequately

57

equipped to complete your journey without assistance.' I am so clearly not. I am not really equipped for a stroll along a trout stream in Hampshire, let alone a tough hill walk in Scotland. But the Celts are supposed to be a hardy people and besides, Mallory went up Everest in a tweed jacket. I think I can handle Applecross in a cagoule.

I am heading for the Applecross Inn where I know there is a session or music gig on this evening, during which, if I play my cards right, I hope to have my first tilt at reciting a poem. The Applecross Inn is one of the Highlands' more celebrated pubs. Actually, the Applecross Inn is one of the Highlands' few celebrated pubs. An unlikely and slightly distressing thing that I have learnt over the years travelling through the Celtic Fringe is that the pubs are terrible. The Irish are almost solely responsible for having us believe otherwise. But when it comes down to it, when you are on the hard road, hitching and walking, without a guidebook, taking the pubs as they come to you, then it hits you that even the pubs in Ireland are not up to much. Sure, the Guinness is always good and they will put ice in your Bulmers. Sure, what happens inside and who you meet make many of them special – 'the craic is mighty' as the tourist brochures now say – but the majority of Irish pubs are, in truth, short on attraction. In the Highlands and Wales, they are worse. In the Isle of Man – where poorly kept beer, grumpy landlords, the sounds of the early 1980s and adhesive carpets are the norm – they are worse still. An average evening in a randomly selected pub on the Isle of Man will have you stopping in a lay-by on the way home, priming your wrist and unwrapping a fresh razor blade. For all the stirring conviviality and alluring atmosphere you get in a Manx pub, you would be better off staying in and watching videos about famine in Africa to lift your mood.

A man who knows his pubs put me on the trail of the Applecross Inn, however. Fergie MacDonald has been a ceilidh bandleader for forty years and there are few venues in north-west

Scotland – pubs, village halls, boathouses, coal sheds – where he has not given his box a good squeeze. 'He is a true Highlander, a Gaidheal,' a friend had said. 'You must go down to Moidart on the west coast and speak with him.' I knocked on his door on a Wednesday afternoon, unannounced and uninvited, and on what was clearly a busy day – there was a stream of stalkers, business associates, family and neighbours needing to talk to him – but I was still ushered excitedly in for tea.

Fergie is only about my height, but he is twice the size, a great barrel-chested bear of a man with legs like trunks of ancient beech. His hands are remarkable – fists of muscle and bone hewn into shape by endless use. When he spoke, his hands flew about like a semaphore signaller on amphetamines, and when he made a point, a hand slammed down on the table top as his bum came off the chair, setting most of the contents of the kitchen quivering. Gaelic is his first tongue, so he spoke English with the airy, delicate pronunciation that I am now familiar with. In some ways, he is an archetypal Celt – of the type that now dominates the popular understanding of the word.

I asked him a question about how Highland culture had changed in his lifetime and within a minute of his answer we were back in 1745 with Fergie's ancestors and the Highland darling, Bonnie Prince Charlie, at the Jacobite rebellion that was so ruthlessly crushed by the English.

'Gaelic culture, Celtic culture, ituh began to die in the Highlands efter the '45. The burnings and the rapes in this veh-ry area were brrrew-htal, brrrew-htal. Yes, we'll no speak Cumberland's name without a spit still,' he said, walking to the back door to curl an oyster out on to the grass. Fergie spoke as if he had been there, on Culloden Moor. The MacDonald family history then roamed on through being standard-bearers to the Clanranald family (lairds of Moidart and much of the Western Isles for centuries) and involvement in the illicit whisky trade. With a gloomy but inevitable reprise, we hit the Clearances, the darkest episode in Highland history that saw the bulk of the Gaelic-speaking crofting community evicted from the Highlands and Islands in the late eighteenth century. They were replaced with sheep, owned by absentee English landlords.

History and in particular family history is fundamental to the Celts. As Robert Louis Stevenson wrote of the true Scot: 'there burns alive in him a sense of identity with the dead even to the twentieth generation.' I am not quite sure why this is but things that happened hundreds of years ago are recalled in songs, in poems and in conversation, with a familiarity that suggests they happened last week. To an Englishman or a Frenchman, this is quite weird. Few ethnicities are subject to their heritage, or derive their identity and sense of belonging from their place in history in quite the same way as the Celts do. If you went into a village pub in Leicestershire and asked a local about, say, the history of the parish church, he would not begin his account with the part his ancestors played in the Battle of Bosworth Field.

Is it because oppressed people recall their history more clearly? Or is it that political history is remembered when it is also family history? Whatever the reason, the Scottish Gaels have a unique ancestral identity and they can feel the fury of things that have gone to dust. The same could be said of any of the Celtic peoples, and listening to Fergie made me realise how little I know about my own family history. A sense of place and identity derived from family history is something I am without.

'And yahr a poo-ht, Paul?'

'It's Ned, actually. Yes, I am.'

'A poo-ht from the Ailah Man. That's good, now. And a rrrr-writer too?'

'Well, yes. And a writer too.'

'Oooh, y'ar a rrrr-writer too! Now, Peter, this is a moost remarkable coincidence. Yah-ra rrrr-writer and am lookin' fur a rrrr-writer, ta ghoost ma memoirs, the life and times of Fergie MacDonald, Highland ceilidh bandleader. So, it would only tek a week uhr two. You must stay here, of course, Donald, and each evening we can have a dram uhr two and I will tell ye the stories. Tis crew-cial y'agree. See uss a Manxman, Jimes, you will hev the humour. Un no one but a Ceilt wud hev ut. How remarkable y'ar here.'

I wanted to say that he had misheard me and that actually I am a waiter from the Isle of Man, not a writer, but there was no use. He was too canny for that, so I had to make other excuses, about long journeys and schedules and festivals to attend. He looked disappointed, but only for a moment. It would have been a lovely job, most likely, transcribing Fergie's stories, but I have Ned the poet to think about. Soon, we had a map out and we were plotting my journey north from Moidart. Fergie told me musicians to visit and the pubs to stop at.

'Ooh, the Applecross Inn,' he enthused, 'has the best food in the wuld, in the hool wuld. Un thee'll wulcume a poo-ht thar too. See, where thur's music, thar is often poo-htree as wheel. And am not wrong either, am not wrong.'

His words are ringing in my ears when I reach the top of the Bealach na Ba, the Pass of the Cattle, at the top of the Applecross Peninsula. It has been a long haul up here and I am beginning to fantasise about food. There is a break in the cloud, allowing me a glimpse of a formidable panorama. The two rugged peaks, Meall Gorm and Sgurr a' Chaorachain, rise either side of me. I see a stag but there is little else up here. No birch or Scots pine or rowan even, just bare moorland and the wind. To the east there are folds of mountains cropped by cloud and ranks of fading ridges. The Lochs are dotted with islands and emblazoned by pools of gold that have pierced the grey. This really is the edge, the fringe, the backside of Europe. On a day like this – the weather is still threatening something awful – it is not a place to linger, though I did read somewhere that children used to cross this peninsula just to get to school, which, I guess, makes me a big southern softie.

*

The village or community of Applecross is small. The village itself comprises one street – a church, a pub, a telephone box and a row of white cottages facing the ocean and the isles of Raasay and Skye. Up the hill above this is a campsite. There is a big house and a few cottages scattered nearabouts, but that is about it. It only takes me an hour after I have put my tent up to take in all the sights before I feel I can justifiably say I know Applecross and repair to the inn.

It really is an inn – two interlinked rooms and a couple of benches outside. Hot from walking, and smelling like a polecat, I take my first pint outside where I can make out the bluish outline of another corner of the peninsula and Raasay beyond, illuminated by the setting sun. The wrinkled sea, lit with purple patches, is lapping the shore at my feet – a fine accompaniment to the notes of the fiddle that are floating out of the pub through the heavy night air. Probes of golden light search out the road from the small windows. I cannot imagine a more perfect setting for a pub, nor a more gloriously Celtic scene. If a hobgoblin ambled past and tipped his felt cap at me, I would merely cock my head back and slosh my pint. Despite there being a change in the weather imminently, which always makes the consciousness particularly acute, I am happy: happy that I am soon going inside that pub to recite a poem.

It is the end of May. I have only been on the road for five weeks but I am leaving Scotland and heading south tomorrow. This night is then a fulcrum of my journey. So far I have managed every move and encounter in it. I have sat in cafés and on buses and in the corners of pubs, observing keenly, scribbling notes in my diary, listening in on other people's conversations, only emerging from my shadow to engage when I feel ready. This is the sort of anonymity that lone travellers treasure, and the sort of anonymity Ned Clague cannot have. The moment I clamber on a table and shout across the top of a pub, 'Listen up. I have a poem,' Ned is out there, known to all and a part-player in the whirling drama of a pub ceilidh.

The problem is getting out there. At the moment, no one knows who I am. No one is expecting me to stand up and read a poem. No one knows there is a poet in the pub. It would be the easiest thing in the world to bunk it, forget the poetry, have another pint and make up a bloody good story from a dimly lit corner table. I have to say it is tempting. But that is not my road, that is not Ned Clague's road. If I am going to get everything out of this summer, if I am going to perform at festivals and get up on stage in front of thousands of people at the Interceltique festival in Lorient in two and a half months, then we have got to get Ned 'out there' now.

'Issors busy as the devil's workshop ee thare,' a voice beside me says, making me leap and spill my beer.

'Am Alasdair.' It is the guitar player from the band.

'Hi, I'm . . . Ned. Great music.'

'Neh bother. Thanks for the pint.' I had bought a round for the band when I got myself a drink, as you should do at a pub ceilidh.

'Yon holiday then, eh?'

'No, not really.' I am not sure what I am going to say next here. 'I'm a . . . a poet, from the Isle of Man, and I'm travelling around, finding . . . inspiration for new material.'

'Aw, very good. I noor sumone from tha Isla Man. D'ya noo . . .' Alasdair says a girl's name but I have forgotten it before I even get a chance to process it. My mind is bouncing around now. Who ever said dissembling was easy?

'No, I don't think so. It is a small place, but not that small if you know what I mean.' I laugh; a small laugh that I am immediately aware most probably indicates that I am hiding a large truth.

The other two musicians walk out, slurping their drinks. 'Ian, Kelly,' Alasdair says, jabbing his roll-up at them, 'thus is Ned, from tha Isla Man. Heza poo-ht.'

They are all younger than me, and coolly dressed for this part of Scotland. Ian, who is wearing a Huggy Bear brown leather coat and has a genteel Edinburgh accent, pulls a joint out of his pocket.

'You perform the poo-hms then, Ned?' he asks, pulling the creases out of the joint and giving it a tap on the wall.

'I do,' I say, with a great deal of unnecessary reverence, like a woman who is marrying the wrong man.

'Fancy doin' one ee here?' Ian asks, turning towards the golden glow and the throaty babble coming from the pub.

'Why not? Just give me a shout when you are ready.' I am keen to change the subject of the conversation so I ask about their gig schedule. I am also keen to find a nappy big enough for a 175-pound baby. They are not actually a band. The three of them were thrown together for a wedding in Ullapool last night and, to make a weekend of it, they rang the Applecross Inn which is well known for music. They all live in Edinburgh and Kelly has played with Fergie MacDonald. The joint over, they agree to go back inside and crack on with the music.

As soon as they have gone, I pull a folded piece of paper out of my back pocket – my latest poem. I am still not even certain that I know it off by heart. The next problem I have is that some lines are in Manx Gaelic. I have pulled them from my phrasebook. Whilst it is good to have them in there, I don't have a clue how to pronounce them and there are sure to be a few Gaelic speakers in the pub. In fact, the poem even has a Manx title: '*Skeallaght ny Feayn-Skeallagh*'. It means 'History or Myth'.

Inside, the pub is heaving. Every table is taken with walkers, sailors and locals shovelling in the excellent food. The bar is three deep with men in thick sweaters waving empty pint glasses above their heads. I order a plate of langoustines, not because I am hungry – I just need to keep my mind off the poem. The band is a strange combination of guitar, fiddle and bongos. They sound good though. Every now and then, the ebb and flow of people clears a small space and someone has a quick step on the carpet dance floor.

I stand at the end of the bar next to Rory McKenzie, who sounds and looks like a character from the film *Whisky Galore*. He

has bright eyes, a grey beard and a laugh that would frighten a sil-
verback gorilla. He is a lifeboat man, he tells me somewhere
between nine and twelve times in the first five minutes of our conversation. He has had a few jars, jugs even, and I cannot help
wonder that you might be better off with plastic armbands if Rory
came to your rescue on the high seas in a storm. He grapples with
my Christian name for a while: 'Ted, is it? No, Ed . . . Bed, Bed?
What canna nem is tha'?' before deciding to call me 'Isla Man',
where, as he tells me with sweet remembrance of things past, he
lost his virginity to a girl from Portadown in a bus shed on
Douglas promenade on a hot summer's night in 1971. A nice
Celtic communing, I think. Fearing further tales of Rory's guide
to carnal knowledge *en plein air*, I excuse myself.

When travelling, it always seems easier to fall into conversation
with the young and the old. I suppose they are less inhibited about
tackling strangers. So it is good to be waved over by a couple about
my age when I am standing in the middle of the pub with my food,
looking stupid.

'Sit here. I'm Angus. This is Jean.'

Angus is a dentist in Aviemore. He is unmarried, wealthy
enough, adventurous and, like all good, modern Scots, he is deeply
in love with his own country. He spends all the free time that he
has exploring the Highlands – rock climbing, mountaineering,
skiing, mountain biking, walking – and he knows the terrain intimately. I am – I hold my hands up here – a complete bore when it
comes to maps, so I get one on the table pronto. Angus is a mine
of information, but I have to endure his peculiar habits to extract
it. Between pointing out great walks and trails across Scotland's
top end, he growls at Jean. She is Australian, younger and clearly
they have not been going out long. While he is then in the middle
of telling me about some famous ice climb on the north face of
Beinn Friggincold, or some such Munro, he suddenly straightens
his back, eyeballs Jean and goes 'Grrrr-gggrrrr-grraaaaah'. She
looks as embarrassed as I am. I just keep on peeling langoustines.

The other peccadillo he has is yelling encouragement to the band. There is nothing wrong with this in essence. Giving it a good 'eeee-yow' when the band change key or up the pace of the tune is an expression of unbridled delight at the music and part and parcel of a good ceilidh. Any crowd that does not respond to the rigours of the music vocally in this fashion is either dead, or, as the Highlanders will tell you, English. But Angus not only yelps out of time with the music or when a song is about to finish, he also makes the noise of a dog having his foot run over by a tractor.

On the dance floor, he is equally possessed. He leaps from foot to foot, whipping his heels up his backside, pogoing and almost cracking his head on the low ceiling. This display of freakish cavorting resembles a Chinese gymnast being chased around a telephone box by a policeman with an electric cattle prod. Poor Jean, who is pressed to dance with him, is entirely without Highland spring. She rocks gently from side to side as you might to a Suzanne Vega song. I give the relationship one month and put my maps away. There is a sudden end to this furious jig then Alasdair wheels round and nods at me.

Shit! I am on.

I am still fumbling in my pocket for the poem when I get over to Alasdair.

'Need a mic?' he asks, putting his guitar down.

'No, please. Yes, thank you. No, no. I mean, I don't think so.' His face briefly mirrors my own confusion.

'Need an intro?' he continues. 'Or willya jes gooferit?'

'I'll just go for it.' I take a big swallow, stand up and turn around. The volume of talking is very loud. Not a single person is looking at me. They are not expecting a poem. They just think the band is having a break and they are taking this opportunity to shout even louder at the person next to them. I am a very long way from having their attention. How to begin, then? I have not even thought about this. 'My king, fine champions, learned druids, great bards and silversmiths, hear me' . . . 'Oi, listen up, you honking mob' . . . 'Now then, will you hear a poem?'

I settle for the latter, which prompts a lone voice in the wilderness beyond the bar to reply 'Ab-soar-loot-lee nought!' Otherwise my introduction makes no dent whatsoever in the volume. There is only one thing for it: I lean back on my haunches and bellow as loud as I am able into the furthest corner of the pub: '*SKEAL-LAGHT NY FEAYN-SKEALLAGH*' and it is as if someone has hit the mute button. You could hear a countess fart. Sixty people are silent . . . for about three seconds, then the peals start coming back but I cannot hear because I am off now . . .

> *Jee banner mee, ghoinney*
> Another tall one he's tellin' ya.
> A pint for a myth et argute loqui
> The ancient spin-doctor, his tongue is cocky.

The chat is already creeping back, but Angus gives it a yelp from the wings. I presume he has just sat on a broken glass.

> Finn the fair one
> Keep yer hair on.
> It's not you, Finn –
> Just the age we live in.
> Tall tales from old men in tweed,
> Tomorrow's driven by reality need.

The pub runs left and right of where I am standing and as I swing to pitch words in either direction, the volume increases behind me. It is like fire-fighting two fires with only one water cannon.

> Dermot of the love spot
> I think not.
> Tain Bo Cualigne
> Who you be foolin'?

> Balor of the Evil-eye
> Anthropomorphic pie.
> The Ossianic cycle
> Are you takin' the Michael?
> Yn Moddey-dhoo
> A black dog that goes 'boo!'

'Dermot of the love spot' and 'Balor of the Evil-eye' – these are figures from early Irish myths. Similarly, the 'Tain Bo Cualigne' or the 'Great Cattle Raid of Cooley' is the wondrous and famous story from a series of part-historic, part-mythic tales known as the *Ulster Cycle*. These are some of the oldest surviving stories in Europe. And this is what the poem is about: the fine line in Celtic literature between history and mythology.

> Warp and weft of a nation's life
> Or bullshit tales of trouble and strife?
> History or myth?
> A draught of forgetfulness on all you non-believers.

There is a natural pause in the poem here, so I have a swig of beer to moisten the desert that is my mouth. Someone begins to cheer and I cannot tell if this is glee because the poem is over or a vote of appreciation. No time to find out, I am off again.

> I been there like, with the suits in the departure
>   lounge
> Sown in by Mannanan's cloak, trying to scrounge
>   the price of a cup of tea.
> I stood t'ward the gale on the pier
> Felt Aonbarr stride by, touched my fear.
> So I feel what I cannot see –
> Explain that to me.
> Stream of origin, crossbred and subjugated
> The Celtic tongue as the myth was elevated.
> When I go spiritual gardening

I meet Phynnodderee and geis and the sons of
   Turenn
And twisted bleeding trees. *Smooinee er shen.*
Degraded myth or history in the making –
If I don't find your god, am I forsaken?

'Yes you fuckin' are!' someone shouts from by the door. I catch glimpses of Rory McKenzie through the forest of faces. He is pointing at me, mouthing 'Isla Man, Isla Man'. I last spoke to him two hours ago and he was lashed then. One more swig of beer and we are on to the last verse, half of which is in Manx. I have to glance down at the piece of paper that is still quivering in my hand, even though the rest of my body is feeling hugely invigorated. I don't know if it is the challenge of holding the crowd, or just hearing my own voice belting out the words, but I suddenly feel physically ready for a wrestling match.

Cheayll me add tagglo Gaelg
Honnick eh ad hene ec y droghad.
Dy jarroo, cur jough da!

I am leaning up and out like the figurehead on a ship, towards the thickest part of the crowd, gesticulating with my fist and looking long and hard into the eyes of the listeners when a girl in the front row lifts up her T-shirt to show me her tits. Two large creamy, blancmange la-las in a creaking grey bra. The sight is enough to put an experienced performer off. The sight is enough to put Bernard Manning off. I hold on tight.

Jee banner mee, ghoinney
Another tall one he's tellin' ya.

A momentary panic. Have I leapt back to the beginning of the poem? I glance down at my piece of paper. No, I haven't. The first two lines of the poem are repeated at the beginning of the last verse.

The sword which no armour can resist.
Present is the child of the past
Darkness to darkness, you're ne'er the last.
The Celts are dead are they? No more to sing?
Think now and ask your mythical king.
This was the work of mighty men
When supernatural forces found the pen.

I am so nearly done. The last two lines. I give it a good lungful.

Sheegyn, ta mee credjal ayndoo
Charrey veen, what about you?

This means: 'Fairies, I believe in them. Now, my friends, what about you?' The idea was to end with a question, so I look enquiringly into the audience to see who is listening. No one. Even the girl who flashed her tits has left. There is some small applause. Ian pats my shoulder: 'Nice one, mun.' A couple of whistles. A cat is being castrated in the corner. Oh, no, that is Angus. But none of that really matters. What matters is that I have done it. I stood up in a pub full of strangers and read a poem. My poem. A few people listened. I didn't pass out. There is no damp circle on the front of my moleskin trousers. No one threw glasses. A girl flashed her tits at me. It is a success. I need a drink.

'A large single malt, please. You choose,' I say to the barman, and he comes back to me with half a tumbler full of peaty-coloured, antediluvian elixir.

'On the house . . . that's for the poem,' he says, smiling. 'Good man.'

4

Dancin' with Mighty Penglaz

The Penzance Express out of London slows to a funereal pace as it approaches the Brunel Bridge just past Plymouth. No doubt there is a speed limit for crossing the bridge, but it strikes me that the train is somehow easing up because it is glad to be leaving England and entering Cornwall, glad to be going home. The bridge, a high suspension over the Tamar River, looks something like the Loch Ness monster in profile and I shift around in my seat to get a good view between the curved pipes and girders. This minor commotion disturbs the tweeded old lady sitting opposite me. Lifted from her mid-afternoon reverie, she puts down her Indian novel, removes her half-moon glasses and looks long and hard up the muddied expanse of river. Then she sighs, a gentle but happy sigh, like the train.

'You're not Cornish, are you?' I enquire in my most polite voice. Certain that my mobile phone will not work once in Cornwall, I have been blathering into it most of the way and I suspect I am not her favourite train companion of all time.

'Huh,' she snorts. 'Most certainly am.' Then she thrusts the small badge on her lapel at me. 'What do you think that is . . . dunderhead?'

The badge – a white cross on a black background (white tin coming from black ore, they say) – is, as I ought to have guessed, the St Piran's Cross. St Piran was an early Christian saint who sailed to Cornwall from Ireland on a millstone and lived until he was 206. He is the patron saint of tin miners. The cross is the emblem of Cornwall or Kernow and something you see about rather a lot these days.

When I get off the train at Bodmin Parkway, the old lady peers at me over her specs and says, 'I hope you learn something while you are here, young man,' like she is talking to a spaniel puppy who is being dropped off at obedience school. Welcome to Cornwall.

A more logical progression of my journey south from Scotland would have taken me the twelve miles across the torrid waters of the North Channel, from the Mull of Kintyre to the coast of Antrim in Northern Ireland. From there it is an easy step either to Wales or to the Isle of Man, and so on, moving south. But there are two inherent problems in that journey. First, the festivals I want to go to do not fit that route. Second, as with the Gaelic languages and their dialects, the culture of these countries meld best with their immediate neighbour and a gentle progress through them would serve to highlight many of the similarities, which is fine, but it would also hide some of the differences. I am trying to find out if there is any real and defined unity of experience among modern Celts the whole way down the western edge of Britain and over to Brittany. I am looking for something that makes it a distinctive place, another country. I need to know if Stornoway and Penzance, where I am ultimately heading in Cornwall, do actually have more in common with each other than they do with either London or Edinburgh. I need to know what sets these realms apart in order to understand what brings them together.

Besides, I also wanted to drop in on my family in Brixton to reassure them that I am not yet entirely off my rocker. This was not a great success. I assailed my pregnant wife with poetry and uproarious tales of late-night pub drinking sessions and then complained about mild bowel irritation: 'You are drinking like a student and you have the body of a pensioner,' she said. 'Never mind Ned Clague, Rob Penn will be dead before Samhain, whenever that is.'

Applecross to Bodmin is only about 600 miles – a distance that you could knock off behind the wheel of a SUV in the Australian outback in an afternoon with a six-pack of Victoria Bitter. But it has taken me two and a half days (excluding the night in the marital suite), three trains, four hitched lifts, one aeroplane and it has cost the equivalent of the gross national product of a thriving Caribbean island. This has nothing to do with the Celts, or the Anglo-Saxons, or anybody in particular for that matter, but I have to make my point here – getting round the British Isles on public transport is sodding expensive.

The Cornish make much of being Cornish. What is amazing – and something that everyone who mocks them for emphasising this distinctiveness should think about – is that they are still doing so in the third millennium. The fiery impulse for independence and the stubborn pride – Celtic traits all over – are as emblematic of Cornwall as pasties and shipwrecks. Cornwall, the claw of England, projects from the mainland as if it is trying to get away, into the Atlantic. It is so nearly an island. The source of the Tamar River, the natural boundary with Devon for most of its course, is only four miles from the north coast. There is a nearby stream which rises and dashes down, north to Marsland Mouth. Were a trench dug between these two sources, a near impossible job since there are hills in the way, then Cornwall would be an island. More than a few Cornish people wish it were.

Questions of ethnicity are always more complex and messy than potted histories suggest. Cornwall's Celtic credentials are based, as with all the other countries', on the language and the fact that the Romans, the Angles and the Saxons never really pushed in and settled here, though they took over the rest of England and regularly popped over the Tamar for tin (for which malleable metallic element the Romans knew of the British Isles long before they invaded). The sense of Cornish independence was encouraged by the creation of the Stannaries (from the Latin word *stannum*, tin), which were tin-mining regions where the communities were so isolated that their customs and conventions were thought to require special jurisdiction. By a charter of King John, the lord warden of the Stannaries was empowered to try in special courts all cases except 'land, life or limb'. There was also a Stannary Parliament, which last met in 1752. Yet, despite this recognition of the individual nature of the county for a brief period of history, at all times before and after the Celts of Cornwall have been marginalised, ignored, defeated (there were a couple of hilarious Cornish uprisings in 1497 and 1549 which barely got out of the tavern) and suppressed by the Normans and the English. The history of Cornwall, like the history of the entire Celtic Fringe, is a story of erosion, of retreat and assimilation and diminution to the point where the language is dead and the county has been so extensively repopulated by the English that it is hard enough to find any Cornish at all.

So it is, I suppose, both remarkable and inspiring that Cornish consciousness is being revived again at the beginning of the twenty-first century. I wanted to lurch accidentally across the train and squash a large cream cake in the face of that lady, but at the same time I am compelled to admire her. She is part of a resurgence of belief in being Cornish, and I forgive her. The silly old cow.

This resurgence is prompted by all sorts of factors: globalisation, structural unemployment, second-home ownership and the fact that every family from Fulham spends all of August letting their Labradors turd above the high tide mark on the beach while they nibble ensalada of scallops pan-fried in ferret musk on the sun deck. The first three factors, in a sense, pressed the emergence of small territories and ethnicities all over Europe in the 1990s. They are not exclusively Celtic, yet Cornwall, or at least the Cornish, have suffered enough because of them. 'Cornwall is a kind of British Tibet,' a Cornishman who lived on my street in London once told me. 'It is far away. It is a very mystical, intensely spiritual place. People who don't live there value it more than the occupying force, that is the English to you. And the indigenous food is equally dreadful.'

Actually, I rather like Cornish pasties and I am eating one as I admire the roll of distinctly Cornish names on the war memorial on the main street in Bodmin. No one would suggest that the Cornish were, how can I put this tactfully, 'over-used' in the Second World War (unlike the Highlanders, who quite simply were – 'The second Clearances' is how Fergie MacDonald described it to me – and the Bretons, who the French used as 'bullet-meat' in the Great War) but the list is long enough: Tregonning, Trembeth ('Tre' is a Cornish prefix and it means 'farm' or 'settlement'), Trethewy, Trewin, Trebilcock. Trebilcock? Now there is a name. Sgt P. Trebilcock. Who said the Cornish don't have a sense of humour?

I imagine for a moment that it is my name. 'Ned Trebilcock, bard extraordinaire, how do you do?' A friend of mine works with a builder called Dwayne Trebilcock. Imagine being his teacher? Every time you tried to tell him off you would lose it. 'Are you flicking ink, Trebilc . . . phhwwht.' 'Sir, are you laughing at my name? Again?' I decide instantly that I have to meet my own real, live Trebilcock so I head off on a tour of the pubs of Bodmin.

In no time at all, I will settle simply for a Cornishman. There are very few about. In three pubs, a fish and chip shop and an Indian restaurant, everyone who serves me is either English or Bangladeshi. When I finally call it a night and start looking for a B & B, I am slightly drunk and slurring my words, which means the first two establishments I call at claim to be fully booked and turn me away. They are both run by thin-lipped, pale-faced English couples. At the third door, I am greeted by another thin-lipped pale-face but he is wearing fluffy purple slippers that are having a bad hair day. Things are looking up.

'Good evening. Are you called Trebilcock?' I ask.

'Oim sooray?' He is a Brummie.

'Are you called Trebilcock?'

'Naw. Smeeth.'

'I have to say it is a disappointment, but I will settle for a commodious room for the night.' A poodle passes slowly between us, on the way to lower its arthritic hips over the variegated cordaeums.

'Itz a beat loight, isn't it?'

'It's never too late, Mr Smith. Never too late to have a fling, for autumn is just as nice as spring. It's never too late to fall in love.'

'Thits a song frum moi woife's favereet musical. Yawd better cum een. Tek ure boots off.'

The living room is like a bad-taste parlour arranged by hip, glossy magazine stylists as an oblique joke at an ideal home exhibition: shag-pile carpet, pink suite, wall ducks, china commemorating royal divorces purchased from the back pages of the *Daily Dribble*, a set of Catherine Cookson novels bound in green faux-leather and embossed with gold, wallpaper with waist-high floral skirting and curtains that could completely unhinge you on LSD. On the sideboard there is a selection of grim family photos and my eyes settle on a girl in a tasselled mortarboard and gown smiling like she has won the lottery and, by way of celebration, popped a pair of lottery balls in her gob.

'That's ewer daah-ta,' Mr Smith says proudly.

'Really? She is very . . . do you think you could show me to my room.'

The problem about staying in B & Bs anywhere on the Celtic Fringe – though it is most acute in Cornwall – is that eight times out of ten you are staying in someone's dream home. What I mean is that the owners have moved here, retired or downsized, to live in their dream home and run a B & B to finance it. Thus, in practice, you not only have to hand over quite a lot of cash, but you also have to love their homes too. You have to pretend to love the rippling carpet, the Kimberley-Clark single sheet toilet paper dispensers, the pump-action bottles of soap, the neatly stacked copies of *SAGA* magazine by the bed, and the doorbell that plays 'Jingle Bells'.

'Do you like our little home, then?' the wife invariably asks as you are trying to press a blunt fork through a slippery processed sausage on your breakfast plate.

'Actually, no I don't and to make my point, I urinated in the bedroom sink three times last night and once this morning for good luck. Okay?' But I never say that. I lower my head, mutter something about 'How happy you must be' and continue chasing the sausage.

'Oir-roit, Meester Clig?' Mr Smith asks when we arrive at my bedroom having done a tour of the house taking in fire escapes, ablution procedures, breakfast roll-call and the failed marriage of his eldest son. The effect of the beer and the over-eager central heating leave me feeling nauseous. 'Full inglish, is it?'

'I think I'll skip breakfast, actually. Goodnight.'

In a bookshop in Bodmin the following morning, I pick up a copy of *Bodmin Moor: The Earth Mysteries – A comprehensive illustrated guide to the alignments, ley paths and anomalous energies at ancient sites in the North Cornwall area* – which is a nice, snappy title. The book is full of slightly bewildering prose ('an harmonious pattern of land and sky and stone') and advice ('leave only your footsteps' . . . 'find this haven of peace in a troubled world' . . . 'glimpse back into a time when humankind had learnt how to be in harmony with the environment and to love and revere Mother Earth'), but it does tow a sort of middle line between archaeology and 'Earth Mysteries' which suits me.

By the time I get up on to Bodmin Moor, beyond the hawthorn trees which are still covered in their creamy white flowers, the rain has set in and the squelch under my feet is intensifying. This is a squelch I know well. The Isle of Man sounds like this. The Western Isles sound like this. In fact, most of the Celtic Fringe sounds like this: the watery, frothing gurgle of a boot being planted on land that is, at best, half earth and turf and half water. This may well be the definitive sound of my journey and, when I am done, Ned's epitaph may read: 'Mind your feet for here lies Ned Clague the Bard – phew, what a squelcher.'

The rain is familiar too. It is a June kind of rain. In terms of the water that it bears, it is somewhere between mist and drizzle. The droplets of precipitation are so thin that they appear to be suspended in the air, rather than tumbling from the heavens. This type of rain barely dimples the puddles or speckles a Rizla, but after an hour of walking in it, I am soaked through several layers of clothing and my skin is clammy white. A friend who lives on the Pembrokeshire coast – so he knows a thing or two about Celtic weather – suggested, before I started this trip, that I get the whole thing sponsored by ibuprofen and Gore-Tex, as I would be standing around hung over in the rain so often. I now wish I had taken that advice. The Irish, as we all know, would call this a 'soft day'. I call it a 'dog day' because you end up smelling like a dog – more precisely, like a wolfhound that has been lost on a bog in County Offaly for several days. The very worst thing about this rain is that it will not shift. It arrives imperceptibly, like a periodic spell of depression (which, in my case, often accompanies it), and when you are deep inside it, it is difficult to imagine that it will ever end. It turns Bodmin Moor into a charcoal drawing that has been smudged by a damp tweed sleeve.

What the hell am I doing here then? Well, I am going to see some standing stones then I am going to visit Dozmary Pool. But why? I have got the fruity guidebook. I could sit in the pub and read all about it over a nice pint of Jenners. The 'why' is not so easy to answer.

The word 'Celtic' inspires today a whole host of images and thoughts, quite different images and thoughts to those that the same word inspired only twenty years ago. In that period of time, there has been an explosion of self-asserting Celtic identities, making the term problematic and ambiguous. I suppose the concept of 'Celticity' has been unanchored. It has become contested. It is no longer specifically an ethnic concept, associated with language. The main confusion has come from the rise and rise of 'Celtic spirituality' or 'New Age philosophies' that promote a rediscovery of the self and claim to have their root in a state of mind that reflects the ways of the ancient Celts.

New Age Celts are pagans, in a religious sense, and they worship – my understanding is pretty shoddy here – 'Mother Earth' as my guidebook has it, and nature. The worship of nature necessarily includes in the modern world a search for the sense of life on earth, a search for the old ways, for a simplicity that we have all too hastily forgotten. The New Age Celts believe that the last people to embody these ways and spiritual beliefs in the British Isles in significant numbers were the ancient Celts. Thus the neo-pagans adopt the badge, and certain accoutrements, of Celticity. The confusion comes from the fact that these people are a hotch-potch of ethnicities and are far from being exclusively from Celtic countries in origin. They are also carefully selective about the aspects of ancient Celtic culture they include in their own. Not least is the oversight that the Celts of ancient Britain reached a golden age, the last great flowering of the Celtic civilisation, under Christianity. This is most notably manifested in the illuminated manuscripts such as the Book of Kells and the Lindisfarne Gospels: these books are the ultimate, concentrated digest of everything that ancient Celtic artistic expression intended, and the zenith of their artistic achievements. Many of the immediately visual connotations of the word 'Celtic' today – curvilinear ornamentation, concentric circles, revolving spirals and whorling capital letters, for example – come from these manuscripts and in an ironic twist they emblazon the T-shirts and jewellery of the neo-pagans. I don't know, it may just be me, but something of the tension of these exciting patterns is lost or devalued when they are so widely reproduced.

Twenty years ago, it was easy to categorise the Celts. There were the ancient ones and the modern ones who occupy the politically created ghettoes of the Atlantic coast of north-west Europe. But now you also have to consider the New Age Celts. It would be very easy to write them off as the children of post-modern culture who have collectively suffered some sort of fundamental panic attack, who can't handle the pace and the surge of twenty-first-century society, who have misappropriated ancient Celtic values of pagan spirituality and the importance of the 'self' to substantiate their drug-soaked lifestyles. But I am not going to do that, tempting though it is. Oh, no. In their own fashion they have contributed to the flowering of the 'New Celtic Age'. I have got to find out about them, include them, and visit places to which they attach spiritual significance. Hence, squelching across Bodmin Moor in the rain when I could be keeping good tavern company.

When I get to the Hurlers, a triple circle of standing stones on a noticeably bleak bit of moor, I read in my magical mystery guide that it is not Celtic anyway. The site predates the Celtic era by a good few thousand years. Great! Like Stonehenge, it has only been associated with the Celts in modern imagination. I get the hump about this but then I read something that I did not know. The legend, and the derivation of the name, is that a group of lads were playing a game of hurling on the Sabbath and they were turned to stone. This is the appropriation of a pre-Christian site by Christian morality, something that is common all over Celtic Christian Britain. What is more interesting is that the Cornish once played hurling. This is something I did not know. The Manx called it cammag and played the game up until the nineteenth century. The Highlanders call it shinty and still play it and it remains the national game of Ireland, where it was invented. It is as old as Irish history and it figures in many epic Irish myths.

I saw a hurling match once, in Ireland. It is a truly mad game, something of a violent marriage between hockey and lacrosse for people who don't care about their teeth. It makes rugby, the most physical game I ever played, look about as dangerous as having tea and scones with your great-aunt. Who the hell else but the Celts would play a game like this? The Australians might, but most of the first settlers there were Irish jailbirds anyway, so they don't count.

As I walk towards the middle of the moor, the cloud lifts from time to time and there are extensive views. The landscape reminds me of the Western Isles. It looks old. It feels restless, like the Cornish people. Eventually, Dozmary Pool comes into sight as I cross the top of Brown Gelly Downs. The pool is most readily associated with King Arthur. You cannot go anywhere in the Celtic Fringe without coming across the legend of King Arthur, though it is kept most vigorously alive in Wales, Cornwall and Brittany where there are dozens of places associated with him, some of which are interesting archaeological sites in their own right while others are grotesque theme parks trading on 'Celtic mist'.

After Arthur's death, the legend of Dozmary Pool goes, Sir Bedivere comes to the lake (though you would hardly call it that) three times with the sword, Excalibur, then throws it into the water from whence comes the hand of the Lady of the Lake to seize it. The hand wheels the sword three times before disappearing with it. (The ancient Celts loved the number three, I have noticed. It pops up in their myths regularly.)

I walk around the pool – it only takes ten minutes – towards the one, low stone cottage that fronts it. Though it is a dim day, there are no lights on in the cottage so I presume it is unoccupied. I am standing directly in front of it, thinking that Dozmary Pool is not exactly the beautiful and atmospheric place I had anticipated, when a figure appears next to me. And I mean appears. The ground at the pool's edge is rough, dotted with rocks, and damp, but I do not hear anything until this person is standing on my shoulder, like he is making ready to pick me up and hurl me in.

'It is a special place, huh?' the voice says, startling me. He smiles a lean, tanned and reassuring smile.

'I don't know. Is it? I would like to see the Lady of the Lake to be sure,' I reply, smiling back.

'The legend of Arthur is not important here. This is a place of healing. It has been for thousands of years. The Excalibur story has it that the lake is bottomless. It dried out one summer a few years ago. Hah!' He laughs and great muscles, taut like piano wire, protrude from his neck. He has the physique of a Tour de France cyclist and there is a central European clip in his speech. His eyes are very, spookily clear.

'I am Walter,' he says, offering a powerful hand which I am invited to place mine in and have it pulped. 'This is my house. You are welcome to camp here. I don't charge.' Round his neck, mounted in a wooden square the size of a matchbox, is a shaped rock – a Stone Age tool, he explains, dug up nearby.

'Do people still come here to be healed?' I ask.

'Sure, all the time. Look, five years ago I broke my back in a climbing accident. Every day I lowered myself into the water for an hour. Three weeks later, I was riding a horse. The doctors were astonished. I was astonished. Like I say, people have been coming here for thousands of years. Who are we to say it has no power because modern science can't explain it? So I can't explain it, or understand it, but it happened. Close your mind to it' – his eyes settle on me now – 'and it won't.' Then he wanders off behind the cottage and I hear geese protesting noisily.

My wife is having a scan of her tummy today. I glance at my watch – about now. There was a problem with the first scan. The probability of the baby suffering from Down's syndrome was way too high for a woman of her age. There is a further test she could have had at that early stage of the pregnancy but this substantially increases the risk of a miscarriage to one in two. After days of agonising, we decided to do nothing. The scan today will tell us whether the baby does have Down's syndrome. I pick up a stone and flip it up and down in the palm of my hand for a minute then I hurl it out into the lake. No white hand comes up like Derek Randall pouching a catch out of the air at midwicket. It just lands in the water – splosh! – that is all. Then I pick up another stone, a smooth, flat grey one, and I pop it into the pocket of my bum bag, where my Beltane crystal and the Barra pebble are. Stones from sacred places are deemed in Celtic tradition to be empowered by their place of origin. I suppose this is a form of spiritual gardening. Feeling slightly self-conscious, I start walking off and with my second stride I hit a rock square on with the toe of my boot and prostrate myself heavily on the floor.

The scan gave the baby the all-clear, which is a colossal relief, but I am trying not to read too much into this. The most amazing thing about Dozmary Pool – and I only realise this long after I have left – is that I had it to myself (once Walter had gone off to talk to his animals). There was nobody else there, on a June afternoon, albeit one that felt like New Year's Day in Alaska. Also, apart from Walter's cottage which was half burrowed into the land like a Welsh hill farm, there were no buildings. There were no cars, no car park, no ice cream vans, no souvenir shops, no guided walking tours, no Land-Rover tours, no wheelie bins, no join the 'Nationalised Trustafarian Fund for Pointless Preservation' welcome committees, no signposts or adverts or warnings or Arthurian replica chess sets in purple quartzite with prancing pawns. There was just me, Dozmary Pool and what I wanted to make of it all. And this, I have to remind myself again, is Cornwall, where tourism rules.

I guess the answer to the small Cornish riddle that causes this vacuum of humanity at Dozmary Pool lies only ten miles to the west of Bodmin Moor, on the north Cornish coast, in the village of Tintagel – a real 'emmet' honey-pot. Emmet is a Cornish term for 'tourist' though it means a bit more than that. It is actually the old English word for 'ant' and it has been subsumed into the Cornish vernacular. It is oft spoken and means something like 'grockle'. Make no mistake, it is not a term of endearment, and as far as the hardcore Cornish go, if your family have not been living on Cornish soil, uninterrupted and without excursion over the Tamar for 700 years, then you are an emmet.

Cornwall, like all the countries of the Celtic Fringe, has never been rich in anything. There was once tin and briefly copper, but they have disappeared and the derelict relics of the mining industry scatter the landscape like the battered castles of a subjugated people. There are still some fish, but the pilchards have gone and only a handful of fishing boats continue to scratch a profit from the sea. Celtophiles everywhere will tell you that their countries have always provided raw materials, whether it is coal or soldiers, for the advancement of their dominant neighbour and imperial ruler. They have always been extracting and never creating. Which leaves tourism in the modern age. It is the only consistent growth industry up and down the Celtic Fringe. The emmet industry is then essential for the economic survival of Cornwall, but it is bad for self-esteem. It is corrosive and corrupting. It sterilises the people who work in the industry. It feeds on ludicrous stereotypes – the innumerable and atrocious homemade 'famine' museums in rural Ireland spring immediately to mind.

Something that the modern Cornishman – and in truth this goes for many a modern Celt – cannot be accused of is failing to capitalise on the renaissance of interest in the romantic image of the Celts. Unfortunately, this all too often spills over into parody – and nothing makes the cash registers ring quite like Celtic parody.

In summer, the pretty lanes, the car parks, beaches, pubs, footpaths and teashops from Devon to the Minack Theatre are rammed to the hilt with emmets. There are stockbroking emmets, with their hip teenage children heading for Rock. There are Cockney emmets cramming pasties into their rubicund faces on the esplanades. There are green-fingered emmets heading for the Eden Project, yachtie emmets in practical shoes, and Brummie emmets on the same coach tour of Cornwall that they have taken every summer for sixteen years. During the emmet season, there are emmets absolutely everywhere, and absolutely every single emmet passes through Tintagel.

I am heading there now and the young surfer who picks me up

in his old French bread van looks concerned. At a crossroads in Trewarmett, he reluctantly tells me that I have to get out.

'Tintagel's that way,' he says, pointing a bronzed arm down a lane with tight sprouting hedgerows. 'I can't go there and if I was you, I'd stay clear too.' It is as if I am heading for Soweto with a Rolex on each wrist. 'That's your warning now. They call it the "emmet enema". Beware.'

The actual history of Tintagel goes something like this: in the fifth and sixth centuries AD it was a trade port, from where tin was shipped to the Continent, as evidenced by the rich remains of Mediterranean pottery which were presumably vessels for carrying the imports. Some time in the thirteenth century, Earl Richard of Cornwall built a dramatic cliff-hanging castle, scant ruins of which still crown the headland beyond the village. And that is about all we know. The associations with King Arthur are solely attributable to one Geoffrey of Monmouth (a Breton brought up in Wales who became a bishop), who wrote the *History of the Kings of Britain*, a great historical work of the twelfth century and much later exposed to be a load of old wives' tales. Not one vestige of evidence to corroborate the legend that Arthur was born at Tintagel has emerged since. But the English perception of the Celtic Fringe is, at best, one of fictional kingdoms of romance, steeped in myth and wizardry. Tintagel fulfils this stereotype perfectly.

Thus this little Cornish village facing the Atlantic has become a must-visit for romance-seekers and legend-lovers, and no one who coins in the cash here would have anyone or anything disrupt that. English Heritage, who manage Tintagel Castle, actually call it, on their flyers, 'King Arthur's legendary birthplace'.

Struggling against the tide, I wade into Tintagel. The first thing that assails me is that every pub, hotel, shop, restaurant, B & B and street has a name associated with the Arthurian legend. The Earls of Cornwall get no mention. So you have King Arthur's Castle Hotel, the Camelot Hotel, Merlin's amusements,

Guinevere's lounge bar, Avalon crafts, Dragon's Breath Gallery, King Arthur's Arms (where Arthur Vision presents Premier League soccer on wide-screen TV), the Excali-bar, Sir Geraint B & B, Pendragon Paraphernalia. I can't find Sir Lancelot's latrines, but I am sure they are here somewhere. It goes on and on.

The only shop I can find on the main street in Tintagel without a Knight of the Round Table prancing in the window is Granny Wobbly's Fudge Pantry which I immediately grace with my custom. With a pocket full of provisions, I head for the castle. It is about a mile from the village along a wide, well-maintained though steep track. In essence, it is no more vigorous than walking round Hampstead but there is still a Land-Rover bus shuttling the infirm and the merely fat up and down the hill.

My first stop is Merlin's Cave which is wonderful, but much like any other sea cave: dank, dark at the back, smelling of decomposing seal blubber and expertly able to echo very crude expletives. I then ascend the steep flight of steps to the castle on the promontory which is only attached to the mainland by a slim bridge of land. The views from the top along the Cornish coast are marvellous. It is a fabulous position. That said, I can think, off the top of my head, of a dozen fortresses within Britain that occupy equally breathtaking positions and which would be empty today. This confirms what I have suspected all along: that we are all here, me and several hundred other emmets in inappropriate footwear, sucking fudge, because of the modern Celtic spin put on the legend of Arthur.

Back in the village I join the throng of boiled sea crustaceans in human form and go shopping. To render some order to the experience, the shops are full of notices that say 'Do not touch', 'No push chairs', 'Please do not sit on this ledge', 'Leave all your money here and shove off home, you emmet'. Inside the shops, the shelves are loaded with an overwhelming tide of distasteful 'Celtic' replication tat. Inside the first 'Gifte Shoppe' a CD called *Celtic Sunrise* is playing. The music prompts me to think of euthanasia. I eye up a wine goblet set bearing the baronial emblems of the Knights of the Round Table and a collection of swords – full-sized weapons – called 'The Lionheart', 'The Conan' and 'The Odin'. There is a 'hand-painted' *Lord of the Rings* chess set next to a tray of jewellery and pottery so giddy with whirling Celtic motifs that I begin to wonder if that fudge was spiked with hallucinogens.

After three shops I have seen enough. There is nothing on sale which is either historically accurate, factually correct or worth buying. The emetic mish-mash of myth, distorted history and Tolkien, all being sold under the misrepresentative banner of Celtic memorabilia, is so confusing that it is no small wonder that the history of the Celtic peoples continues to be utterly misunderstood. Feeling a little sick (of course, that could be the pound of Granny Wobbly's fudge that I have wolfed), I totter out of town.

Like Brittany and to a lesser extent Wales, the map of Cornwall is dotted with the fabulous names of dozens of Celtic saints – Petroc, Gwethinoc, Breock, Issey, Cadix and Finbarr to name a few – most of whom were never recognised by Rome and whose names are unheard of outside the Celtic Fringe. Many of these itinerant gospel spreaders, like St Petroc for example, were Welshmen who had been educated in the monasteries of Ireland – which wraps up into a nice little Celtic parcel. What is also interesting about these pilgrim saints is that they were very adept at performing miracles. In all their stories, what we would call 'magic' is interwoven with the Christian faith; for the Celts this was a happy marriage. The saints also conveyed knowledge of herbs and natural remedies for ailments that were the inheritance of an older lore, which through them was not entirely lost in the Dark Ages.

The period AD 450 to AD 600 has been dubbed the 'Age of the Saints' within the Celtic Fringe, because so many of them were on the move (Irish monks were taking the gospels to Scotland at the same time), though it is possible to see the voyaging saints as part of two greater migrations: that of the Scotii from northern Ireland to the Isle of Man and the west coast of Scotland, and that of the Welsh and Cornish to Brittany.

The Christian saints in Cornwall have recently been celebrated with the development of a long-distance footpath called the Saints' Way which runs from Padstow to Fowey. It may or may not have been a footpath frequented by miracle workers in the Dark Ages, but it is undoubtedly a route that generations of travellers – traders, drovers, pilgrims to Santiago de Compostela – heading between the Celtic Fringe and continental Europe would have taken in subsequent centuries, when sailing round Land's End remained risky.

On another day of filthy weather I set off along it. Once again, so much is familiar: the rain, the stone four-hole and wheel-head crosses beside the way, crimson and pink valerian sprouting from the walls, St John's wort which is blooming yellow just now, and bell heather, the nectar from which the ancient Celts apparently used to make ale. In the lush gardens, beyond the hedgerows, are camellias and rhododendrons and stunted palm trees, which thrive in the temperate climate that the Gulf Stream brings to the Celtic Fringe. I see swallows flying low, so worse weather to come, and I hear the high-pitched call of a wren. One of the weirder Manx and Cornish folk-beliefs was that the wren's feathers would protect people from drowning and they hunted this tiny bird until the nineteenth century.

In Lanivet, I feel that I have finally arrived in a Cornish village. The pub, where there is a darts competition going on, is thick with Cornish accents. I mention this to the barman and he says, 'Wherv ya bin, boy? An ah coast? Ain't no Cornish dine thur noo. Ain't no Cornish can afford a live an ah coast anymore. Em Cornish at is left is dine Redruth un Camborne. Youz wanna git dine thur, boy.'

I take the advice. I abandon walking the Saints' Way in the morning, as casually as I began it, and I head south-west along the industrial, scarred spine of Kernow.

Most people talk about Redruth and Camborne the way people talk about downtown Detroit or the East End of Glasgow. Actually, Redruth is very nice. From 1740 to 1860 it was a hugely prosperous place, sitting in the middle of what was then the richest mineral ground in the 'Old World'. The Victorian Age brought fine buildings, the railway and prestigious institutes that teach mining. At its peak, the area around Redruth, including the granite heights of Carn Brea, Carnmenellis and Carn Marth, produced two-thirds of the world's copper. In 1866 labour-intensive copper mining collapsed overnight (copper deposits were found near Lake Victoria and tin was found in Malaysia) and a third of the mining population migrated to the corners of the British Empire where their skills were still needed. One does not readily associate Cornwall with a great migration, but the number of Cornish Societies in Australia, for example (the largest Cornish festival on earth takes place near Adelaide), is testament to the fact that they sailed in their thousands.

Not much has happened in Redruth since. Most of the shops on the high street look like they last opened in 1866. It is the sort of place where people faint if you pull a twenty-pound note out of your wallet. The single addition, it seems, in the last hundred years is the Library of Cornish Studies, which is superb. I spend a happy afternoon in here, rummaging in interesting pamphlets and setting the poor librarians off on searches for poetry books that I subsequently realise I have invented in my own tiny little mind.

The B & B I book into is run by a Cornishwoman; in fact, everyone in Redruth is Cornish. There are no emmets. It's bliss. She sounds perfectly okay when I telephone but I discover she is as mad as a cut snake when I get to the front door.

'Hi, I telephoned about the room,' I say innocently enough.

'Can you sing?' She actually sings this, throwing her shoulders back and waving at a gawping pedestrian.

'Um, well . . . one song. "Don't think twice, it's alright" by Bob

Dylan. That's it, and I warn you, I don't sing that very well. But I am a poet, from the Isle of Man.'

'He'sa bloody port with no tail,' she yells back down the hall into a room where laughter is mixing with Elvis Presley.

'Is it karaoke night?'

'Naw. It's our Ben's birthday. He's a' – she starts singing again – 'a singer on a cru-uru-uru-ruise ship.' Then she stops suddenly and continues perfunctorily, 'Anyway, he's awv un tha Caribbean. Yous look ahright. You'd better shift in.'

Twenty minutes later, after two plates of bacon, eggs, sausages and chips, three cups of tea and a large vodka and Coke, I am standing on a chair in a pink afro with a blow-up plastic guitar thrown over my back, having sung the Bob Dylan song, reading a poem. I read '*Skeallaght ny Feayn-Skeallagh*' and they, Pam, her two sisters and three children, fall about laughing. I had never really thought of it as funny, but there again, I have never had to recite it in a pink wig.

At 7.30 p.m., after two more tumblers of vodka, I have to go out to meet the parents of a girl I knew when I worked as a solicitor. I am greeted there by the sound of popping corks. Very kindly, they invite me to stay for dinner and by the time we sit down at the table, the old boy and I have had a bottle and a half of wine each. I spend forty minutes forking risotto on to my lap and then I walk into two doorframes trying to leave. I came to talk to them about Cornwall and how it has changed but I can't remember a damn word either of them says. The ten-minute walk there takes me an hour back. I get lost once and I stop for a snooze on a bench, but just as it would probably be if you stumbled into a ghetto in Detroit at night, it is as safe as houses.

It takes me another week, but I finally work my way as far south as the Land's End peninsula: a place, like the sea, where death is ever-present. There are ancient barrows and chambers and burial stones galore. I spend a couple of lugubrious days wandering around here, but all the time I am heading for a place that is related to birth, which is a cheering thought.

Madron Well has been venerated for at least 1,400 years. This much we know, though it is not unreasonable to speculate that the site has attracted worshippers of some description for much, much longer. As with so many Celtic places (particularly sacred places that were later subsumed for Christian use) no one is sure where the name derives from but it is most likely either from Maduin, a Breton priest who died in the sixth century, or it is named after Mabon ap Madron, a pre-Christian Celtic deity. It is a baptistery well and it is still in use today, or so I have been told. Children are baptised at a small stone font within the low, remaining walls of a tiny chapel.

In modern times, it has evolved into a rag well. According to superstition, tying a piece of cloth that has been next to an injured or diseased part of the body on to a tree near a healing well will lead to recovery from the affliction. As the cloth naturally degrades, so does the illness, which means if you tie a piece of Gore-Tex up, you should be right in a thousand years.

The pagan Celts worshipped water – springs were portals to the 'otherworld' – and when Christianity reached Britain, innumerable wells and springs were kept in use as places of reverence. The whole of Britain is actually dotted with places like Madron Well, though many were destroyed during the Reformation and it is in the outermost reaches of Britain and Brittany where they have survived best, in their traditional form, encouraging what is a curious mixture of early Christian and late pagan worship. The reverencing of sacred springs has proved to be the most persistent pagan practice in these isles.

I reflect on this when I arrive at the muddy path that leads away from the road. My legs are tired from walking on the moors all day. There is a beaten-up old signpost to the well, but nothing else to indicate that a site of worship of such longevity is here. I head along the path. The moss-covered boughs of old trees and hawthorn bushes crowd about the track, creating a tunnel where the air is perceptibly heavier. I have read about the numen or *anima loci* of ancient places in, let me say, unscientific books. The *anima loci* is the 'place-soul' you might find at a revered site, as opposed to the plaice and sole you might find in a good fish shop. It is the spirit of a place; the personality and qualities that a locality has and which come into being when we acknowledge or honour them. And if you think this has the whiff of the David Ickes about it, if you think this is the sort of mumbo-jumbo that goes with mung beans and Carlos Castaneda, then worry not, because so do I.

At least, so did I. I have to say that within minutes of starting along the track towards the well, I am transposed from the lane and the moor and what I have been thinking about all day. The whole world out there completely recedes. I do not know if, because of all the walking and the camping I have been doing, I am getting more in touch with my senses and with nature. I do not know if, because of what I have been reading about and whom I have been talking to, my Celtic psyche is developing – but walking down the footpath to Madron Well, I feel something. A spirit? Perhaps it is simply that I am in a beautiful place and in the right mood. The air beneath the canopy seems to go taut, as if a storm is coming. My breath quickens. I look over my shoulder and snag my rucksack on a branch, which makes me jump. There is something around me. Perhaps goddesses do dwell here? Perhaps the centuries of veneration and the hordes of ancestral worshippers have left the place with a distinct aura that is strong enough to register with human sensory perception? My skin is tingling. Why not? After all, I feel something when I walk into, say, Canterbury Cathedral or Hagia Sofia in Istanbul. The sanctity of places causes us to withdraw intellectually and emotionally from the power of our senses, somehow making the past more important. What I am experiencing is a tangible feeling – magical and really rather odd. And no, I have not been taking drugs.

Before I reach the spring, the votive rags tied to the trees begin. One or two stray ones, then a few dozen, then as I near the end of the path, a cloud. There are not tens of rags as I had expected, but tens of thousands of rags tied to the two dozen trees in the short distance between the spring and the walls of the chapel. The rags are every colour. There are strips of cotton and silk, tears of handkerchiefs and scarves, a sock, a black stocking, shoelaces, single threads of wool, tinsel, clothes labels, pieces of tissue, hair bands, beads, a strip of leather, a tartan thong, some grey underpants, pieces of rope, a bra, a Sainsbury's receipt, plastic bags, the bottom of a pair of jeans and a piece of tissue with what looks like blood on it. This may sound like the produce from half an hour rummaging on a rubbish tip the size of the Scilly Isles outside São Paulo somewhere, but viewed collectively, hanging in the trees, it does not look like rubbish. It looks like what it is: a vast collection of votive rags hung by eager visitors.

There are even some handwritten notes wrapped up in plastic. Unable to restrain myself, I uncurl a couple: 'I wish with my heart that Sarah and I can sort things out and spend the rest of our lives together,' reads one, 'I wish that my Mum recovers from cancer,' another, and a third, 'I hope my GCSEs is all A.' Er, not in English, my lad, unless the examination board really surpass themselves with cock-ups.

The stream flows through the chapel and a small granite stone font. I sit here for what seems like a few seconds, but it is actually half an hour before I realise that I have been off on a wild daydream. I was thinking again of Walter at Dozmary Pool, and then of the procession of ages that has walked the same narrow path from the road to here, and sat in this very same spot in the hope of being healed. Today, everything we learn encourages us to rationalise all that we see against what we know. The breadth and depth of human knowledge breed in us an arrogance that leaves us reluctant to let go of this interpretive approach and simply experience things. Madron Well, like Dozmary Pool, has been a place where people's most crucial needs have been satisfied for thousands of years. Who am I to say that it smacks of nonsense now?

I pull a fuchsia handkerchief (a legacy of the first and last time my wife allowed me to operate the washing machine independently) from my pocket and tear a strip off. So what do I wish for? I feel pretty healthy, now that the bowel irritation has cleared up. I wonder if I can ask for the return of the Ashes, or world peace. Could I perhaps elevate the quality of my poetry? 'I wish that my poetry sings in the ears of the innocent like the song of a skylark at the Lorient festival in August, and if that can't happen, please can I not be bottled off stage.' No, it has to be the baby again. This is, after all, a baptistery well. I choose my branch carefully and tie a knot, making my wish.

As I walk back down the path, stooping and scrabbling to pass through the tunnel, I wonder if this ability to 'simply experience' is something that the modern Celts feel especially able to do. Certainly, there is a great deal of magic – I cannot think of a better all-encompassing word – the length of the Celtic Fringe. There is a high incidence of people with 'second sight', who have premonitions. All of the six countries have their own fairies – *sheegyn* as they call them on the Isle of Man, as in my poem. Belief in these 'Little People' who inhabit another world but who may enter ours is habitual and unquestioned throughout the Celtic Fringe. In Cornwall there are 'tommyknockers': sprites who live down mineshafts and at sea; and in Scotland there are 'brownies' and 'boggarts'. In Wales the fairy people are known as the 'Tylweth Teg' and in Brittany there are the 'korigans'. In Ireland there is a plethora of Little People but the most famous are, of course, the leprechauns.

There is a famous Fairy Bridge at Ballalona on the Isle of Man on the road between Castletown and Douglas. I must have been over it a thousand times in a car with my mum. Now, just so you know where we are coming from here, I have to tell you a little bit about my mum. She is a magistrate, a qualified lawyer, a former teacher, a former member of the Board of Education that oversees the island's schools and a current member of the Financial Supervision Commission – all in all an intelligent and immensely capable woman by anyone's standards. And yet, on each and every single occasion we have ever been over the Fairy Bridge, she has greeted the Little People. Every time. And what is more, I have always had to do the same. Oh, yes. Everyone in the car, actually, has to utter a cheery greeting: 'Good morning, Fairies . . . Good afternoon, Fairies, thank you for the lovely weather.'

When I was an obnoxious teenager, I obviously rebelled against this and one day I refused to greet the fairies. Mum, canny like a hungry cat, unearthed the plan before we got to the bridge. As she was adamant that the wrath of the fairies would not be wrought on her motor, I was deposited by the side of the road before the bridge after a brief row. Invigorated by this snub, I stood on the bridge and invoked the fairies to desist briefly from fornicating with their sisters and uncles and other next of kin and come up on top of the bridge to swivel around on my rigid middle fingers. Alone in the pallid sunshine, I jumped up and down, fists in the air, swearing abusively at my feet like a man looking for an extra's role alongside Jack Nicholson in *One Flew Over the Cuckoo's Nest*.

Feeling a great deal better, I walked beyond the bridge and got back in the car. That very afternoon, I lost my tennis racket. A brand-new tennis racket. The same tennis racket that John McEnroe had just won Wimbledon with. A birthday present that was eight days old. I left it on the roof of the car and never saw it again. That night, I slept in the draught of an open window and woke up with a crick neck, which kept me in bed for two days. My mum patiently nursed me and though she never once mentioned it, she knew. My mum, the epitome of an accomplished, cosmopolitan woman, knew that this was the work of the Little People, who I had been so foolish to cross.

The gloaming light on top of the moors is beautiful when I arrive in the village of Madron, a mile or two from the well. At the bus stop outside the pub, I meet Maeve, who has lived here all her life.

'My son wus baptoised ar the well fifty-four year ago. Un people still ar,' she tells me. 'Dactor's son wus baptoised ere only a few year ago. Thas the last I 'eard af. But the well'as bin tiken over by witchcraft now. Thez covens that meet up thar, there are. Az bin vandulised wit the devil's work.' New Age pagans, I think. They are moving in. I notice that Maeve is beginning to eye me in a funny way, then the Penzance bus pulls up and I leap aboard.

The Golowan festival takes place in Penzance and it celebrates midsummer and the feast of St John (*Gol-Jowan* means 'Feast of John' in Cornish). Contrary to what many people choose to believe, the midsummer solstice was not a crucial day in the Celtic calendar since it is not one of the quarter days. Yet it was, and still is, a time when people gather, usually on high places, to light bonfires. Throughout Cornwall a chain of bonfires is lit one after another on hilltops from Land's End to Kithill on the Devon border. For the Highlanders and Islanders and people on the west coast of Ireland, St John's Eve was the night when the seals or 'selkies' came ashore and turned into men and women. On the Isle of Man, Midsummer is Tynwald Day, the biggest occasion in the Manx calendar when politicians gather on a mound in the centre of the island and the new laws are proclaimed in Manx. Interestingly, Tynwald Day is celebrated on 5 July, or 'Old Midsummer's Day'.

The discrepancy arises from the change from the Julian to the Gregorian calendar in 1752. The Westminster government ordered that the calendar in Britain be adjusted by eleven days to bring it into conformity with the rest of Europe and to ensure that the vernal equinox occurred on 21 March every year. Many places on the Celtic Fringe ignored this. As late as 1900, families on the

Isle of Man celebrated Christmas on 5 January. In the Preseli Mountains in Wales, they still do. All along the Celtic Fringe, this discrepancy lingers. There are lots of Beltane celebrations on 12 May and 12 August (the old quarter day of Lughnasa) remains a key date.

Golowan is an old festival, though I could not find anyone to tell me its origins. What I do know is that it died out in the 1860s when, as one of the festival organisers related, 'Penzance was gentrified by the arrival of the railway'. The railway and the hordes of tourists that it brought were the death knell for much that is distinctive about Cornish culture. Golowan was revived as a schools community project in 1991. Then, just Mazey Day or Midsummer was celebrated, but such is the current mania for all things Cornish, and I suppose festivals in general, that it has grown into a ten-day party which attracts 70,000 people to Penzance. There are Cornish language workshops, civic parades, public debates on local affairs, theatre, storytelling (the Cornish are famous raconteurs), processions, parades, male voice choirs (as with the Welsh, two great passions of Cornishmen are rugby and singing) and lots of bands. The stated aim of the charitable organisation that runs the festival is to 'advance education for public benefit through the promotion of art and culture, with particular but not exclusive reference to the art and culture of the Celtic regions of Europe'. So it is a bit of a pan-Celtic love-in as well as a contemporary crowd-puller but at its heart it is an authentically Cornish affair. And that heart is Mazey's Eve, the night of Celtic ribaldry that I have specifically come to Penzance for.

I start the evening at the Dock Inn, a lively boozer that smells of tobacco and rope and rusted chains, of tidal water, of the sea. It is the full beard show inside. Leaning against the bar waiting to order a pint, I count nine gloriously unkempt, gratuitously abundant beards. If I include the bar lady, that makes a round ten. It is like an Open University physics lesson on the TV. The beard nearest me – a great brown thing with grey tips that looks like a brush for scouring industrial machinery – appears to have a mind of its own, moving independently of the man sporting it.

Beards aside, it is a heterogeneous crew slaking their thirst hard on this sunny June evening. No two haircuts are the same. No two people are dressed the same – not even the young. No two people laugh the same way. The badges that bind them are more subliminal: worn wraps of Golden Virginia, half-revealed tattoos on hips and forearms and necks, the absence of black apparel (too urban) and the 'I've lived a bit' faces. There is a buzz – an eagerness to get to the bar, an energy in the conversation, a top edge to the laughter – that speaks highly of a pub, even though it is Mazey's Eve and everyone is out for a big night. The Dock is a great 'Fringe' scene and I love it.

It would be a good venue for a poem, but it is early and there is no band playing. To initiate it, I would have to clamber up on the table and silence the whole pub myself, spontaneously. Part of me wants to do it – I guess that is Ned Clague working in alliance with the two pints of strong Cornish ale I have already had – and part of me is screaming, 'No way! They'll strip you, cover you in tar and fling you in the harbour. Don't do it!' Despite my relative success in the Applecross Inn, I am just not sure if I have got the balls for it here. To take my mind off it, I sit down to chat to one of the beards.

'Airz, um fur Penzance. Iz uh good pub, the Dark. Look at em awll. Looks like the sixties never ended, eh?' There is a fellow in the corner opposite us dressed in riding boots, a black kaftan and a medieval crown with, literally, brass knobs on. I point him out.

'Thaz Pody,' Dave says. 'Eez in the mock mayor elections later arn.'

Ah, traditional Mazey's Eve mayhem when the people of Penzance elect a mock mayor for the year ahead. I have read about it.

'We like ar tradition ere,' Dave goes on. He clearly thinks I am English and I decide to let that run for a while.

'Why is that?' I ask. As is so often the case among the Celts, it is extremely dangerous to judge anyone on appearances. At first glance, I would have said Dave was a fisherman; there are actually quite a few boats working out of Penzance still. He has a strong Cornish accent and the sleeves of his thick sweater are rolled up to the lumps of his biceps, revealing Popeye forearms. Yet he talks like an intellectual, and I have set him off.

'See, we live awn the edge ere. The edge of un island that is arn the edge a the world's greatest landmass. Yes, there az bin trade in tin fur two and half thousand year an some emigration an mail boats to America, bud ir don't amount ta much. See, most a the major events in 'istory az passed Cornwall buoy. History is thin, then. No much as appended ere. Nor az many ideas and innovations come frew ere. You need people comin' a goin' fru thaht. So ar traditions, ar old ways un ar lores important in a way tha jus ain't ta you. You av yer institutions – church, state, aristokreceipt, Mark un Spencers – but thas nat fur uz. We av air community un ar lores instead.'

'I am from the Isle of Man, actually,' I butt in.

'Whoa,' he guffaws. 'Yurah bugger, aren't yer. We be smugglin' buddies thenz. So you know what am sayin' anywaze. You be down the marquee fuh the lections then?'

I walk along the quay where there is a funfair. Nobody is going on any of the rides and gangs of kids are standing around counting the number of cigs left in ten-packs. At the end of the food stalls is an old wooden, barrel-shaped caravan. The hoarding says: 'Lulla Corla, leading clairvoyant as seen on TV. Lulla is the seventh daughter of a seventh daughter. She can make and unmake luck. She is a consultant on many problems.' I have never had my fortune read before, but I walk straight up the steps without so much as consulting myself.

'Yes, I have a gift,' Lulla says, putting down a bacon sandwich and rubbing grease on to her dress before she clears a chair of debris for me to sit on. She pulls a cloth from the small table beside her to reveal three crystal balls. I wonder if they are windows on the past, present and future.

'No, small, medium and large,' she says. 'Which one would you like me to look into to tell your fortune?' This business is more prosaic than I had expected.

'Er . . . large, please.' It is like ordering a pizza.

'That's twenty pounds. Please pay me now.'

'Twenty quid. Blimey. And how much is the small one?'

'These crystal balls are over two hundred years old, young man,' Lulla snaps back.

I want to ask if they were a christening present or to suggest that the loan might have been paid off by now, but I don't. And then I panic that she may be reading my thoughts. If she can read my palm, why can't she read my forehead?

'The small one is ten, but for you I will offer the medium crystal ball for ten pounds.'

That was going to be my counter-offer. She is reading my thoughts. I have never haggled over my future before and my stomach tightens just as it does at that moment when the roller-coaster cranks to a halt at the top of the hill.

'Done,' I say without conviction. Lulla shuffles forward on her chair and leers over the crystal ball as if she is about to ingest it in her bosom. Her cheeks grow even brighter, like a pair of New Zealand apples, and the light from the ball illuminates the flecks of colour in her eyes. Suddenly, I am not sure if I want this moment. I want to keep the small talk going. I want to say, 'Six sisters and six aunties, eh? Christmas must be hell,' but she is off.

'I see you are a bit of a romantic. You will have heart problems when you are older. Your ancestors have bearing on your life.' She pauses. Well, you could disclose that lot to a dung-wallah in Delhi zoo and be pretty confident of being right. I merely snort.

'There will be three great loves in your life.' I raise my eyebrows when she glances up at me. My wife is my second love and I have no intention of making it three. 'They are not necessarily all people. One could be something rather than someone.'

'What, like a small farmyard animal?' I proffer. This does not get a laugh, which is fair enough because it is not very funny. Lulla looks more intense than ever. She leans nearer the ball, bringing her eyes very close to her hands like she is ducking apples.

'Two generations back, on your father's side . . . no, this is not clear . . . yes, I think it is your father's side. Two generations back there is a male who influences you. You have his spirit in you. There will be a crisis in your life. Then, he will guide you or advise you. This crisis will be a time when you nearly lose your life, and this spirit will save you. You must listen for his voice. Perhaps you should find out about this person now, so you are better able to heed the advice he gives you. This is important.'

I nod with what reverence I can muster.

'I see you travelling across the seas. Not once, not twice, not three times. Many times. I cannot tell how many times. Across the seas, there you gather things, information. This information you bring back home, for your work.'

Well, that could make me a spy, a scientific researcher at an AIDS charity or a scout for a new Asian babes pornography channel, but it is, I have to admit, a pretty good description of a travel writer, which is what I am. I start sweating and I want to apologise for the quip about the farmyard animal.

'Any questions?' she asks, letting a huge breath of odorous air pass between her chaotic teeth and up my nostrils.

'Yes, one. Will I be a famous poet?' She peers again. There is a long pause.

'No.'

'Oh.'

'But . . . wait . . . ah, you will have success by writing other things, through using the pen in other ways' – I am thinking bus shelters and graffiti here – 'This is how you will make your living, with the pen. But not with poetry, no. You will write poetry for your pleasure, but not for financial gain. The only person who likes your poetry will be you.'

Suddenly I have a dozen questions but Lulla is pressing a plastic star into my hand and giving me a big squeeze with one of her meaty paws ('the left hand, it is closer to the heart') and I am gone, tripping out of the door and wiping my watery brow as Lulla goes back to her bacon doorstep.

Inside the marquee, the chairman of the Golowan Decorum Committee introduces the candidates for mock mayor to a crowd that quite honestly sounds like the start of a donkey race on Blackpool beach. There are five men, one woman, a transvestite and a dog called Buster up for the title, all attempting to engage with and carouse the public, ostensibly trying to impress upon us that they are 'totally unfit and unsuitable to be mayor of Penzance' and so capture our vote. Votes are registered on a wooden clap-o-meter, and thus not even measured. The chairman effectively chooses the winner, so we are only here for the ritual. Each candidate – they include Pody, the 'Prat in the Hat' and Helga, a fourteen-stone goddess with pewter wings – takes their turn on the stage to deliver their manifestos.

It is a lunatic affair, but it is impossible to ignore that there is a serious side to this. The Irish go in for this sort of hellzapoppin' high jinks. In Kerry, the citizens of Killorglin choose a goat each year to be King of the Puck Fair, which is thought to be Ireland's oldest festival. Beneath the japing and the hilarity, there is something serious in these ridiculous acts. They are expressions of rebellion and disrespect for the institutions of the English. They show a desire to undermine any authority imposed on them. In this sense, they are markedly Celtic.

When the voting is taking place, and the maelstrom is at its most raucous, as we are yelling and whistling at the man with the clap-o-meter, it hits me how very Cornish this evening is. It is these people around me now who have kept the sense of Cornish independence alive for 2,000 years, these people who believe they have a prior claim to the islands of Britain over the English, who believe their language will be spoken again, who claim an inalienable right to their sovereign parliament, who refuse to offer allegiance to the monarch, who wholeheartedly and vehemently believe they are different.

This, I realise now, is serious shit. And then I make a very big mistake. The dog wins the election and in the cheering I turn to the bloke standing on his own next to me and with whom I have only yet traded glances and I say: 'Good result. As Adlai Stevenson said, "People get the type of government they deserve." And you have got a dog. Hah!' Well, I am the only one going 'Hah!' He stops cheering. He stops clapping. Somehow a small space in the crowd forms and he is standing square in front of me, this great beefcake of a Cornishman, looking at me as if I have just absent-mindedly driven over his favourite sheepdog in a new silver Audi with personalised number plates. He is absolutely furious. I know what happens next. A 'thunderflash' goes off in my face then I am lying on the beery floor, picking pieces of teeth and strips of pellucid lip out of my mouth, wondering how I get hold of some morphine before the shock wears off and the pain of having a broken cheekbone kicks in. A Cornishman fractured my cheekbone once before. He whipped an uppercut into my undefended face when I was getting off the ground on a rugby field. It was a profoundly unpleasant experience. And I am about to go through it again, because of my big mouth, because I mocked the mock mayor elections, because I am not fucking Cornish.

Then – and I shall remain perpetually grateful to this man for all of the rest of my days no matter what whips and scorns are thrown at me – Dave pops out of the crowd beside me. He very quickly surmises the situation, shoves his beard in this bloke's ear and they are both gone, through the crowd that quickly engulfs the space they leave. I have no idea what Dave said. He may have said, 'Leave it out, Killer. He's one of us,' or it might have been, 'Not in public, Gnasher. We'll give him a good shoeing together on the quay, later,' but I don't really care. I still have one perfectly intact cheekbone and one, though it is set a bit funny and missing a couple of chips, that functions well enough, all of which is more than cause for a celebratory drink.

It takes three pints of Mazey's Ale before I have a hold of myself again, and the best bit of the evening is still to come. On the street outside there is a band loosening up. They are dressed in white with sashes and hats with flowers in. There are four accordionists (or 'box players', as Fergie MacDonald would say), a bagpiper, eight fiddlers and a few drummers. When they pick up the first tune, the crowd of 200 people fall in behind. At the front, leading this heady parade round the narrow streets above the quay, is Penzance's own ''obby 'orse', the mighty Penglaz, an extraordinary, demonic, prancing eight-foot-tall creation covered in a cloak of torn black cloth with a long wooden snout that snaps at the crowd as it swells around him. Behind Penglaz is a man in a tailcoat, bowler hat and sunglasses who carries a large, brass baton with which he beats time for the band and the dance. The crowd all link arms and the Serpent Dance has begun. We snake through the streets, curling back on ourselves, looping in and out of other parts of the chain, crashing our bodies into whatever is there as the human chain halts and lurches about and across itself, dodging Penglaz, whooping and cheering and kicking up our feet, processing through the night.

'Za rare mad do!' a lady blurts in my face as she swirls past.

Halfway up Chapel Street, full of drink and riding on the euphoria, I duck out of the serpent and clamber up a wall.

'Penglaz, people of Penzance,' I yell, 'I have a poem for Golowan.' It is near hopeless. My voice is lost in the frenzy of the band and the shrieking dancers. I press on with the poem, but I must look like a nutter barking enthusiastically from the wings. When I finish, I have almost lost my voice, but the dance goes on. In the vertiginous confusion, I understand that if I am to captivate festival audiences laden with drink and teetering on the edge of euphoria, then I am going to have to up my act. I need to create a performance if Ned's poetry is going anywhere. Like Penglaz, I need a costume.

5

Manx Kilts and Ceilidhs

'So you are among your people,' a desk-bound London friend had said to me when I rang him back in May from the top of Quinag, a sculpted sandstone mountain that towers above the magnificent coast of north-west Sutherland. 'I expect you will be happy since the Celts are a work-shy race of slackers, just like yourself. All kilts and ceilidhs and not a worthwhile job between them.'

This is not an untypical English view of the Celts, though my friend's vituperative comments might have been a reaction to the fact that I was surveying the glory of the Highlands whilst he sweated out a hot day in a windowless office in EC2. What interested me though was the reference to 'kilt' in ready association with 'Celt'.

The kilt, everyone knows, is a garment that Scotsmen are proud to wear. But it has drifted, it seems, in the late twentieth-century wave of Celtomania to become a badge of pan-Celtic identity. Today you can find men from all the Celtic realms sporting the tartan plaid. Even the Cornish are up to it. At the Golowan festival, I saw half a dozen men in Cornish tartan kilts.

The kilt as we know it today is actually of relatively recent design: early eighteenth century most probably, though it was not popularised as the national dress of Scotland until the time of George IV. Purportedly, an Englishman designed the modern kilt in 1725 – one Thomas Rawlinson, who owned an ironworks in Lochaber. For a hundred years or so prior to this, Highlanders wore a profuse garment called the 'belted plaid' (the Gaelic term is *feileadh mór* which means 'big wrap', though *plaide* is also a

Gaelic term for 'blanket' or 'rug'). Before that, Highlanders most likely wore the *leni-croich* and the *brat* – the saffron shirt and mantle that the fellow getting handfasted at the Beltane festival in Edinburgh was decked out in – but the point is that the kilt did not derive directly from the animal-skin loincloths that cavemen wore, as some people like to believe (and if you have ever been to a real Highland ceilidh, it is not difficult to see why they do). The belted plaid was a voluminous piece of cloth that wrapped around the waist and folded over one shoulder. Think Liam Neeson in the movie *Rob Roy*. As one can imagine, the machinery and the fires at the ironworks posed something of a danger to this flapping garment and all that was contained therein. Rawlinson then, allegedly, cut off the material above the waist and tailored what was below to create the modern kilt – an altogether more practical garment that would not get between a Scotsman and a good day's work.

I say 'allegedly' because the more reliable evidence suggests that such tailoring was done well before the time of Rawlinson, who merely documented it. Furthermore, no Scot will give you flowers and champagne for suggesting that he thank an Englishman for his national dress. The notion causes apoplectic uproar north of the border, something akin to the reaction you might get from an Englishman at the suggestion that Bobby Charlton's parents were, contrary to popular belief, Pakistani, or that St George was an Armenian whoopsie and the only dragon he beat up on was his long-suffering, sexually starved wife.

For a time in the eighteenth century both the belted plaid and the kilt were worn, and for a time neither were. In 1746 (the year after the Battle of Culloden Moor), an Act of Parliament made the wearing of any form of Highland dress illegal. It was thought that in being forced to wear English garb, the Highlanders would be subdued. Also, the functionality of the belted plaid – clothing and bedding blanket in one – was thought to allow men the freedom to join a rebellion at a moment's notice. Finally, and here is the funny bit, the English claimed that the plaid encouraged indolent living because Highlanders pulling a 'sicky' could fling the blanket on a heather hillside and idly blow the day.

The Act was repealed in 1782 and a combination of Walter Scott's romantic writings and the heroic feats of the Highland regiments in the Napoleonic Wars effected a wave of sentimental Jacobinism which culminated in the royal visit to Scotland of George IV (a short Kraut with a taste for pageantry, you understand, who needed to get a bit of British popularity behind his buttocks) in 1822. Both the king and the Lord Mayor of London wore kilts, which promptly became the Scottish national dress. The king and the Lord Mayor also wore flesh-coloured tights which thankfully did not make it into the patriotic costume. Clan tartans as we know them today date from about this time too.

Kilts and tartan grew quickly to become, along with bagpipes, the symbols most readily associated with Scotland and they got everywhere, and I mean everywhere. Now here is a fact that will win you no friends at parties: Neil Armstrong had a square of tartan in his pocket when he walked on the moon. Fascinating? Not really. Fortunate? Yes. I mean, imagine if he had taken a set of bagpipes instead . . . 'That's one small step for a man, one giant step . . . oh, shit. I've got the bellows snagged on the gantry . . .'

The Scots then, and the Highlanders certainly, have some history in the wearing of the kilt. And the rest of the Celts? Well, no. Pipers in Irish regiments of the British army wear a saffron kilt and there are small pieces of historical evidence to suggest that mantles bearing some resemblance to the *feileadh mór* were worn on the Isle of Man in the seventeenth century, but it does not amount to much. In truth, the kilt is an artifice for the modern Celt. It is a badge of otherness, worn as an emphatic statement which says: 'We are not English. We are not French. We are Celts and we wear skirts.'

Obviously then I need to wear one. It will, I surmise, advance my mission in many ways. First and foremost it is a costume for the poetry readings. It is also a statement of my overt sympathies towards pan-Celticism. Furthermore, it may also be a good talking point, particularly if I pick an obscure tartan, which will get conversations going in pubs and at festivals. Finally, I suspect that if I look more like a Celt, then I may feel more like one too.

The one glitch in my cunning plan is the Manx tartan. It is awful. Goodness knows who thought it up. The palate of colours is supposed to be representative of the Isle of Man, so you have blue for the sea, green for the hills, purple for the heather, white for the cottages and yellow for the puddle of vomit you have just parked at your feet. Actually, the yellow is for the gorse, but you are beginning to get the picture. I have witnessed people laying their eyes on Manx tartan for the very first time and it is as if they have been cutting jalapeños and absentmindedly stopped to take an eyelash off their cornea. Ouch! It prompts the same sort of bodily reaction as smelling salts or sitting on a drawing pin. If items of clothing could possibly be subject to the same judicial system that their wearers are, then Manx tartan would be up for GBH. It hurts. When I was a kid, my dad had a Manx tartan tie, which he wore to parties hosted by people he didn't like.

I have managed to assure myself that the kilt is a fine garb for a bard, but – and it is a big but – can I, dare I, wear a Manx tartan kilt? This is the question that I am wrestling with as I make another mother of a trans-Britain journey from Penzance to Ramsey, Isle of Man (two trains, two buses, a taxi and one plane. Cost? Not bad – the equivalent of a two-week holiday for a family of five in a private fully staffed villa in Mauritius in the high season) via my lovely and insightful wife ('You don't look well. You will look even less well if you wear Manx tartan.'). Once again, it is an irregular course to be taking about the Celtic Fringe, but I have no choice. Yn Chruinnaght, the small but perfectly formed inter-Celtic festival on the Isle of Man, has already started. I am on the final leg of this journey when my mum phones.

'There is another Manx tartan and guess what? It's okay,' she says. You see? Even my mum, a true Manx patriot, finds the Manx tartan fundamentally upsetting, but that's only half the story. Over the years I have been the smiling recipient of some of Mum's 'okay' clothing, which, once unwrapped, turn out to be the sartorial equivalent of hara-kiri. I am not falling for this. 'It is called Manx hunting tartan,' Mum goes on.

'Right,' I say. 'And what are the colours of the Manx hunting tartan, I wonder? Orange for Mr Fox, crimson for the colour of Lady Fauntleroy's cheeks, brown for the beagle turd and mustard . . . because . . . because it goes so very badly with the other colours? And don't tell me, you get a matching car rug and a botany turtle-neck sweater free with the kilt.'

'Don't be stupid,' Mum says. 'It is brown, olive and gunmetal grey. Believe me, it is quite nice. Anyway, I rang the shop. They only do bespoke, but they happen to have a kilt in the hunting tartan in your size and I bought it for you. It will be here when you arrive for the festival.'

Well, I am a pretty odd shape, even by Manx standards, so if they have one made up in my size, I should take that as a sign. It must have been made for me. Where would I be without my mother? Left to my own devices, I would have happily procrastinated over buying a kilt until the eve of Samhain. Then I would have bought one – and they are not cheap – worn it once, and found space for it at the back of my cupboard where moths would have dined on it in saturnalian splendour for two uninterrupted decades.

Manx hunting tartan it is. I have absolutely nothing against hunting, but the irony that there happen to be no foxes on the Isle of Man is not lost on a scintillating wit like mine. There is, however, a drag hunt on the island, which I love the idea of. It is very 'Raj' and very silly – tearing round the countryside risking permanent disability in pursuit of a deadly trail of aniseed vapour. If Wilde will forgive me, it is not so much 'the unspeakable in pursuit of the uneatable' as the 'unspeakable in pursuit of something which may help one's flatulence'.

The Scots say that you have to grow up wearing a kilt. I always assumed that this was a measure of the pride they take in their national dress and a means to discourage others from dabbling in the tartan, by which they distinguish themselves. But having had my wafting piece of 'plaid' on for a full fifteen minutes now, I feel inclined to concur that there is something in what they say. To put the sentiment another way: wearing a skirt takes some getting used to.

Actually, the skirt bit I feel I can deal with, despite the fact that I have legs that would have secured me a small part in a Victorian freak show. (One of my nicknames at school was 'sausage legs'. There, it's out now.) But it is going gorilla in the underwear department that is more challenging. I read that 'going gorilla' is a term which has recently made it into the *Oxford English Dictionary*. I do not know if this is indicative of the fact that more and more people are wandering the streets of Britain without underwear, or if a small but determined number have been at it for a very long time. There are, of course, times in everyone's life when going gorilla is quite acceptable: coming back from the beach in a pair of jeans after a late night skinny dip; when a humorous classmate has hoiked your pants out of the changing room window; or going down La Croisette on a Vespa. I could go on. But going gorilla in a skirt is a whole new world.

Mum was right: the tartan is absolutely fine. It is quite staid and you would not find Billy Idol prancing the pogo of revolution in it, but in the sort of condition I am in right now, staid is good. Standing up straight, the kilt reaches the middle of my knees, which is the correct length apparently, and it fits comfortably round my middle. It is just that when I bend over, I have absolutely no idea where the rear hem ends. I do not know if people stand-ing behind me can see my two misshaped legs respectably covered

in tartan or if my bum shows and, to borrow an old Blues metaphor, people are 'looking right into the New Year'.

Also, when I walk the great number of folds flap disconcert-
ingly around the backs of my thighs. I know this is all a measure
of my inexperience, but considering I am going to be dressed like
this on stage, giving my first poetry reading at a festival in just
under half an hour, I think I have good cause to feel disconcerted,
if not truly petrified. It may be rash to think that Ned Clague can
pull this off, but, as I am terribly aware, the lighted half of the year
is flying by. It is the middle of July, almost two and a half months
have passed since Beltane and the next quarter day, Lughnasa, is
only two weeks away. Feeling the need to move my poetry forward,
I'd telephoned the organiser of the Yn Chruinnaght festival.
'Sure,' he'd said, 'we'll fit you in. I'll get you on stage between the
bands on Thursday night, about 8 p.m.'

Yn Chruinnaght festival (it means 'the gathering', especially a
gathering for Celtic arts and crafts) was revived in 1978 by Mona
Douglas, a remarkable lady who devoted most of her life to the
survival, revival and promotion of all things Manx. She was also
a rather good poet. What she appreciated was that music and
dance were as integral to Manx cultural life as eating and drinking. The problem she faced was that for a hundred years the
Church, whose influence on the Isle of Man was pervasive, had
frowned upon such frivolous activities, and they had been forgotten. The leg-up she needed to establish a permanent Manx cultural festival came in the form of a resurgence of interest in
pan-Celticism in the 1970s.

The pan-Celtic movement was, and is, an attempt by the Welsh,
Scottish, Irish, Manx, Cornish and Breton peoples to recognise
the special nature of their shared Celtic heritage and to maintain
it through a network of cultural links. At the very heart of this are
these festivals, which evidence the recurring theme of the Celtic
instinct for community. Pan-Celticism is not an entirely modern
phenomenon. The destruction of the last vestiges of the indepen-

dent Celtic nations in the 1700s and developments in linguistics and archaeology at the same time started the ball of Celtic Studies rolling and laid the foundation for the histories of the ancient Celts. From the earliest stage, it fed an emerging national self-consciousness, especially in Ireland where the roots of Irishness were already being sought in an idealised Celtic past.

The idea that one could write a joint history of the ancient Celts (as opposed to individual histories of each country) only emerged at this time. No one had previously thought of themselves as 'Celtic', despite the survival of the languages. It is interesting that this Celtic identity was surfacing at the same time as the identity of the 'British', in the modern political sense. Both were creations of the eighteenth century.

However, the first real heyday of the pan-Celtic movement was in the period 1880 to 1900. A lot of shit went down in the Celtic countries in the nineteenth century – famines, migrations, the Clearances, pernicious and active suppression of the languages, industry failures, mass unemployment – all at a time when there was a widespread belief among the English that the Celts were a people of stunted intelligence. There were actually surveys and experiments to prove that people with Celtic surnames had smaller skulls than people with Anglo-Saxon surnames (which scientific lunacy still lingers today in jokes about how 'tick' Paddy is).

There has been a belief amongst the English throughout history that they belong to a higher order of human being. This assumption of superiority was (and, let's face it, for ample-bottomed, thin-lipped *Spectator* readers in monogrammed slippers, it still is) an article of faith for the empire and an essential part of subjugating and homogenising the dominions. In the late nineteenth century, this way of thinking was de rigueur in London. It was also racist and for the Celts it was the icing on a mountain-sized cake of grief. It prompted them to act.

National societies for the promotion of the Celtic languages were formed: Yn Cheshaght Ghailkagh on the Isle of Man,

Kowethas Kelto-Kernnack in Cornwall, the Gaelic League in Ireland and so on. The Celtic Congress was formed. It quickly grew in stature, and even hinted at the notion of a future federation of autonomous Celtic countries as an aim. The movement was inevitably political as well as cultural and it grew with the rise of national consciousness. In Ireland, the Celtic revival made a defining contribution to the development of nationalism.

Yet, for all its rallying cries to the people, the nineteenth-century movement was not a popular one. It was an intellectual and elitist one crafted out in ivory towers and middle-class drawing rooms, led by academics and antiquarians who were removed from the peasant societies on the Atlantic seaboard. On the ground, there were few expressions of inter-Celtic fidelity. In Clydeside, in the iron-making districts of south Wales and in the coalfields of Pennsylvania, where Irish, Scots and Welsh workers were pitched together, they were happy knocking six bells out of each other. Deep suspicion tainted the regard people of these nations had for each other. During the industrial boom in the Welsh valleys, for example, the Catholic Irish were frequently looked upon as the scabs, the strike-breakers who would work for next to nowt. In Glasgow, probably the world's most Celtic city at the end of the nineteenth century, migrants from Ireland lived uneasily with Gaels from the Highlands and Islands. They even fought over who had the rightful claim to the term 'Celtic', and the Irish won one battle in this struggle when they named their football team, created in 1888, Celtic.

It took nearly a century, a massive decrease in the number of speakers of Celtic languages and a reasonable distance from the major events of the British twentieth century – two World Wars and the break-up of the empire – for the movement to become popular throughout the Celtic Fringe. In the 1970s, fuelled by the rapid decline of organised religion, post-imperial guilt, stress on the notion of 'Britishness' and environmental concerns, Celtomania kicked off again. By the time I was going to Yn Chruinnaght as a teenager, it was on a roll.

Yn Chruinnaght has never been an ambitious affair – and in that sense it is authentically Celtic – but to a teenager in Ramsey in the early 1980s it was big. It wasn't so much the major event of the summer; it was the summer. A week-long knees-up in a marquee on the promenade with music, dancing, dancing girls, dancing girls from several foreign countries, exotic costumes and a wild array of mad-looking adults who were far too captivated by what was going on to care about under-age drinking. It was great.

I had no idea what it was all about, of course, and I cared even less. I had absolutely no sense of Celtic consciousness. To me this was merely a gathering of the 'weird beards' as we called them. Burly men who spoke hilarious languages that no one understood, least of all the people they were speaking to. There were troupes that danced like cats on hot tin roofs being sprayed by machine-gun fire. There were costumed musicians who looked like they had just stepped out of Mr Ben's changing room. There were even – and you can't imagine how funny this was aged thirteen, after a quarter of vodka and two cans of cider – men in skirts.

Little did I know then, as an enthusiastic but breathtakingly ignorant teenager, that I would, twenty years on, be one of those men in skirts. As I walk up to the door of the Grand Island Hotel, to hit Yn Chruinnaght 2002 for the first time, the one light and reassuring thought I have is that some kid full of snakebite is going to need his underpants changing when he catches a glance of me in this kilt.

The Grand Island Hotel is very much home ground for me. It is 500 yards from my parents' house. I worked as a waiter here one summer – the Kiwi chef called me the 'Manx Manuel' – and I have been drinking in the Ayres bar regularly since it was last refurbished, around the time the Task Force set sail for the Falkland Islands. There is no venue I know more intimately, yet I am feeling distinctly nervous. This is partly because there are people here who know me. The Isle of Man is a very small place. I am just getting used to being Ned Clague and I am increasingly aware that I need this 'guise', as it were, to perform. I could easily be stripped of it here when some friend of Mum's from the Bride Church harvest festival flower-arranging sect recognises me. And if I know my luck, it will not be in a deserted car park at 3 a.m. No, it will be as I am extolling the virtues of the tetrameter and describing how being peripatetic adds a liberating dimension to my verse with an Irish poet of higher repute when the flower arranger butts in.

'Ooh, is it? Well, I never. It's Robert, isn't it? Robert Penn? Rosemary's son? Gosh, I haven't seen you since . . . let me see now . . . since you dropped a plate of Cod Mornay in my lap when you were a waiter here. So how are you? What are you doing?'

'I'm a dancer in a gay nightclub in Berlin. Hasn't Mum told you? She's struggling with it. Would you excuse me?' is how I will reply, but it will be too late. Cover blown.

So all in all, I am knotted up like a little ball of elastic nerves about this evening. And I am late too. I feel strange, frightened perhaps, as I regard my white knees walking up the steps of the hotel. I push the swing doors open and feel the warm air tickle the hair on my thighs. The reception area is busy with people drinking, talking loudly and milling. Music is coming down the corridor from the ballroom. I have a quick glance to take all this in and a deep breath. Here goes. Then I set off, but before I get two paces into the room, a large lady – Cornish, guessing from her accent, and wearing glasses the size of scallop shells – steps into my path and bellows thirty feet across the room, 'Ahoy there, Highlander, show us yer love lance!'

My immediate retort should be: 'Only if you show me your Cornish camel coat first' but I hesitate. The truth is, you simply can't play at wearing a kilt. It is like wearing white tie: you must throw champagne bottles and swing from chandeliers; like wearing lederhosen and long socks: you must pour beer on your head and kiss other men; like wearing a pimp suit: you must freebase cocaine and slap your bitches. It is all or nothing. It is all or go home and change. Ned Clague is all. Rob Penn is nothing. I choose all. I stop halfway across the foyer, face the woman and lift the front tartan hem skywards like the soldiers in *Carry on up the Khyber* scaring away the rebellious natives. She wrinkles her nose, nods respectfully and disappears into the crowd. It is a chilling moment.

But not as chilling as taking the stage. It is only minutes later – I have got a pint but I have certainly not regained my equanimity – when I meet the festival organiser.

'Perfect timing,' he says. 'You're on. Need a mic?'

The ballroom at the Grand Island Hotel is big. I know this because I used to have furniture steeplechase races round it with other waiters when we were supposed to be polishing wine glasses. This evening, the wooden dance floor is clear, but the rest of the room is full to bursting. Every bit of space is taken up with chairs and every chair is occupied. I reckon there must be 200 people but I may be wrong. I am too busy trying to prevent my anal sphincter from submitting to unconditional surrender. It is touch and go. As I am fiddling with the mic, the last person on stage being, I presume, Robert Wadlow, I glance around the crowd. It is a bloody SAGA outing. This is not how I remember Yn Chruinnaght. 'Okay, folks. Eyes down for a full house,' I want to say. Then panic kicks in. I am not sure if I can even remember the poems. I guess there is only one way to find out.

'*Fastyr mie. Kanys ta shiu?*' I say. That is 'Good evening. How are you?' in Manx, which civility is met by 200 stony faces and exam room silence.

'I have a couple of poems for you. Do interrupt me if you're about to die and need a doctor.' I don't say that. I just crack on with the first poem: 'Port of Ness'. Halfway through, I am sure I hear someone snoring. A few people, probably everyone who can, get up and wander out. At the end, six people clap. I count them. One of them is an old boy in the front row who has been staring at me with blazing eyes, like a Welsh sheepdog. Rabies, I speculate, which makes five clappers. I feel shyer than a borrowed suit.

I consider skipping the second poem, but something urges me

on: I am not sure if it is pure pig-headedness or the flashing vision of me on the stage at Lorient in front of thousands. The only good thing about this situation is that my mum and dad aren't here. Like a teenage girl going to her first disco, I banned them from coming. I raise my shoulders and fill my chest to give 'Skeallaght ny Feayn-Skeallagh' a good airing. As it happens, I do remember it, though I am not sure if this lot would notice if I veered off into a Brotherhood of Man song in the middle.

'Gura moar mie ayd. Thank you very much,' I say at the end, thinking, If you are all still alive in ten minutes, there will be a band on. There is some applause and a whistle, though I suspect this is to get the attention of old sheepdog eyes in the front row. All in all, it is not a dazzling performance. Nobody dashes off to phone the newspapers: 'Hold the front page, there's a new talent arrived.' The festival organiser says, 'Well done' in Manx and tells me where my Manx pronunciation is out. A sweet-faced old man totters up and bores me with his story about a windy day on north Lewis. When I finally get to the bar, I am eager to drink and sulk, but there is further torment due.

'Hey, look who's here,' a northern English accent booms behind me. 'It's the Cockney Celt.' He is pissed and he has a couple of mates in tow who, for reasons currently eluding me, think he is funny. He slaps me on the back.

'So what happened, like,' he continues, 'wuz the Roarmans cum through Lundun an all the bloomin' Celts leg it, like, west. But there's wun oo ides. Un ere ee is! Live un well un performin portray int Isle a Man. It's bloody amazing.' He slaps me on the back, again. I want to disappear. He has noticed something I have been struggling to hide all along – the faint trace in my voice of a London accent, which I barely know I have but which is as obvious to a northerner as a simpleton is to a conman.

'Actually, I am from Ramsey,' I say, reluctant to keep this one going, but seeing no other way out. He spits beer across the bar when he registers what I have said.

'Tha cuda fooled me.'

'Clearly I did. Which makes you a fool.' The last thing I want to do is announce who I am, but I just can't face hours of this bloke's jibes.

I tell him where I live and one of his mates, a Manxman, says, 'Heck, yow muss be Rawsemary's sun. Then there's nuttin wrong with yawr Manx creh-dentials.'

'Well, thaz still the Cockney Celt ta me. Will yav a pint?' the backslapper says. He is called Paul and he turns out to be very entertaining, despite the fact that he calls me the Cockney Celt all night. ('Ah knaw, ah knaw,' he says, 'am as much fun as lumbago.') He knows lots of English folk songs and has sung informally for years but he really impresses me with a story about being barred from a vegan soup kitchen. He went overboard at a festival his daughter took him to and when he had a 'whitey', he took down half the stall and a vat of mung bean stew. Not bad for a man of fifty, I think.

Together we drift into the main bar where there are a few musicians warming up. There are musicians in every corner of every room, practising before going on stage, trading songs with musicians from other countries, just jamming. When they go quiet in the bar, Paul starts a whisper of 'shhh' and when everyone is looking up, he cups a hand over one ear and starts to sing. It is a lovely song. There is applause and then we all return to the drinking and shouting we had let up on. It was daft to assume it, but I had expected everyone at these festivals to be Celtic. But here is an Englishman, albeit a Lancastrian so near enough to the Isle of Man, singing English folk songs that are well received.

Back in the ballroom, a few hours of drinking and talking nonsense later, a Scottish band called Mak-a-Rak-it are doing just that. When I met the drummer earlier, I asked where they were from and he said Fochaber.

'Hang on,' Paul interjected, 'he only asked where you wuz from.'

'Aye. Fochaber in Morayshire.'

The dance floor is full of young blood now. An Irish lady drags me from my chair. We are dancing some sort of reel though it feels more like a game of rugby: part Highland fling, part pub fight. Everyone except me seems to know what he or she is doing so I rely on my Irish escort for direction. She flings me round like a Frisbee, spinning me through the mêlée and dashing round the back of the crowd to catch me. Every now and then I glimpse an empty chair but before I am able to determine my precise trajectory to reach it, her hand fastens round my waist again and I am whirling dervishly across the boards once more. You could sail the Fastnet Race in a gale and not feel as queasy as I do when the music finally stops.

'There y'are now,' my partner says, delivering me to a seat like a nurse in an old people's home. 'Oid say ya dance with erl the hagility of un old pig what is unfahtunately dead. But I luv de kilt. Oim Patricia.' Then she is gone, back amongst the twirling bodies, linked to a man twice my age and several times more nimble.

Next up on the main stage are Tan ha Dowr (Fire and Water) from Cornwall – a group of dancers and musicians who specialise in Cornish step dancing. As anyone who has had the misfortune to sit through a performance of *Riverdance* will know, step dancing is seriously physical stuff. It also combines grace and artistry, but it is the invigorating athleticism that sets it apart and which enthrals me.

Step dancing is as central to Celtic culture as the music it is performed to – the definition of a ceilidh is, after all, a gathering for music and dance. This is a fact largely overlooked outside the Celtic domain (at least until the advent of *Riverprance*), no doubt because the music travels much better. But to the modern Celts, if you can dance well you are a king or queen. Which makes me a jester.

It seems most likely that the step dancing tradition (eight measures or bars of music are called a 'step', hence the term) originated in Ireland, though all the Celtic countries (save for Brittany where dancing is equally popular but distinct) have their own traditions which have been practised for centuries. There are many records of dances in Ireland in the mid-1500s though the tradition probably dates back much further. As with the music, the poetry and the language, the eighteenth and nineteenth centuries were tough times for step dancing in Ireland, by then a widespread tradition and part of every form of social gathering. Throughout this period, step dancing was kept alive in rural Ireland by 'Dance Masters', itinerant teachers who taught dancing subversively in kitchens, barns, pub cellars and at the informal Catholic 'hedge' schools. The Church and the English suppressed it for the familiar reason that it encouraged individuality and community ties, but also because of the wild abandon that it often resulted in. Rather like a 'raver' cutting loose to the sound of low-down, dirty house music and reaching an elevated stage of consciousness and extreme pleasure in the physical turmoil of dancing, so step dancers are transported. As a description of dancing in Ireland from the late Middle Ages has it: 'in every field a fiddle and the lasses footing it till they are all a-foam.' Foaming lads and lasses. Yes, step dancing has much to recommend it.

I read somewhere that prior to the twentieth century, you could tell what village a Manx boy or girl came from just by the way they danced, so attached was each locality to its own steps and style. All that changed with the codification of dances, a process initiated by folklorists who saw so many unique dances dying out, and continued by bodies like the Irish Dancing Commission founded in 1929. So out went the distinctive regional dances and the dances on barrels and on soapy table tops and in came costumes and hard shoes (now with fibreglass toe tips and hollow heels, for louder 'clicks'.) Standardisation has meant that there are in Ireland, for example, only four types of Irish music and their associated dances. They are jig, reel, hornpipe and the set dances.

Within those types there are hundreds of dances in different tempos but I begin to get a bit lost when I delve deeper. I am no musician. As with my 'dead pig' dancing, such a miscomprehension of all matters musical does not speak well of my Celtic roots. Should a dancer say to me, 'This is a jig in four four time', I am not unlikely to reply, 'Good-oh. What's with the stutter?' and I have to admit that before this journey began I thought an 'up-tempo hornpipe' was a lesbian love-aid.

The Manx have always been famous for their singing and yet people will completely break with decorum in church and move pews mid-way through a service rather than endure my vocal bludgeoning of a hymn. So, as I say, my musical abilities do not bear the hallmark of a great Celtic heritage, but right now this does not bother me. I am just so relieved that I did not choose to travel the Fringe as Ned Clague, sizzling step dancer. Sure, me in a kilt blathering in Manx is quite comical, but me in fibreglass shoes doing the Michael Flatley would have been the highlight of Yn Chruinnaght for everyone who witnessed the perineum-splitting performance.

The Cornish girls are flying at it now. There are three girls dancing and – I have seen this before, particularly in solo performances by Irish men – the body posture is bizarre. The upper body and arms are rigid, as if the dancers are locked out on parallel bars between dips. I think this might have something to do with the fact that many of the dances came from ships, but I guess it is also to do with placing emphasis on the movement below the knees, where I have to say, things are really going off.

Many of the dances were originally courtship dances and there is something erotic about the paradox between the apparent freedom and the taut, uncompromising accuracy of the steps. Feet are flying in all directions in rhythm and the room is full of the 'clicks' and 'clacks' of their shoes drilling the wooden floor. 'Footing it till they are all a-foam' – I could not put it better myself and I now know what the good men of the cloth were trying to suppress.

I may be reading too much into this – I have had a fair bit to drink by now – but it strikes me that this curious form of dancing, half corpse in a coffin and half epileptic fit, is illustrative of something wider about the Celtic psyche. Does it say that the love of their culture can never be straitjacketed? Does it intimate that their emotional make-up is a mixture of opposites, effusiveness and total denial? Or is it merely indicative of one outstanding fact: that the Celts are barking bloody mad?

I wish I could write that the Isle of Man is situated at the very geographical heart of the Celtic Fringe. It would make the point I want to make so much easier. Even someone who knows as little about geography as the average American citizen would sniff out a 'pork pie' if I tried to suggest that it does. It doesn't. Brittany buggers it up. However, if you draw a line from John o' Groats to Land's End the mid-point is on the Isle of Man, near enough the very top of Snaefell, the island's highest hill, and the exact spot where I am standing on a clear, blowy day.

There is nothing quite like a stiff walk up a mountain to cure a hangover. All right, so there is a fry-up, a Bloody Mary, ibuprofen, more sleep, a massage, gel eye-packs, a glass of Old Doctor McCardle's Celebrated Python Juice and a shag which may prove to be more popular in a nationwide survey, but a stiff walk up a steep hill does it for me. And no, I don't need to be thrashed with a bunch of gorse when I get to the top, thank you.

As with walking up any hill anywhere along the Celtic Fringe on a windy day, walking up Snaefell is a gamble inasmuch as I had absolutely no idea what the weather was going to be like at the top when I set off. The skies coming off the ocean may deliver cloud so thick that paper aeroplanes can't get ground clearance for take-off, or you may get a day of such dazzling brilliance that you can see the whole world, as I can today. Well, the whole Celtic world. Okay, a lot of the Celtic world.

Snaefell is only 2,000 feet above sea level, but as I have walked from sea level, I feel that I have earned my 'piece', as the Scots like to call a sandwich, when I arrive. I lie in the heather beneath one of the radio masts for a few minutes. When I have wolfed my lunch, I scuff up the bare ground around the trig point with my boots, trying to find a vaguely prepossessing stone to slip into my pocket and add to my set. I am still not quite sure why I am doing this – gathering stones. I remember how, in Evelyn Waugh's novel *Brideshead Revisited*, Sebastian wanted to bury gold everywhere he had been happy so he could return when he was old and miserable, dig it up and remember. I am taking a stone from each place where I have been happy, or at least moved, and I am hoping that whenever I look at the stones, I will remember. Not that I am going to load my rucksack with a thousand rocks and turn my journey into a commando marathon. Certainly not. Restrictions apply. I am allowed one stone from each of the six Celtic countries.

When I have found a stone and scraped the dust and mud off it, I wander across the summit to take in the stupendous view. I can just make out Snowdonia over seventy miles away to the south. To the north, so close I feel I could pick them up, are the purple-headed hills of the southernmost tips of Scotland, the Mull of Galloway and Burrow Head. To the east, and almost as close, are the proud peaks of the Cumbrian Mountains and in the west the curvaceous tops of the Mountains of Mourne. Inside this bluish outline of hills and promontories is a silver ring of sea, distressed into abstract patterns by the wind. Inside that again, and right at my feet, is the faintly rhomboid shape of the Isle of Man.

Though I cannot actually see Cornwall, in a way I can sense it because the Isle of Man looks so like it. In fact, the Isle of Man looks rather like a little bit of Scotland set down in the sea, as much as it resembles Wales and Ulster too. Immediately around me are the upland peat bogs covered now in blooming heather and brilliant yellow gorse. There are a few coniferous plantations but otherwise not much in the way of trees. Below the plantations are the solitary, low, whitewashed cottages with slate roofs, surrounded by dry-stone walls partially covered in the lichens that love the damp, clean air. Beyond them, winding their way further down the hill, are the lanes that snake through the tiny fields divided with hedgerows of hawthorn and blackthorn. The lanes are bordered with sod banks covered in ferns, foxgloves, fuchsia bushes and montbretia. They are lanes that could lead you almost anywhere along the Atlantic seaboard on an unbroken journey the entire length of the British Celtic Fringe.

I have walked up Snaefell dozens of times. I even, for reasons which I cannot now remember, spent one New Year's Eve up here in a terrible gale. But seeing the situation of the Isle of Man, in the middle of the Irish Sea, (almost) in the middle of the Celtic Fringe, is helpful. I am just beginning to get the whole picture of the Celtic Fringe rather than seeing each country by itself.

Much of history is geography. So geography – the earth's form, the physical features, climate, population and the distribution of flora and fauna – matters. The geography of the Celtic Fringe is distinct from that of much of England and lowland Scotland. For a start, it has been so little modified by invasion, in comparison. The Vikings who sailed through the seas that surround me now, looking for spoils, were the only invaders really to impact on the Celtic Fringe. In the Isle of Man, they had a profound influence on the institutions, the way of life and the place names (the name Snaefell means 'snow mountain' and is of Scandinavian derivation), yet even their legacy has faded to a subliminal degree. It remains, of course, yet it is the Celtic culture that the Vikings disrupted that we remember, celebrate, revive and write poems about today. Why? Because of where the Isle of Man is situated, because of geography.

The peoples of the Celtic Fringe are all so very different from each other, but there remains much that binds them. At the heart of this is geography: the damp land they walk, the salty air they breathe, the rain that floods their fields, the flowers they smell, the hedgerows they fall into on the way back from the pub, the soil they till in an age-old fight against adverse natural conditions that has bred a race of people who understand the value of man's effort to win through, the traditional industries of agriculture, fishing, weaving and mining and, today, tourism are all the same because they share this geography.

This means that today there is a unity of experience along the Celtic Fringe that you just cannot ignore, no matter what you think about who the ancient Celts were and how their bloodstock has been diluted. And this means one thing: the weird beards at Yn Chruinnaght are on to something.

'Look ut it as therapy,' Jim, a real weird beard, says as we prise our way through a drunken crowd to a pair of free seats. I am back in the Ayres bar for the last night of Yn Chruinnaght and it is heaving. It is past midnight now and it has been an action-packed evening. The repertoire of bands from the different countries and a host of dance troupes doing their different interpretations of an epileptic fit on a b-b-q have all been on stage. I also caught a Manx poet called Vinty Kneale (pretty much every Manx surname begins with C, K or Q) reading some of his poems in a side room. He is a well-known character on the island and Mum had told me about him. Very much in the tradition of a village bard from the Western Isles, he is a plumber and his poems, in a sort of modern Manx dialect, are about odd people and village folklore. Caution is a leading trait in Manxmen and Vinty read his poems without much ardour. But they were fine poems and the Manx accent – like the Hebridean accent, the voice lifts at the end of sentences – renders itself well to spoken poetry. I asked him afterwards where he got inspiration for his poetry: 'I write about what's around me,' he said. 'About the little things that happen to me and the people you meet every day. There's material enough there.'

I have been struggling for a few weeks to find a good idea for a new poem. I must have started a dozen poems which have all been abandoned. I have been chasing grand notions, verses to summon a sense of Celticity. This is way above me. I should be writing simple poems about simple things, not trying to shoot the poetic moon. So Vinty cheered me. An even greater boost came later on when some Cornish girls summoned me to their corner table in the bar, not to view my love lance at their leisure, but to hear a poem. Like a page three girl turned actress, I thought, I am finally being appreciated for my art.

'Reet, thar we goo,' Jim says, squeezing in between a Breton fiddling with his oboe and a Welsh dancer who has fallen asleep upright in a chair, still in his waistcoat, plus fours and white stockings.

'Aye, see utz a strange foam a mut-wall therapy, all of us Celts geetin a-gether. Un I find tha, along wi a lahge amoont af alcohol, ut works veery, veery wheel. See, isolation breeds fear, un wher all fuckin skird, big man. Skird a tha future, skird a tha whole fuckin global revolution.' Jim is a Highlander by birth, but he has lived in Glasgow all his life. He reminds me of Spud in *Trainspotting*, galloping along on a hastily consumed wrap of 'Billy Whizz'. He has what you might call a 'lived-in' face, but let's be clear about this, there is lived in and there is lived in. Jim is not lived in in the sense of a new bijou studio in Canary Wharf owned by a finance director who drops in from time to time when he has meetings in London. No. Jim is lived in in the sense of a 'haveli' in Varanasi, somewhere near the ghats, that has been continuously occupied by no fewer than thirty members of the same family of funeral pyre tenders for 3,000 years. His pub philosophy has not been gained from books. It is the amalgam of ideas grasped during the few moments of lucidity that he has had in a decade of propping up the bar. That said, some of it makes good sense.

'Isolation brids fear, ama right thar? Right. Si all this tek about lanwage un culture un whe'ever, is shite. Pan-Celtic, pan-Rangers, I'll pan you! Ya here cuz ya fuckin skird, same as me. Right?'

'But what about nationalism,' I reply, 'new identities, the end of English and French suzerainty, the emergence of a centrifugal Europe? This is the future of the Celts and we all need to help each other through what is likely to be a volatile and unpredictable period. That's why we are all here.'

'Jesus, yoo doo talk some shite, mun,' Jim replies, straightening his kilt out. 'Un whooz thus French bud called Suzi?'

His gaze drifts away from me. I have lost him now. He is no longer listening. The whisky has kicked in or the vodka has kicked out or something. I may as well be talking about the radioactive isotope of strontium present in the fall-out of nuclear fission.

'Noo what? Fur a Celt you can be fuckin boring sometimes. Now, see tha Welsh bud over thar, in a green dress?'

'What about her?'

'Ah believe her father was a goat. Nother pint, mun?'

He is getting up and squeezing past the dormant dancer when he checks and swings round at me with his forefinger out. Jim is my height, but every time he stands up, I can't help but think how short he looks. I guess it is the kilt. It may make big men look bigger, but it makes small men look like hobbits.

'Wanna noo whas really, really important? Whas at the total fuckin core a all this?' He waves towards the bar and the crowd. 'The real reason wha we all come a-geether? Scots un Welsh, Manx un Bretons, bleedin Irish un all a um? Well let me tell yoo, cuz a sense tha yoo doo nought fuckin noo. It's a see who artchly huz the whitest buttocks.'

'What are you talking about, you bloody haggis?'

'This, pal. Listen. The central purpose a this gatherin is a find ouht what mun a which prood Celtic nation has geet the snowiest cheeks. Iz time fuhr the whitest buttocks competition. You get tha pints, mun. Aal gee tha committee a-gether.'

I have owned my kilt for three whole days. The aggregate time spent wearing it is about fifteen hours. I have barely even spilt beer on it and here I am lined up with Jim and Dan in my first ever 'Who's got the whitest buttocks?' contest. The adjudication panel are sitting behind two tables shoved together with paper and pencils that Jim nicked from hotel reception. From left to right, they are Sean, a squinting Irishman who is, remarkably for this time of night and our condition, still wearing a jacket and tie, Jacques, the Breton *bombarde* player and self-appointed chairman, and Mary, a pretty, young Cornish dancer who, quite frankly, I would rather not show my 'bahookie' (as Jim likes to call his arse) to, and if the way she is shifting in her seat means anything, she is not anxious to see it either.

The competitors are myself, Jim and Dan, the only other person in the Grand Island Hotel awake, drunk and stupid enough to want to be involved. He is a big Cornishman, shaped like a sodden old leather rugby ball. His kilt is Cornish – black and white, like the St Piran's Cross, which makes me think of the old lady I met on the train to Cornwall. Oh, if she could see us here. I am certainly learning something about the Cornish now. If his arse looks anything like his face, then it will be a terrifying sight and the adjudication panel may need sick bags. The barman, with a deadpan and very Manx face, asks if he should put a doctor on notice before we begin.

'Naw,' Dan says, 'iz post-traumatic struss syndrome they need tuh worry abut. Call a psychologist.'

After some debate we settle on the rules. Shape, lift, texture and viscosity are to be ignored. The sole criterion judgeable is colour. The whitest pair wins. We are all to lift our kilts as one, and the judges have thirty seconds to inspect.

'Gennelmern,' Jacques says, 'yer tam begins nur.' As one we lift up our kilts.

Mary laughs like a frightened child. Sean says, 'Dan, are ya hoidin any weapons a mass destruction up dere, now?' Jacques makes some notes. After half a minute, we lower our kilts again and there is a round of applause from the small crowd that has drifted down to our end of the bar while the judges confer.

'Ze praz for ze snowiest chics,' Jacques says grandly as if he is about to award the Légion d'Honneur to a war veteran, 'geurs to . . . Gim.'

Jim is delighted. It makes his big night. He is almost tearful. It looks for a moment like there will be an acceptance speech.

'Thas the rewurd for tekkin all ma holidays un Clydeside, where the sun ne'er shines. Get it?' he shrieks, thumping me in the chest. But I am elsewhere for the moment. Standing there, clutching my kilt around my waist, two lines of a poem came to me:

> I've got whiter buttocks than you
> You're a joker man, mine have gone blue.

I snatch up Jacques' pencil and paper and start to scribble:

> The damp detritus of a big old night
> Strafed cross the pub, hell of a sight
> Old Jim clutching his dram, face agog,
> Fat Jacques and young Mary having a snog
> The fiddler's done, the box player lilts
> And pale men from the north lift up their kilts
> 'Och, I've got whiter buttocks than you.'
> 'You're a joker man, mine have gone blue.'

6

On Brandon's Height

The key determining influence in the geography of the Celtic Fringe is the Atlantic Ocean. It goes by a thousand different names – the Minch, the Sound of Sleat, the North Channel, the Irish Sea, Inishtrahall Sound, Bantry Bay, Cardigan Bay, Mount's Bay, Baie de Douarnenez, Golfe du Morbihan – but in the end it is all one continuous stretch of ball-freezing Atlantic water. The ocean sculpts the coastline; it brings a fragment of the temperate Gulf Stream which affects the flora; it was a highway for 3,000 years; from it came enough food to support an industry; goods were smuggled over it and, for most of the time, it delivers the weather. The sway the Atlantic Ocean has held over the Celts of western Europe has been profound since they first slung a hook into it or launched an animal-skin boat on it thousands of years ago. And though that sway may be in decline – it is no longer a highway, there are no fish left – its influence remains a key to understanding the modern Celts.

The best way to get a handle on it, in my opinion, is to get in it, which is precisely what I do when I reach the sea below the village of Dunquin at the end of the Dingle Peninsula, the westernmost point of mainland Ireland and the very edge of Europe. I have been swimming in the Atlantic all my life. I remember those summers as a kid when we played in the sea for hours, when the sun always shone. Didn't it? Of course it didn't. If you think upon your childhood beach holidays at the great British seaside as endless days of Cretan sunshine, building sandcastles grander in conception and execution than the Red Fort at Agra, then you are suffering from selected amnesia psychosis and it is time you

stopped smoking pot and drinking gin. I see no evidence – meteorological, ornithological, neurological or otherwise – to substantiate the ridiculous notion that summers were warmer when Abba
were big. As far as I am concerned, the only difference between the
terrible summers of the twenty-first century and the terrible summers of the 1970s was, back then, I had no balls. Thus I could sit
in the sea making baby dolphin noises for eight hours in any given
day whilst my parents fastened their parkas and drew their beaver-
skin caps close about their heads. I can say this with confidence
because pretty much every time I have swum in the Atlantic Ocean
since my nuts lowered themselves away from my body to catch the
breeze has been like an initiation test to join the Inuit SAS.

So it is today. Getting in is, of course, the worst bit. Personally,
I prefer the diving technique. Once in your swimming trunks it is
important to assuage all testicular suspicions that something
awful is about to happen. Ideally, you want a strip of mink stuffed
down the front of your shorts which you whip out at the last
moment before you plunge from the rocks. Splatting into the
Atlantic Ocean may be the self-induced equivalent of a frontal
lobotomy and you do run the risk, if you are over the age of
twenty-six, of suffering an immediate and terminal cardiac arrest.
But on the up side, your balls are so desperately dazed and confused that they remain largely in the same place, albeit now the
size of garden peas.

The alternative approach is to wade in and as there are no rocks
that I can reach, this is what I have to do today. Thankfully, it is
sunny, but the innumerable drawbacks to this option remain. First,
you have to negotiate an underwater footpath made up of stones
and seaweed, holding your grip with toes that are fast gaining the
dexterity of frozen chipolatas. This first stage alone can make the
hunkiest of beach bums sound like a eunuch entering a snake pit
on a Japanese game show. With one hand cupped hopefully over
the front of your shorts and the other raised like a rodeo bull rider,
you proceed. I find, during this stage, that it is comforting to make

the noise of a gypsy woman giving birth to a washing machine. I can't explain why. I just know it helps.

At the point where the water laps the knuckles of your cupped hand, you really should dive. A good belly flop will turn your stomach the colour of beetroot and sting, usefully diverting attention from the alarm bells of pain going on elsewhere in your body. If you do not dive, and you do take another step, then you have reached the point of crisis. When your balls hit the water, they do not exactly stir gently from luxurious repose like an old man being woken by a familiar nurse in the conservatory on a sunny afternoon in autumn. Rather, they depart the scrotal sac with the same sort of velocity and purpose that Alan Wells displayed coming out of the blocks in the 100 metres final at the Moscow Olympics. One nanosecond later, your balls arrive in your thorax like the weight hitting the bell on a fairground 'Test Your Strength' machine that has just been smote by Desperate Dan – Ding! – bruising your tonsils severely on arrival. If at this point you find you can still breathe, then you can swim about. And though it still feels like you have fallen off a boat in the Bering Straits, things can only now get better.

Well, you would think they could only get better. The beach I am on is adjacent to the jetty from where boats depart for the Blasket Islands. It was deserted when I arrived – no boats, no passengers, just the seaweed sluicing around in the clear water and a few gulls. But when I have completed my impersonation of a hairy Duncan Goodhew, I turn around to swim back to the beach and I see two men stripping off. When they are down to their birthday suits, they start waving at me and shouting 'Hi! . . . yah! . . . yah! . . . hi!' They are Germans or Dutch or Austrians or something. It does not really matter. They are continental, they have their kit off and they are bringing their swinging truncheons towards me.

When the ferryboat to take us to Great Blasket does arrive, there are twenty of us waiting. It is like an EU youth convention. I can hear people speaking French, Italian, German and something else. The two girls speaking something else are – I ask – from Slovenia. What – and this really is a question that needs to be asked – are all these Continentals doing spending their summer holidays in the wettest, most expensive country in Europe? Getting Europeans to visit Ireland is a PR coup on a par with getting people to smoke tobacco or vote for Margaret Thatcher.

As we set off, I go and talk to the skipper, looking for a bit of Celtic bonding. He is my age and from Dunquin. He worked as a fisherman on boats on the Isle of Man when he was a teenager. And now?

'Well, am at this ferry service in the summer months and in the winter, oim away ta Thailand.' He spots a copy of *The Islandman* by Tomás O'Crohan on top of my bag. The book is an elegiac account of the last generation of crofters on the Blasket Islands – a way of life that changed little from the time of the ancient Celts to the twentieth century. It could be set anywhere along the Celtic Fringe from the Pays Bigouden in Brittany to the Isle of Lewis and it romanticises the image of the noble peasant in a way that has done much to colour the modern view of the Celts.

'Now daunt be getting aal nustalgic erbout this,' the skipper warns me, pointing at the book. 'Ut wus er bitt-her struggle air people hed. Awey y'are now. Enjoy Great Blasket.'

Nostalgia for this simple way of life is a modern malaise and a middle-class one at that, but walking along the ridge of Great Blasket over the peaks of Slievedonagh and Croaghmore on a heavenly afternoon, it is a difficult one to resist. The island is only three miles long, but the western seaward end of it feels like the end of the world. Here I pitch my tent. Good sense would have you camp at the sheltered end of the island, among the sod and stone ruins of Tomás O'Crohan's community, away from the prevailing wind. But when I walked up through it, there were already a dozen tents up and I suspect that the sandy beach there – where the New Year's Day hurling match took place in O'Crohan's day – will be like a nudist colony on the Côte d'Azur by now. My innate Celtic modesty and a desire really to get to the edge have driven me on to here.

Tent up, I sit in the heather sipping whisky, watching the sun sink into the silver-coated sea behind the fabulously named outer island of Inishvickillane. Just to the north of me is Inishtooskert, which could be the name of a ballroom dance. I scribble some notes for a poem and reflect on how happy I am to be here. This journey has already taken me to some of the most beautiful places I have ever been, nearly all of which have been facing the Atlantic. Somehow I manage to convince myself that the reason this beauty touches my sensibilities so profoundly is because I am, deep down, a Celt. Me and Tomás O'Crohan, living on the edge, tolerating the rigours of Atlantic life. The earnest, earthy, devout Celt – a man who would polish his shoes and put a suit on to hang himself – that's me. By the time I scramble into my sleeping bag, I have drunk a lot of whisky. As I zip up my tent, I feel a breath of wind on my face and I see a blanket of violet cirrus high in the western sky. Heavenly, I think. How lucky I am.

When I wake in the night, my first thought is, Why am I flying a B-52? The sound – an incessant grey wall of deathly moaning that makes my eardrums tremble – can mean only one thing: someone has unlocked the gates of Mordor. The Nazgul are abroad and they are coming for me. A mother of an Atlantic storm has moved in. A mixture of inexperience and sheer stupidity tells me to go outside and see what is going on. As I stand up, a gust thumps me in the solar plexus and carries me off my feet. At the same time, my tent starts to move off down the hill. It is a desperate moment. Leaping barefoot through the soaked heather, I manage to dive back into the tent and fix it to the earth with my own weight though it continues to shake like a jelly on top of a tumble dryer. The noise is so continuous and all-consuming that I can't even squeeze thoughts through it, thoughts like, What do I do now?

For the Celts, like many primitive peoples, the dead were to be feared unless they were buried or burnt with appropriate ritual. Thus they feared those who were shipwrecked along the hazardous Atlantic coast. In a number of places on the Celtic Fringe, the wind is known as the 'calling of the dead' and it is thought to be the voices of drowned seamen speaking out their own names. Eventually, there is a pocket of silence and I do my best to turn the tent away from the wind and peg it out. For the rest of the night, I lie in my sleeping bag unable to sleep. It is a hellish few hours. I speculate about what Tomás O'Crohan would have done on a night like this. He would probably have played badminton or rowed across to the mainland for a pint.

Dawn brings little relief. By the time I have my tent back in the bag – an activity combining the disciplines of judo, gymnastics and pig-wrestling and surely something that has a place in the vogue for new fitness fads – the rain is lashing down in barrels and the cloud is set thick on the ridge. With a rucksack on my back, providing the sort of extra lift you would get from a Buck Rogers 'jet pack', I nudge my way back down the island. I can only just see my feet and despite the sort of post-anaesthetic disorientation this causes, I can still sense where the footpath drops in one swift 1,300-foot flight into the sea. Here, I am forced to crawl.

The three miles takes several hours and I feel as if I have just come down from a solo ascent of K2 without oxygen when I reach the north end of the island again. It is clearing up. The wind drones on, but there is blue sky again. On the beach is a scene of muesli-munching pan-European utopia that would make Jacques Delors squirm with *plaisir*. I head straight for the boat.

It is late afternoon before the swell has gone down and the boat can finally make the crossing. In a final act of meteorological menace, the wind drops completely and I am served up as lunchtime dim sum to the midges. I tell the skipper about my encounter with the massed ranks of drowned seamen.

'Tis the loife here yet,' he says, steering the boat towards Slea Head and letting the current take us forcefully towards Dunquin.

'Tha weather here is in cantrawl ar us all. It twill change sohfast that it is little wunder that the people wus superstitious.'

It has taken me all day to get from Dunquin to Cloghane, though the villages can only be ten miles apart as the crow flies. The problem is that Mount Brandon lies in the way, a great cloud-catching beast of a mountain that really ought to be away in the middle of the country somewhere, not protruding straight up at the sea's edge. Rather than repeat my Great Blasket experience, I chose to come round Brandon rather than over – and I am heading up there tomorrow anyway – on a journey rather longer than ten miles, along lanes full of tourists on bicycles and hire-car traffic jams.

In O'Connor's bar in Cloghane, there is a fug that you could cut into slices with a knife, wrap in tissue and give to the patrons to snack on as they stagger home. Pipe smoke, drying tweed, alcohol fumes, the smell of stew, the steam of potatoes, the hot air being talked, the odour of merriment and the honest tang of the earth and decent humankind. I am not saying that it would taste any good, but it would give sustenance, for sure. This fug has a tangible texture that my skin senses as I drop down the step from the pavement into the bar. It fills the vacant spaces of the room like gel and I have to work my way through it to get to the counter. It is a fug that fills me with joy. I am back in an Irish pub, and life is mighty.

I have been to O'Connor's before. It is a precious gem of a public house, an unreconstructed old-time Irish boozer that compels you to settle in for a session. I am glad to be back. My glee is heightened too, now that Yn Chruinnaght is behind me. It was very difficult to throw myself into what I was doing on the Isle of Man. Ned Clague was in chains. All the time I was nervously tiptoeing round in the fear that I might meet someone I knew. This sort of low-level deceit leaves a bad taste in the mouth. But the reality is that if I said to everyone I met on this journey: 'I am Rob Penn. I am half Manx and half English. I live in London. I work as a journalist and I am writing a book about YOU!' that would get me nowhere. I want people to behave entirely normally and talk about whatever they want and if I have to be Ned Clague for that, fine. No doubt someone somewhere will be outraged when they read all about it in the book. Maybe one day, I will walk into a pub in a remote corner of the Celtic Fringe and one big and beefy fisherman will get up and punch me into the following week, but I will have to worry about that then. For now, it is time to let Ned Clague go a bit.

Weaving my way back from the bar between the voluminous love handles – they come with the Guinness, I guess – I am looking for a seat when I see an old lady beckoning me. She pats a stool beside her.

'Well, oi door like ah man in er kilt. Oim Nora un oim seventy foive so daunt be getting any oideas erbout chattin me up niw. Would ya loike ta hear a joke?'

'I certainly would, Nora.'

'Well, it is loike this niw. Mick Murphy is a semi-hilliterate man from Brandon village un wun deh da fellow gauze down to the job centre in Dingle to look for werk. At the desk, the clerk says, "Name?" "Tis Mick Murphy," Mick says. "Eeghe?" "Twenty-three," he says. "Sex?" "Awnly de wunce in Ballybunion".' Nora slaps me on the knee and screeches. 'Now look,' she goes on, recovering and looking across the bar, 'there's my sun un I hev to gore home. See you hed yur chance to chat me up and yer blew it. Next time, I will tell yer a dirty joke.' She re-ties her scarf and she is up, shouldering men twice her size apart as she hobbles across to the door.

When I am back at the bar again, a man with a crimson face and a tweed cap pushed so far back on his head I assume it is Velcroed on says, 'I hawp yar not here for de hoi-land games and will be sufferin sum terrible disappointment on account of arriving in de wrong pleace.'

'No, no, I am in the right place. I have come to walk up Mount Brandon tomorrow.'

'Domnach Crom Dubh,' he says, his face breaking into a glorious smile. 'Well, well, *Céad mile failte*. Oim Mickel.' A hundred thousand welcomes. The Irish are neither frugal with their welcomes nor their thanks.

'Domnach Crom Dubh' means 'Crom Dubh Sunday' – I read this but I have not heard it said before – and Crom Dubh is the Gaelic name for the god who lives on top of Mount Brandon (or Slieve Dagda as it was known before Christianity). Tomorrow I am going to walk up the mountain, I hope in the company of others, in a ritual that has been nearly continuously celebrated for at least 2,000 years.

It is the time of Lughnasa (pronounced 'Lunasa'), the ancient Celtic quarter day and a festival associated with the reverence of high places. The actual night of Lughnasa, 31 July to 1 August, is next week but when the early Celtic Christian Church adopted the pagan rituals of the Irish Celts, the celebration was moved to the Sunday before 1 August. Tomorrow, as we set off for Mount Brandon, people will be marching up hills all over Ireland. Most notably, thousands of shoeless penitents will be scaling Croagh Patrick. The word '*Lunasa*' has passed into modern usage and is the Irish Gaelic word for 'August'.

Lugh (pronounced 'Loog') 'of the Long Arm', 'the Shining One', is one of the most important personified, pagan deities of the ancient Celts. He is a central figure in some of the great Irish epic myths and he commanded numerous cults associated with high places, across Europe and the Celtic world. Thus he is remembered in many place names from Lyon to Léon in Spain and Luguvallium (Carlisle).

Lughnasa, the quarter day, is obviously named in honour of Lugh. It is a pre-emptive festival to celebrate the winning of the harvest, a struggle that is symbolised by the conflict between Lugh and Crom Dubh, the mountain dweller, controller of the elements and acquisitive harvest god. In early Christian times, St Brendan, hence Brandon, replaced Lugh as the adversary in folklore.

Whether or not it is a pagan or Christian festival does not matter to me. What is interesting, though, is that for people who live in the small villages around the base of Brandon, climbing the mountain at this time of year is an act of reverence that connects them directly with 2,000 years of their ancestors. The Beltane festival I went to in Edinburgh may have lacked a certain authenticity but the Lughnasa celebrations in Cloghane do not.

Out of all the Celtic countries, Ireland observes the festivals and rituals of the ancient Celts the best, and this is why I have come here for two weeks around Lughnasa. The journey from the Isle of Man to the west of Ireland was relatively straightforward in the general scheme of this trip, and in passing from the Ayres bar to O'Connor's I feel that I have barely missed a beat.

'Will you be walking up the mountain too, Michael?' I ask.

'Well, there will be sum dedicated sools who will accompany you there,' he replies.

'I have a poem to read at the top.'

'Ah, yer'll be very welcome then. Sum years there has bin a little music at the top. Is it a good pohm now?'

'You will have to come to the top to find out.'

'Oi tink Crom Dubh himself will desoide. If tis an earful pohm there will be thunderbolts chasin yer down all the way ta the sea. Will ya hav a pint to encoorage ya in yer mighty task? The lady with the white face us it?'

'Yes, a Guinness would be fine, thank you.'

'Moi woife says tis better to pair-tronise the airts than tis to pair-tronise de bookmakers. There will be sum music in a little whoile un here. I horp yer will not be dashin awee tee yer bed.'

I must admit that I was hoping for a good day. I should know better, of course. I have spent enough time on the Atlantic seaboard of Britain and Ireland to know that one must always expect the very worst of the weather. Go to bed prepared for squalls, gales and horizontal sleet and you might be happily surprised the following day. Then again, you might not. On my previous visit to Cloghane, we had squalls, gales, horizontal sleet and impenetrable fog for four days in August. My wife, my son and I sat in O'Connor's for four days and four nights, going slowly mad. We all got flu. Vicky and Lucas went home early. The only single redeeming feature of the holiday was that my son learnt to enjoy pubs, and to this day if you offer him a choice between an hour snuggling up on the sofa to watch the *Teletubbies Omnibus* or an hour in the pub with Dad, he will always choose the latter. He is only two. Respect.

On that occasion, we had also come to walk up the mountain. So in hoping for a good day today, I was banking on the fact that I had sat out my quota of days of pain at the bottom of Brandon. But no. O'Connor's is about sixty feet above sea level and when we – the dedicated souls – first gather outside the pub, the cloud is on us. It looks like a scene from an educational mountain-rescue video, warning strictly against going hill walking on a day such as this.

There are about forty of us when we gather in the car park at the start of the track that leads up the east side of Mount Brandon. The crew seem mostly to be Irish men and women originally from the Dingle Peninsula, though they have returned from the furthest corners of the country for this weekend. There are also an English couple on a walking holiday and a man from Brooklyn who speaks like Marlon Brando in *On the Waterfront*. I am loitering at the back, slightly self-conscious in my kilt in daylight hours, when I meet John-Joe.

'You look fit. Yes, you look fit fur it. Ar ya then?' he says.

'I'm as ready as I can be. I'm Ned Clague, from the Isle of Man. How are you?'

'Aw, very good now. Very good. Oim John-Joe. We will have us a foine day now.'

'Have you been up the mountain before?'

'Many toimes, many toimes. I grew up in Ventry oer d'other

soide thar. I bin up on Domnach Crom Dubh too. Tis a foine day ort. Der may heven be a little entertainment at the top. There was sum musicians wun year.'

'I look forward to it. I have a poem for the top too,' I say, trying to appear casual. I have decided to spread the word early – to 'out' myself as it were – so I do not change my mind on the long walk up. There will be no shirking today. I am going to read a poem at the top come what may.

'Very gooht, very gooht,' John-Joe rejoins enthusiastically. 'Thet will spur me on durin the ascent. Tis a good pohm now, is it, Ned? For tis an oarful long way oop jus to be hearin a bad pohm.'

John-Joe is rigged out like a walker from the 1950s. The complete absence of hi-tech kit is refreshing. His capacious shorts remind me of post-war FA cup final footage. They would have been worn by players called Len and Stanley who competed for the trophy and two shillings in prize money, with a ball roughly the same weight as a prize-winning marrow.

When everyone is ready, Tony O'Callaghan, one of the guides and an experienced walker in these mountains, introduces himself. He explains briefly the festival. People from the village walked to the top of Brandon on or around this day from pre-Christian times until the 1860s when the Catholic Church put a stop to the event because it was celebrated too frivolously, or, as Tony puts it, 'The hoolies made a lot of roistering and fighting.'

John-Joe nudges me and says with eyebrows raised like an unfinished Romanesque arch, 'Now I daunt gnaw execly whut roisterin is but I fancy there will be sum efter yer pohm, eh, Ned?'

The Feile Lughnasa was revived in Cloghane a few years ago, Tony goes on, as a community festival, which is no doubt what it would originally have been. There is, he explains, one senior gentleman from the village – he has already set off – who has made the ascent of Brandon on this day every year of his life.

'Ear ya ready then?' Tony asks and there is a cheer to cast off the damp. Up we go.

The guidebooks say that Mount Brandon is one of the finest walks in Ireland. Not today it isn't. On a good day it affords wonderful views as you ascend, back over Brandon Bay to the mouth of the Shannon. Then when you near the top, the extraordinary panorama of Ireland's peninsulas opens up to the south. As we walk up, all I can see is the wet path and John-Joe's nuclear fall-out luminous legs striding away from me into the mist. What is uncanny is that, even when visibility is this poor, there is still a sense of the grandeur, a feeling that awe-inspiring scenery lies beyond the Tupperware shield that surrounds us. When we turn up a steep ravine, the walkers bunch up and there is great merriment, despite the arduousness of the task.

When I reach the top after three hours, well over half of the walkers are already there. John-Joe looks as fresh as the moment he started.

'John-Joe, see how brand new you look. Was your father a mountain goat?' I ask.

'Grandfather,' he replies, winking and handing me a hip flask.

The pinnacle of Brandon is 3,127 feet above sea level and we are well and truly buried in the cloud now. Shades of grey whirl around us, tossed about by the gusting wind. Michael Ó Coileáin, another local man, leads me over to the holy spring. It looks like a pool of stagnant water but he insists it is fine tasting and we both slurp up a palmful. I join about a dozen people who are crouching within the knee-high remains of what the Manx call a 'keill' and the Irish call an 'oratory', a tiny, single-chamber stone building where early Celtic Christian missionaries endured the rigours of solitude. These buildings appeared in barren parts of Ireland and north-west Britain in the fifth and sixth centuries. The diminutive remains of these chapels still litter the landscape of the remotest parts of the Celtic Fringe: so much so that when you come across the quiet dignity of a keill, you really know you are on the edge. The design is ascetic, pure and severely simple. There are those who say that architectural design along the Celtic Fringe has progressed little since.

We all share our biscuits and our chat. Despite the conditions, it is remarkably convivial which makes me wonder if there is anyone who is able to enjoy bad weather quite like the Irish. I am having such a good time that I completely forget that I promised to read a poem. Tony raises his voice to explain to us that it was on this spot that St Brendan looked out over the great expanse of the Atlantic and had a vision of the 'Land of Promise', a vision that prompted him to depart on a seven-year expedition which earned him the title 'the Navigator', despite the fact that he got lost a lot and he never found the Land of Promise. I suppose it might have diminished the effect this powerful allegorical voyage had on the Christian flock if he had ended up as 'St Brendan the man with absolutely no sense of direction whatsoever'. Then I hear a lovely, thick Kerry accent from a cluster of bodies.

'Hoo is the por-ht then?' It is Paddy Moriarty, who runs the post office in Cloghane. He is the man who has trod the path up this hill on this day for sixty-five years. He won't remember me, but last time I was in Cloghane he proved to be a genius at entertaining my one-year-old son on our occasional sorties outside O'Connor's. He steps towards the edge of the oratory where he can be better heard.

'Hoo is the por-ht then?'

John-Joe has his eye on me now. I stand up.

'I am.'

'A por-ht from the Aisla Man uz it? Well, yor moast welcome. There's nor bitter man.'

I could just stand where I am, in the dug-out oratory, but as I look round, John-Joe is waiting to catch my eye and he flicks his head at the big pile of rocks and stones. In for a penny, I guess. When I am halfway up the mound and scrabbling with the loose stones, John-Joe shouts, 'Now daunt be looking oop his kilt now. Ya will net be hevin nor vision a da Land a Promise or da Isle a Delight.' Everyone laughs and a hail of gags start.

'We already hev,' a lady interjects, 'und thet is whoi Geraldine is smoilin.'

'Noh, noh, ignorance is bliss,' a man shouts.

'Young man,' a rather proper Irish lady enquires, 'is anything worn under there?'

I have been waiting for this one – it is the oldest kilt gag of them all. When I get to the top, I steady myself and stand up straight. I look in the direction of the enquirer and say, 'Certainly not. Everything works perfectly well, thank you.' More laughter. Then a hush goes round. I have been in two minds about whether to read my new poem, 'I've Got Whiter Buttocks Than You' or *'Skeallaght ny Feayn-Skeallagh'*. I have settled for the latter, as it is about Celtic history and it seems far more appropriate to this scene. I take a couple of deep breaths and take all this in.

Here I am in my kilt standing on top of a rocky mound beneath a great wooden cross, atop a mountain in the west of Ireland, above the Atlantic, on Domnach Crom Dubh. There is silence save for the whistle of the wind in the rocks. Rain is running down my face in rivulets. Poets and storytellers and musicians and holy men of one description or another have stood on this spot on this day for centuries, propitiating the gods with their words. For the first time since this journey began, since Beltane, since I was on top of Cader Idris in fact, all of this feels distinctly right. Being Ned Clague feels right. This is what Celtic poets do. I am supposed to be here. I want to read my poem.

I raise up one hand and thrust it out as I throw my voice into the clouds:

Jee banner mee, ghoinney
Another tall one he's tellin' ya.

At last I feel comfortable with this poem. I know it backwards and forwards and so I can concentrate not on the next line but on how to draw the detail out of it, how to place the emphasis and how to keep people listening. For the first time, I get lost in the rhythms of it. For a moment there is just the poem. No crowd, no Mount Brandon, no buttocks clamped like an industrial vice, no me – just the words of the poem rattling around in the firmament, searching for an ear. I think this sort of detachment from the poem means that I am enjoying myself, though it may simply indicate that I am sober. It is a freakish feeling. The wind has a blast and I stoop to steady myself, rising again to my not exactly great height for the final two lines:

> *Sheegyn, ta mee credjal ayndoo*
> *Charrey veen*, what about you?

To my surprise and delight, there is rousing applause. The one dog with us, an ageing retriever, goes mad. He starts barking and leaping 360-degree aerials, like a ghost has passed through him or the postman has just gone past on a motorbike wearing a suit made of dog biscuits.

'Oid say he had a soight up yer kilt there,' one man says, shaking my hand and pointing at the dog. Paddy and John-Joe and others all come over to shake my hand. When the banter has died down again, John-Joe sings a song in Irish Gaelic. The area to the south of us now, where John-Joe was born, is a Gaeltacht or Gaelic-speaking area. It is his first language. A couple of people then goad a young man called Billy into singing a song, which he reluctantly does. He does not have a great voice, but just hearing Gaelic sung up here is enough for us to sit and listen.

In all, we are on top of the mountain for an hour. Michael and Tony start walking slowly off the top and everyone gathers up their kit and rubbish. It has been a special time, made so perhaps by the easy company of strangers and the fact that we have salvaged something memorable from a miserable day.

Walking down, we pass out of the ravine and on to open hillside where the cloud has lifted. There is a fine view of Brandon Bay.

'Ther'yare,' Billy says. 'Thas frum the gods, for de pohm.' Billy and his friend Kieron are both Gaelic speakers. We walk and slip and tumble our way down the mountain together. Billy has just finished a degree in Celtic studies in Dublin and he has moved into the Gaeltacht that John-Joe is from at the end of the Dingle Peninsula, in order to speak Gaelic daily. The truth is that there are not many places where you can do this any more. The number of Gaelic speakers in Ireland today is a fraction of what it was a century ago and the Gaeltachtai are under constant threat.

'Tis immigration ut is tha problem,' Billy says, clambering over a knackered old stile. 'Dar wuz a toime when de peepel movin in here were wilcome. But now? Will, we gnaw de damage to de culture an de language dat de immigrants can do.'

This is a familiar story that I have heard in every Celtic realm that I have been to so far. James Boswell wrote, on his trip to the Hebrides with Doctor Johnson in 1773: 'The loss of an inhabitant leaves a lasting vacuity; for nobody born in any other parts of the world would choose this country for their residence.' How times have changed. The isolation that the remote parts of the Celtic Fringe offer has become an attraction rather than a discouragement in this technologically advanced age. 'Live local – work global' is the slogan that the Western Isles Council has adopted, trying to attract businesses to the Outer Hebrides. Artists, creatives, smallholders, downsizers, capsizers, New Agers, Old Agers – they have all found synchronicity in the gentle pace of life and the cheap homes on the Celtic Fringe. Unlikely as it may seem, this modern immigration has turned places like West Cork into a Babel of nations. In the Western Isles, I met Americans, Canadians, English, French, Dutch and Austrians who were all residents.

Even Wales is catching on with non-Welsh bankrupts, ex-drug addicts, organic producers and ageing hippies finding happiness tucked away in the remote valleys. These days, the Isle of Man draws dodgy businessmen in droves, as well as legitimate bankers and insurers. At an economic level, this immigration is good, perhaps necessary. The Isle of Man, an unkempt island gasping for financial breath when I was a kid, is now rich. There are jobs for everyone and the young no longer have to leave to find work. At other levels – culturally, ethnically and, in particular, linguistically – immigration is usually damaging. Many of these Gaelic-speaking areas of Ireland and Scotland, like the one that Billy lives in, are so fragile that it only takes a handful of whitewashed cottages to fall into the hands of (usually well-meaning) incomers and the language has gone. And when the Gaelic-speaking areas are gone, the language becomes the academic curio that it is in the Isle of Man.

The other effect is that incomers push property prices up. You don't have to be Alan Greenspan to work that one out. A week ago there was a story in the Irish press about Bill Clinton looking for a house on the west coast. All the papers ran features on what a million pounds will score you in Kerry these days – not much is the answer – and I mention this now.

'Aw, Jesus,' Kieron says. 'Oi wes walkin dorn de street in Tralee et lunchtoime, un de chokes of h-istonishment det wuz echoin aught er de pubs as de gents were reading der papers wuz funny. Twuz us if dey'd herd news dat arl de Guinness in Oirland was finished.'

Our discussion about the erosion of Celtic identity in Ireland goes on and I tell Billy and Kieron about my journey to meet the modern Celt. Kieron says, 'Yu'll struggle ta foind im here, in Ireland, now. Not efter what's happened in the lest ten years. But un trooth, whet political, cultural and linguistic connection de modern Oirish hev with the erncient Celts doid in de seventeenth century, wid de Plaintation. Un what's left a dat collective Celtic consciousness? Net much, oid say. What der is, is in de music, de imagination, in de pohr-try, eh, Ned?'

Halfway down we meet a late starter coming up, another walker with the outward appearance of a Bolton Wanderers left back circa 1952. He stops when we reach him and he addresses me in Irish Gaelic. Quite correctly, he is assuming I will be able to understand him as a Manx speaker, only I am no Manx speaker, sadly. I grasp a couple of words – poet, Isle of Man – but my Manx remains hopeless. Gracefully, he smiles and translates.

'You must be de poht from de Aila Man. I hem sorry that oi missed yew at the top.' Clearly my notoriety is descending the mountain quicker than me.

'Ah, twas a rear performance,' Kieron says, laughing.

The three of them speak in Gaelic for a minute then we set off down with promises to save some mutton pie. Kieron asks about the Manx and how I am learning it. My use of it in the poem is misleading – it implies somehow that I am much more familiar with the language than I actually am. I own up.

'But ya ha good *blass*,' he says. This is a huge compliment from an Irish speaker. *Blass* is a lovely Gaelic word that literally means 'taste' or 'tang' and is used to describe how it is to hear someone speak Gaelic. My head swells.

When we reach O'Connor's at 4 p.m., my legs are tired, but it is a good feeling – like the luxurious after-effects of designer drugs. Kieron and Billy lean their staffs up outside the pub. I have coveted them as I slipped and slid my way down the mountain, rubbing Irish earth into my buttocks.

'Ya need a stick,' Billy says. 'Der moighty fur hill walking un I tink it ud gore wid de rig. Yer wud hev a blackthorn stick now. De blackthorn is de por-ht's stick.'

Guinness has barely tasted so good but chewing my mutton pie – apparently a traditional meal served on this day – contains all the merriment of eating cardboard boxes. The only difference is that the pie is harder to swallow. Kieron and Billy fall on their pies like hungry dogs, whilst I am desperately looking down the street for a hungry dog to fall on my pie. The highlight of this repast is the cigarette I spark after I have slipped the remnants under the table.

The people of the Celtic Fringe are not great foodies. That is the biggest understatement in this book. By and large they are complete food heathens with palates that are delicate like elephant dung is delicate. I am not sure why this is, but for the modern Celts, eating is not a criterion of identity. It is not aimed at satisfying a psychological need. A meal is not an occasion for exchanges or ostentatious acts. Eating is an elemental need that is perfunctorily satisfied, so that the drinking may begin in earnest. You eat, you have a crap and you get down the pub pronto. It is the sort of utilitarian approach to filling your belly that people would recognise in the Australian outback, where you sit down at the 'trough' and you have a 'feed' (or if you are really going some, you have a 'growl') of 'tucker'. Simple.

If you adhere to the French gourmet Brillat-Savarin's famous dictum – 'Tell me what you eat and I will tell you what you are' – then the Scots are a nation of battered and deep-fried Mars bars, the Irish mutton pies, the Welsh unidentifiable breaded things, the Cornish soggy pasties and the Bretons boiled hams. Yes, even the Bretons. Each and every Celtic culinary treasure is a school dinner that you would happily forge your mother's handwriting or eat soap to avoid consuming. Celtic cuisine is like English food before the River Café. No, before Elizabeth David. It is hell.

My Celtic credentials fall woefully down here. I like food. Not only is my mum a fabulous cook, but within two minutes of my home in Brixton I can eat Italian, Thai, Indian, Japanese, Indonesian, Ethiopian, Peruvian, Mediterranean or Caribbean cuisine and most of it is excellent. As they say, once you've tasted paradise, nothing else will do. I know that to a tough Scot, caring about what fills the space between the layers of pastry makes me a homosexual of the highest order. I have done my bit on this journey. I have eaten black pudding rolls with 'brown', spam sandwiches, jumbo saveloy, pea fritters, breaded faggots, unidentifiable boiled things and deep-fried haggis. I can count the number of good meals that I have eaten on one finger: that was at the Applecross Inn, where an Englishwoman ran the kitchen.

The whole food thing leaves me with an ache – and I am not talking about the stomach ache I have got from that mutton pie.

It is the ache of credibility. Does a true Celt really care whether he sprinkles Maldon sea salt or custard powder on his tuna osso bucco with chorizo lanyards and pecorino? The answer has to be . . . *non*!

'Y'up fur another mutton pie, Ned?' Kieron asks, wiping a broad forearm across his grease-soaked beard.

'No thanks. It was, er . . . no thanks.'

If one of the premises for being a Celtic poet on this journey was to ask how deep the fabled love of poetry runs in these people, then that is being answered today. People keep coming over to say how they enjoyed the poem on top of the mountain or, having heard about it, how they wished they had been there. When John-Joe says goodbye, he gives me his address and asks me to send him a copy of the poem. The little tourist office at the end of the village also wants a copy to go on the wall.

The word even reaches the girls of the village and when we are outside the pub for the Lughnasa parade, a couple bound up to me.

'Is it you, da poo-ht den?' a girl with emerald eyes and dark hair asks. I can hear Billy and Kieron snigger. Enough has been written about the brash air of Irish women. They are not especially beautiful, but they can disarm you quicker than a police Alsatian. It is something about their ability to assess desires without regard to social expectations or moral imperatives. The usual effect that their immediate intimacy has on me reminds me that I am at least part Teutonic. What usually happens is my face goes crimson, I start speaking like Emlyn Hughes and I drop my pint.

The very best defence against Irish women and the way to avoid public embarrassment in these situations is to find out their names before the carefree flirting carries you away into legless-la-la land. You see, their names are usually so hideous as to have the same effect as a thimble of iodine in your pint or a wash in a bidet of iced water: Nora, Coleen, Maureen, Eileen, Hairychineen. But if you don't find out their names fast then you are in big trouble, for it only takes a moment for their charm to work. My wife is like this. She is not Irish but she has red hair and she spent a lot of time in Ireland when she was growing up. I think it rubbed off. The first time we met, I fell for her, unconditionally. And I mean unconditionally. If she had said there and then, 'As a small test of your commitment you have to spend the next six months on a desert island with ten years of Lithuanian Eurovision Song Contest entrants,' I would have agreed.

Modern Irish women are, it seems, merely the latest incumbents in a long lineage of brash, butt-kicking, charismatic Celtic women. That lineage starts, of course, with Boudicca, Queen of the Iceni, who gave the Romans a good seeing to in Colchester. Then there is Queen Maeve, from the Irish epics, and Grania, Deirdre and Findabar – all legendary women. Ammianus Marcellinus, a Roman historian, wrote in the fourth century that it is dangerous enough to fight a Celtic warrior, but sheer lunacy if his wife is around too.

So I am not then the first fool to go limp at the 'Oh, shit, I haven't looked in a mirror for months, I'm probably not wearing any knickers and boy do I scream when I am shagging on the bathroom floor' manner that Irish girls all seem to have. On this occasion there is the flash of a red bra strap and a stunning smile, and I am all over the place. It is brain/mouth bypass time. I have the IQ of an eight-year-old and I start speaking in non-sequiturs. The conversation goes something like this, though I cannot be sure as my brain is deluged with hot blood and Guinness.

'Oi said is it youz da poht then? Oive heard earl about ya.'

'Yah, hi. I'm Red. Nob's a nice plum on Tuesday. I roodled a port bottom on top of Brandon main tin. Salamanca, Salamanca, why don't we all spank her? Look, I'm sorry about this. Can I go potty now?'

'You're dribbling.'

'Diddle I? Yes. It's the mutton pie. Also, I have a strange disease of the larynx. I live close to Sellafield and I have a disease of the larynx and a brain the size of a peanut. Hah! A peanut. You have lovely tits. I mean teeth. You see my uncle's a dentist and I know a bit about teeth . . .'

She has gone, with a flick of densely curled hair. I can't blame her. I just don't know how I managed to get my wife to stick around for the first ten minutes. I recall John Wayne playing Sean Thornton in the film *The Quiet American*. Thornton succumbs to the beauty of Mary Kate Danagher the very first time he sees her. Mickaleen O'Flynn, who is driving Thornton's trap at the time, says wisely: 'Tis awnly a mirage brought on by yur terrible thirst.' So I have another pint, or eight.

When I try to leave the pub some time after 2 a.m., my legs are useless. I cannot be sure if it is the walking or the drinking. As I seem to be the first person to exit the pub, I lever my way from shoulder to shoulder across the bar. As I am passing unsteadily through the door, an old fellow who I recognise from up the mountain grabs my arm. 'Fair play to ya, Ned,' he says, boring into me with brilliant eyes. 'With that apparition oop thar today, yer will pass into local mythology. See, even the dogs out in da street air callin your name.'

I dare not tell him they are actually moaning with bellyache, from bolting the remains of my mutton pie.

7

The Merry Monk of Mayo

Guinness distinguishes itself as an excellent drink in many ways, but its single most important contribution to the way of life in Ireland is what is familiarly known as 'the settling period': the minute or two that a three-quarter-poured pint takes to swell in creamy waves to the top of the glass, leaving the body a solid, monochromatic black. Actually, it is dark ruby and not black, but Irish pubs are so dimly lit that you can never tell. And if you must know, the creamy waves are nitrogen bubbles surging to the surface where they gather tidily in the white hat. The settling period is an integral part of the 'two-part pour', as recommended by the brewery and anyone who knows anything about drinking the black stuff, and it makes for a greatly superior pint than one that is sloshed to the brim in one go. But the settling period is more than just the key to a good pint. It is an Irish cultural phenomenon. It is a hiatus in time, a pause in the day, a moment of repose. It is Ireland's meditation.

There are plenty of things you can do while you let the nitrogen surge. You can take a piss, inspect the dusty prints on the walls of the pub, count the whiskies on the top shelf, send a text message, admire your nails, re-tie your shoelaces, lose yourself in thought, check your change, fiddle with the receipts in your wallet, sing a verse of the Marseillaise or vigorously scratch your arse. But if you actually know the ways of an Irish pub, then you do what is expected of you: you begin a conversation with the other man standing at the bar. I do not think that I am stretching things here when I say that from this settling period, directly from this change of pace in your day and the social interaction with strangers that follows, stems the now globally accepted notion that Irish pubs are the most convivial on earth.

One of the pleasures about starting a conversation in a pub in Ireland is that there are no ground rules. As it happens, the Irish are just as predisposed to talk about the weather as the English are, but the point is that you do not *have* to open with a meteorological comment. I once read a long-winded academic essay on the importance of exchanging pleasantries in peasant societies. The argument went that in countries or regions where the fabric of rural life remains intact, people more readily interact in commonplace situations. This is not rocket science: there are fewer people around, and you see them less often in the countryside. In urban situations, where everyone has one eye on the clock, this need is eroded. Imagine trying to say a cheery 'good morning' to everyone on the London Underground at rush hour. You would never get to work and you are sure to be handbagged by some secretary from Essex who is hung over and running late.

However, I feel it is more complex than a mere rural/metropolitan thing. I am sure that the need or the will to exchange pleasantries is more pronounced along the Celtic Fringe than it is in any other place I have been to, and that includes some pretty remote spots – the Australian outback, the Kara-Kum Desert, the Mid-West of the USA and the Anatolian plateau. In Ireland, in the Western Isles or in Brittany it seems that you never pass anyone without exchanging some words, no matter how banal they may be: 'How are ya?', 'Night's coming on,' 'Winds have changed,' 'Raining again,' 'Life is tough,' 'Your flies are undone,' 'Spank me daily, my friend.' In Ireland, I have noticed that even car drivers wave or 'tick' each other with a half-raised, crooked finger when two vehicles pass on a lane. What's that all about? 'Hi, there and thanks for not driving into me,' 'Enjoy your journey now,' 'Oive hed eight points and if yer dawnt tell the garda, then I warnt tell about the potcheen in yer boot.'

What I am trying to say in a round-about way is that by the time you get to the pub of an evening in Ireland, you have already exchanged pleasantries with 12,500 people and commented on the weather close on a quarter of a million times, so you don't have to mention it now, whilst your pint is settling. Pleasantries are done with, which means you can start a conversation about whatever you want.

So, as the pint washes around in the goblet and the barman turns to the till with your cash, you can breeze in with, 'Remarkable that they managed to cross a hamster with a cat in Madagascar recently,' or 'Roy Orbison was the greatest,' or '*The Oxford Book of English Verse*, 943 pages. I say "too long"' or 'I do adore a mango in the morning.'

Only in Ireland will the man on the bar stool next to you have an opinion on any of the above, which he will immediately share, displaying an anxiety that suggests that this is the very matter that has been niggling his private moments all week. Elsewhere in the world, this same man would say, 'Look, you freak, you clearly need help. Now, leave me alone.' A decade ago, when I was not well accustomed with Irish pub behaviour, I was at a bar in the Wicklow Mountains waiting for my pint to settle. The man next to me grasped the extent of my ignorance of Irish pub custom. He sensed that I was not going to begin the conversation, so he averted his gaze from 'never-never land' and said to me, 'Chemokenesis is de wurd fur some h-increased h-activity that will happen in h-an h-organism when h-a chemical h-agent is h-introduced.' I was bruising my brains for something that might make a faintly intelligible retort to this extraordinary statement when the man on my right perks up and says, 'Now I taught he wuz de brave fella whut was always leapin' buses on his mortarbike.' This made things much clearer and I chipped in, 'Oh, I thought it was a rare arrangement of planets in the zodiac at mid-winter.' We all then, as one, looked up at the top shelf, pursed our lips and nodded gravely as if someone had just explained Nietzsche to us.

And so it is that I am standing in the Merry Monk, an unprepossessing pub on the main road out of Ballina in County Mayo at a quarter to ten on a Tuesday evening, waiting for that first pint to settle, and I look at the man on the bar stool next to me and I say, 'Isn't it remarkable that the common slug has made a revival in the uplands of Peru?'

'Yes it is,' the man replies, without looking up, turning his pint in his paws. 'Dey muss be resilient fellows, de slogs. Han example to us arl. If we could only but resemble dem in dear deeds a little, we wud be a better people fair it. Where is it y'are from den, to be knowin soh mutch about dese slogs?'

'The Isle of Man.'

'Ah, the haila Man, is it?'

'Yes, the Isle of Man.'

'Ah, is it?'

'Yes, it is.'

'Ah?'

'Ah.'

'And wud ya say dear's been sumting of a reveival in da fahtune of slogs in da haila Man?'

'Actually, I only know about the slugs in the uplands of Peru.'

'Ah. I see.'

Having spent a lot of time in Irish pubs in the last week, I know this conversation is going somewhere. I have, perhaps, been spending too much time in Irish pubs. But when it is raining – and this is, I heard on the radio, the wettest summer in Ireland for a century so we are talking wet like a bastard of a monsoon in Bengal – what else is there to do in Ireland? Do a tour of grotesque modern bungalows with Doric-columned porches painted pistachio? Go bog snorkelling? The truth is, when it is raining, and that is every day at the moment, there is bugger all to do in Ireland except drink. And anyway, why not celebrate what is good about a country?

As Oliver Reed so eloquently put it (he was talking about life in general, not just Ireland), 'The nicest people I ever bloody well meet live in pubs.' I could not agree more. So, ignoring the advice

of my doctor, my dietitian and my wife (my little axis of evil) I
have been living in pubs while the rain washes the countryside
clean of my trail, making the Emerald Isle even more emerald than
it normally is. My pub crawl has taken me from Kerry to Mayo,
via Tipperary, Laois and Offaly as well as several other counties
that no one has ever heard of and I have already forgotten. It has
been a ball, and I am now shaped like a ball, a recently punctured
one that is bulging in some places and sagging in others. On the
up side, my alcohol tolerance is peaking which means I can drink
from dusk to dawn with these bibulous Celts, something that will
stand me in good stead at the festivals to come. Furthermore, I
instinctively now know when a conversation in a bar is going
somewhere.

'I'm Rob,' I say. 'Can I buy you a pint?' For no reason other than
laziness, I have been dropping my bardic pseudonym from time to
time. When I am not reciting my poems, it does not matter, though
tonight, I immediately realise, it may.

'Tank ya, noh. Oim P-J. Oim just after getting a point a milk
fur de wife. Oi found meself persin de poob un so I am stopped
for de wun point. Werk on yerself now.'

'Work on yourself?' It is a curious phrase. It suggests that one
should go about drinking with the same sort of calculated vigour
that one usually reserves for getting fit, or dieting or learning the
Highway Code. This sort of encouragement to reach a higher
stage of drunkenness is the last thing I need. I have been manag-
ing very well without it, thank you.

The Merry Monk is not just another randomly selected pub on
the unsteady path of a poet through Ireland. I am here for a good
reason. Flushed with my success atop Mount Brandon, I am keen
to perform again. I have to perform again. Lorient is looming,
fast. I will be in southern Brittany in under a fortnight. I still only
have three poems to my name, but I am not too worried about
that. If I can perform them well, then three is enough. I just need
to get some more gigs under my belt. In a pub in Athlone, I saw a

notice about a series of *seisiúns* of music and arts organised by the national cultural organisation Comhaltas Ceoltóirí Eireann. A glance at a map and I realised that Ballina was vaguely on the route that I proposed before I started my crash course in living like Oliver Reed. (I cannot help feeling sad that he never made a 'self-help' video about living in pubs. It would have been a joyous antidote for everyone who never got on with the *Jane Fonda Workout*.) So I telephoned the organiser of the Ballina *seisiún* to say that I was a poet from the Isle of Man and could I come along and read a couple of poems.

'Delighted,' he said. 'We start at 10 p.m. We'll have a couple a hundred in so be sure to bring copies of your published work to sell.'

'Great,' I said. My voice suddenly sounded distant like an echo on a long-distance call in the 1970s. 'Will do.'

Published work? Oh, shit, I thought. He thinks I'm the bloody poet laureate. How am I going to pull this one off? I wanted to call him back and say, 'Look, I'm terribly sorry. That was a hoax call. You see, Ned Clague is an insubordinate alien living inside me. He is psychotic and dangerous and forever trying to set up gruelling and embarrassing events in public for me. Me? I'm Rob. I am very nice and very timid. I like ponies and warm milk. I am sorry for the inconvenience. I need to go and lie down now. Goodbye.' I resisted making that call and for the last three days I have carried in my head an almost continuous vision of me standing naked but for my kilt on a podium, facing 200 people who are manically chanting, over and over again: 'Show us your published work, Ned! Show us your published work!'

When I was a student, we invented an imaginary game show called *Paranoia Paradise*. We were working on the perverse truth that secretly everyone loves a little paranoia. Contestants on the show would be made to eat a golf ball of Humboldt Gold or some such other pungent weed before entering a reality situation to confront their greatest fears: a sort of *Big Brother* meets *The Magus* scenario. Back then, being on a podium in a kilt in front of a chanting crowd might have been my *Paranoia Paradise* scenario. But not now. I don't smoke pot any more. Well, I don't smoke pot like I used to. And I am here, aren't I, in the Merry Monk?

My thinking is: if I can't explain why I have forgotten my published work, then I might as well pack up and go home to the bosom of my family and try and get some work writing for the 'lost cats' page of the local newspaper. Besides, there are a host of excuses as to why I have failed to bring copies of my published work to the Merry Monk. 'I am making a long journey on foot and I can do without the weight.' 'I have just begun a new body of work and everything else has gone on the bonfire.' 'There's been a hold-up in printing the seventh edition. Remarkably, edition six sold out last spring at a literary festival in the Crimea.' 'My American publisher has insisted all copies of my work be withdrawn whilst the accusations of plagiarism are settled in court. It must be very embarrassing for Seamus Heaney, I am sure.'

I have been rehearsing them all day, trying to determine which is the most convincing. However, they may not be needed. It is now only minutes before ten o'clock and apart from P-J, the barman and myself, there are only two other people in the pub. And a dog who is hogging the hearth. Clearly, I have got the wrong night. I explain to P-J that I am here to read some poems and I ask if there are, by any chance, two Merry Monks in Ballina?

'Ah, a poo-hit? Tis grand,' he says, nodding at the barman for a refill. ''Twill be busy enough now for the recitation.' With that the door swings open and the band walk in. Half an hour later, the pub is rammed. I meet Peter, who I spoke to on the phone. He has completely forgotten about the published material, so I don't mention it. He has completely forgotten that I was coming along, but that is no matter.

'Air ya in fur the noight?' he asks. 'Whet is it ya do again?'

'I'm a poet. I have a couple of poems to read.'

'Ah, yes. Very good. Oil give yer the nod.'

Something that I had only half anticipated is how very normal it is to have a poet read in a pub in Ireland. You don't have to go to an Arts Centre with lots of women in baggy purple sweaters, or to a furiously trendy bar that is empty, to hear performance poetry. You can catch it in your local. That is not to say every pub in Ireland has a resident poet, nor that poetry would run Sky Sports a close second in a poll of pub entertainment, nor that pubs would close down in their hundreds if the league of poets went on strike. However, the Irish familiarity with spoken verse may well make them unique among races.

Back at the bar, P-J (now savouring his third pint by my counting) introduces me to a number of his friends: 'Da fella's a poo-hit from da haila Man. He's in fur a recitation.'

No one bats an eyelid. Davey, Vincent, Dermot and Gerry – they all respond in the same way: 'Aw, very good. Well yur welcome here.'

In an analysis you would have to say that of all the countries of the Celtic Fringe, Ireland remains the most 'Celtic'. The culture here has been least affected by invasion and erosion over the centuries, starting with the fact that no Roman legionnaire ever set foot here. The colossal contribution, far out of proportion to the size of the country, that Irish men and women have made to literature and poetry in English (quite apart from in Irish Gaelic) is testament to the Irish love affair with words that dates back through the supremacy of Irish medieval poetry to the oral tradition of the ancient Celts that began hundreds of years before Christ. All of which makes my task tenfold easier. Reciting poetry in Irish pubs is like playing a football match at home. I am almost feeling relaxed about it, not that this stops me from working up a bit of Dutch courage with a few pints.

The music, which has been going on for an hour or more now, has stopped and I notice for the first time how roaring the volume of conversation is in the pub. P-J is flapping at me from round the corner of the bar.

'Yer man wants yer,' he says, waving towards the band. I realise that my name is being called out over the PA system. 'We're vehry loocky to hev in de poob tonight' – it is Peter's voice – 'a poo-hit erl de way from de haila Man, Ned Cligg. Forks, a warm welcome, please.'

By the time I get over to him, the moment's silence and the light ripple of applause have passed. Peter hands me a cordless microphone and it feels fleetingly like karaoke time. I am not accustomed to mics, but clearly I have no option in here. Just being heard at the back of the pub is going to be a problem. But a more immediate problem is at my feet. I had not noticed this, but the members of the band are all teenagers and they have clearly never seen a short man in a skirt doing karaoke-poetry before. It starts with a barely restrained titter, but when one of them gasps for air, making the sort of strangled sound of someone flying a microlight swallowing a blackbird, they all completely lose it. I check no one has slipped a mirror on to the floor between my feet, and try to carry on as normal.

I kick off with 'Skeallaght ny Feayn-Skeallagh'. A big hush goes round the room when I begin. I have read and re-read this poem into mirrors in B & B bathrooms. I have proclaimed it from bus shelters and whilst idling by the side of the road hanging my thumb out. I have it sorted now. There is an ebb and flow in the level of the back-chat going on in the pub and it only takes a hiatus in the poem followed by a foot stamp and a roar to get the silence back again. The tittering around me, however, hardly abates. At the end there is a healthy round of applause. When I give the mic back to Peter, he tilts his head in appreciation and asks if I will read another in a while.

At the bar, the lads are proudly clapping. There is a pint on the bar, 'Fur de recitation', P-J says. The lady who runs the B & B across the road where I am staying pops up beside me.

'Ooh, very good, Ned,' she says, 'very good.' I hadn't expected to see her in here, though she was intrigued by the kilt when I walked through her garden in it.

P-J leans forward conspiratorially and twists his eyebrows to ask a question. 'Ned Clague? Is that loike a pen name?'

'Sort of, P-J. It is what is called a bardic name,' I reply, trying to look convincing.

'Shoite,' he says, 'yer bleedin famous, airn't ya?'

'No, P-J. I'm not.'

'Y'are too,' he says, giving me a big wink. 'Oi knew it. Oi may nat be awverly fehmiliar wit de literary world, but oi naw dut to be hevin a beardic name wud signifoi dat de poo-hit hin question wud be a famous wun. Tis loike a boxer. When he is gettin to be a good foighter, then he will hev himself a nickname. An I gnaw a bit aboot boxin now.'

There are more pints and toasts, the best of which is:

> Your health and a long life,
> May you have a wife to your liking,
> A child every year,
> Land without rent,
> And may you die in Ireland.

Davey says it in Gaelic and then translates it for me. At some point I say to P-J, 'I thought you were only having the one pint?'

'And will ya look? Airn't oi hevin awnly de wun pint now?' he says, framing his Guinness with outstretched hands. 'But oi tink oi ud better fawn da woife and h-explain dat it is terkin an earfully long toime to drink it.'

When I go back up for the second poem, the pub is a little rowdier and I am a lot more drunk. I am feeling very . . . fluid. On the spur of the moment, I decide to have a go at my new poem: 'I've Got Whiter Buttocks Than You'.

'Will you hear another poem now?' I yell over the heads across the bar. 'It's a poem about wearing a kilt and it is called "I've Got Whiter Buttocks Than You".' The band loses it again and there is a cheer from the lads. I have the poem on a piece of paper in my pocket and I place this on the table, just in case I lose my way.

In your *feíleadh beag*, or your belted plaid
Yon spirit of the Highlands embraces your lad.
So it's fine for carousing or dancing a reel,
But it's death to Butcher Cumberland that your
    buttocks do feel.

There is another rowdy cheer. They are listening now.

My blanket, my dress – I'm ready for action.
Pugnare in nudo. Look'ye here, pretty Saxon.
I've got whiter buttocks than you.
When I've chopped off your head, what will you do?

I think it has clicked that it is a song of rebellion, a poetical and musical genre that the Irish have almost made their own. They really are listening.

When the war pipes do drone,
If it's the tone of the moan
That'll never leave you alone, then shout
'I know where I'm from. Sassenach gi' out!'

For this last line, I take the mic away from my chin and shout it out as loudly as I can.

I walk the bienns, I trace the sky in the lochs
Cold air on my bahookie, naked in ma socks
Yes, I've got whiter buttocks than you.
Think on it, now. You know it's true.

I point and glare at the crowd. I am galloping a bit here, getting ahead of myself in the enthusiasm.

Tis a matter of national pride, it's the tartan ID
A hero's mantle, that exclaims 'forever free!'
Bonnie Charlie to Begbie, Rob Roy to Joe Jordan
In our pleated skirts, we'll give the English a-maulin'.
It is worn by the clans of bearded freaks

Who all claim the prize for the snowiest cheeks
I've got whiter buttocks than you.
Where the sun never shines, the wind blows true.

There is raucous laughter. I pause and glance down at my piece of paper, and then I have a swig of Guinness. Someone starts to clap, so I snap the mic back up.

The damp detritus of a big old night
Strafed cross the pub, hell of a sight.
Old Jim clutching his dram, face agog,
Fat Jacques and young Mary having a snog.
The fiddler's done, the box player lilts
And pale men from the north lift up their kilts

'Ga awn then,' someone shouts.

'Och, I've got whiter buttocks than you.'

I pause here and look all the way round the pub. I can take as long as I like. They all know there is another line coming. There is still plenty of nattering going on at the back of the pub, but around me it really looks like people are listening. Even the kids in the band have stopped sniggering.

'You're a joker man, mine have gone blue.'

'*Gora mie ayd*,' I say, raising my pint glass above my head. There is a wave of applause.

'A rebel song,' Peter says when I return the mic. 'Yerl hev free points in hare all noight now.' He is not wrong. I am not allowed to put my hand in my pocket ('Or even hup yer kilt,' as Davey puts it) again. When the band packs up, the pub thins out. Soon it is just P-J and me at the bar again. He is telling me all about his boxing career when the publican shuffles us off our stools at 2.30 a.m. We stagger out into the drizzle like a pair of Polish sailors on leave. So often as a journalist, meeting people is all about contact without consummation, or information without attachment. As Ned Clague, this is probably even more so; anxious not to be unmasked, I do a great deal of hovering around the thin layers of deceit that I am spinning, fearful that the comfort of a hastily formed friendship will reveal me. But tonight has been different, not least because P-J has the most engaging characteristics of the Celts – patent sincerity, complete lack of affectation and that strangely disarming charm that visitors to Ireland fall head over heels for. It has been a grand night. When our ways split at the end of the road, we shake hands vigorously. As I turn away, P-J stops and says, 'Aw bollocks. Now didn't oi forget that point a milk.'

8

The Lughnacy Games

Cú Chulaìnn (pronounced 'Ker Kullin'), or the Hound of Ulster, went to study weaponry in the Land of the Shadows. There, Cú Chulaìnn fought Princess Aoife, the fiercest warrior-woman in the world, in single combat and he defeated her. She then went to him and when she left she was pregnant with a son. These things happen.

'Call the boy Connla and give him this golden ring,' Cú Chulaìnn said. 'Let him follow me to Erin. Charge him under "geise" [a magical injunction] that he must not make himself known, nor turn away from any man, nor ever refuse a combat.'

Seven years later the boy went to seek his father. The Ulaid, the knights of Ulster, were assembled on the beach and they saw the boy out on the sea in a bronze boat with golden oars. In the boat was a heap of stones, which the boy was using in a slingshot to stun the sea birds flying above. Afterwards, he revived them and sent them back to the air.

'If the grown men from his country came here,' said Conchobar macNessa, King of the Ulaid, 'they would pound us to dust. Let him not enter this country.' Condere, son of Echu, who was known for his eloquence, was sent to him.

'Where are you from and who is your family?' Condere asked.

'I will not identify myself,' Connla replied, 'and I will not turn away either. Go and ask the Ulaid whether they wish to come against me singly or in a host.'

Conall of the Victories went then to meet him, saying, 'Delightful are your games, little boy.' But the lad slung a great stone at him which knocked Conall head over heels and before he could rise, the boy bound him up with the strap of his shield. And so man after man was served; some were bound and some were slain.

'Send for Cú Chulaìnn,' King Conchobar eventually said.

Cú Chulaìnn was playing with his wife, Emer. 'Do not go!' Emer said. 'I am sure it is Connla, your son, who is there.'

Cú Chulaìnn answered, 'Silence. It is not a woman's advice I seek regarding deeds of great splendour. Whoever is there, I would go for the sake of the Ulaid.'

Cú Chulaìnn went down to the shore then: 'You will die unless you identify yourself,' he said.

'Prove that,' said the boy. The two of them struck at each other. The boy performed a hair-cutting feat with his sword, leaving Cú Chulaìnn completely bald.

'The mockery is at an end,' Cú Chulaìnn said. 'Let's wrestle!' The boy stood on two pillars of rock and threw Cú Chulaìnn down between the pillars three times. The lad never moved his feet and they sank into the stones up to his ankles. Still wrestling, they fell into the sea. The boy ducked Cú Chulaìnn twice and he would have been drowned on the third ducking when he remembered the Gae Bolga, and he drove this weapon (that only he knew about) through the water into Connla, and the boy's innards fell out at his feet.

Then Cú Chulaìnn saw the ring on the boy's thumb. He took the boy in his arms and carried him to the Ulaid, saying, 'Here is my son.'

'Now show me the great warriors that I may know them and take leave of them before I die,' said Connla. He put his arms around the neck of each man and kissed them in turn. Then he bade his father farewell and died. Cries of grief were raised and for three days not a calf of the cattle of the Ulaid was left alive. This was the only son Cú Chulaìnn ever had, and this son he slew.

It is a tragic story and it comes from a remarkable collection of tales called the *Ulster Cycle*, centred on the epic events of Cú

Chulainn's life. The collection was probably first written down by monks, the earliest Celtic scribes, in the eighth and ninth centuries AD, but it may date back (there is plenty of correspondence between the texts and archaeological evidence to substantiate this) as a series of oral tales to several centuries before Christ. That's old. In fact, the *Ulster Cycle* is possibly the oldest vernacular epic in western European literature. So put that in your pipe, eh? The *Ulster Cycle* is part of a corpus of ancient Celtic literature that includes, among other things, the *Fenian Cycle* and the *Book of Invasions*. This body of literature has been described by people who know about these things as 'one of the marvels of civilisation'. Yet outside Ireland, few have even heard of it.

I am only finding out about this stuff now, and I don't want to bang on but it strikes me as odd that literature of such obvious greatness should be so overlooked in the British Isles (in favour of, for example, Greek mythology). Come to think of it, the whole history of the ancient Celts has been pretty well overlooked, and that includes their art and the influence that Celtic culture and languages have had throughout the islands of Britain.

I struggle to remember it clearly, but I am pretty sure that chapter one of the first 'History of Britain' book I ever opened began with Caesar arriving on the shores of Kent in 55 BC. Sure, it was a notable event: Caesar pulled his cloak close about him, peered into the drifting rain and said, 'Sod this. I knew we should have invaded Sardinia.' But what starting at this point means is that almost 1,000 years of the history of these islands – rich, fascinating Celtic history that is no minor prelude – have been axed before you have even got going. It suggests that before Caesar pitched up with his baths and his town planners and his road builders, there was nothing in Britain but bearded, bibulous, half-naked heathens who collected heads and had the cultural finesse of a troop of baboons in the mating season.

The tales of Cú Chulainn suggest otherwise. The blend of romance and realism, heroism and humour, cultural history and epic myth distinguishes ancient Irish literature. It is this corpus of literature that perhaps best embodies the spirit of the ancient Celts. Any historian will tell you that elements that have entered into a nation's make-up in remote times endure through all of its history, and stamp the character of the people. Reading the *Ulster Cycle*, it strikes me that this may be particularly so for the Irish, and perhaps all the Celtic peoples. Put another way: there is a historic stream of life coursing through us all, but in the case of the Celts it is a river.

Cú Chulainn is a kind of Superman figure and the tales are full of feats of extraordinary athleticism (catching stags, leaping castle walls), skill (bringing down birds with his slingshot, planing trees with his fingers) and magic (Cú Chulainn had a sword which spoke), not to mention the glory he attains in battle. These are violent and bloodthirsty tales which also explore the themes of triplicity (the number three), sacred cauldrons, shape-shifting, anthropomorphism, the veneration of human heads, sex and erotic symbolism. (In one tale of the *Ulster Cycle*, Cú Chulainn meets a girl he rather likes and, peering down her cleavage, he says, 'I see a sweet country. I could rest my weapon there.') It is all wonderful fuel for a boy's imaginings.

But nothing in these tales compares to when Cú Chulainn descends into his '*riastradh*', or 'battle-fury'. He undergoes a transcendence out of this world – think the Incredible Hulk here – and amazing things happen: the muscles on his neck stand out like the head of a young child, one eye is engulfed in his head and the other protrudes like a telescope, foam pours from his ears like fleece, the beats of his heart are like the lion's roar as he attacks a bear, flecks of fire stream from his mouth. One description ends like this: 'in virulent clouds, sparks blazed, lit by the torches of the war-goddess Badb. The sky was slashed as a mark of his fury. His hair stood about his head like the twisted branches of red hawthorn. A stream of dark blood, as tall as the mast of a ship, rose out of the top of his head, then dispersed into dark mist, like the

smoke of winter fires.' Cú Chulaìnn really loses it. I suspect that
only someone who has been to a Rangers versus Celtic football
match will know precisely what Cú Chulaìnn went through.

Though Cú Chulaìnn is barely known in England, he has
always been a much-loved hero in Ireland. A statue of him com-
memorates the 1916 Easter Uprising at the General Post Office in
Dublin. Upon this statue, the protagonist in Samuel Beckett's
novel *Murphy* tries to kill himself by repeatedly head-butting the
buttocks of Cú Chulaìnn. He is the subject of muralists on both
sides of the Troubles in Belfast and there is even a brilliant Pogues
song called 'The Sick Bed of Cuchulainn'.

Despite his supernatural ancestry, Cú Chulaìnn is held up as a
figure from early Irish history and the confusion is forgivable
inasmuch as the tales about him do entwine aspects of historical
fact and, as I mentioned, correspond with archaeology. (Some say
that the continuing Irish habit of mixing fact and fiction stems
directly from this ancient literature.) Not least of these historical
accuracies is the situation of the fort where King Conchobar and
the Ulaid lived in the *Ulster Cycle*, and where Cú Chulaìnn would
have returned to rue the death of his son (though let it be known
he also killed his half-brother and his best friend, so he probably
did not rue too much).

The fort is called Emain Macha and it still exists, which will be
no surprise to anyone who knows Ireland well. I doubt there is
another country where myth is wedded so closely to the soil, and
where place names are so charged with legendary associations. I
know Emain Macha still exists because on a damp early August
afternoon I am standing on top of it. The flat-topped glacial hill
or drumlin is surrounded by a large ditch and a bank. On top of
the hill and immediately beneath my feet is an artificial mound
from where there are extensive views, even on a grey, misty day,
across the county of Armagh.

There was a huge archaeological dig at Emain Macha (or Navan
Fort as it is also known) in the 1960s. They came up with more

questions than they answered. What we do know is that the site was occupied for thousands of years, but in the few centuries before Christ it was at its most remarkable and important. A unique structure was created here during that period: a wooden building with five rings of oak posts, 130 feet in diameter. This, one must assume, was a ceremonial structure for druidical inaugurations, tribal gatherings and big, big piss-ups – the usual stuff. At some stage around 100 BC, the whole thing was burnt down. Nobody today knows why. It was then filled with limestone boulders and the whole mound was carefully layered with soils, other deposits from a variety of environments and turf. So what is all that about? This ten-foot-high cairn was clearly built to last. It has probably not changed at all since.

The archaeologists did dig up pottery, amulets, decorated jewellery and, get this, the skull and jaw of a Barbary ape, which means one of two things: in the second century BC the Irish were trading with North Africa, or the Barbary apes were formerly party to a great seafaring tradition and *Planet of the Apes* is all true. However, as with most Bronze and Iron Age monuments, there is not a lot here other than the grassy mound. Emain Macha may be one of the oldest prehistoric sites in all of Britain, but it has far greater symbolic significance as the abode of the Kings of Ulster, and the court of Cú Chulaìnn.

Curiously for people who have such a strong sense of their own identity today, the Irish have no love of history in the conventional sense. As an Irish journalist I once worked with put it: 'We have no national ambition. So what would we need history for?' Committing history to paper gives it permanence and credibility with future generations and it is always written down by the victors. The ancient Celts never wrote anything down before the monks came along and little enough after, hence the oral tradition. This is why most of what we know about the ancient Celts comes from archaeology and classical historians. However, the English (or the Angles and Saxons as they were) were at it from the time of Bede in the early eighth century, who wrote the first history of these islands and in so doing gave the English a Roman historical context and destiny which they have not yet managed to slough off, hence the flawed history book I read as a boy.

The Irish, and the Celts in general, have been mistrustful of history ever since Bede. But history combined with myth, fantastical deeds, cult heroism and battle-furies – history veiled in a thin cloak of mist just as Emain Macha is today – is different. The Irish cannot get enough of it, which is perhaps why Emain Macha is so unusually atmospheric for an archaeological site. And I am not saying this because I have just been reading about the Hound of Ulster, nor because the site could be a 'mesocosm' linking the underworld, the earth and the sacred cosmos, nor because I have just found three apples arranged neatly in a small divot at the exact centre of the top of the mound (a Lughnasa gift of first fruits for Lugh? An offering to the spirit of the druids?), I am saying this because it is what I feel.

I wander around, alone, for half an hour. My shoes are soaked through from the moisture in the thick grass. Low cloud drifts across the plains to the south. It really is very enigmatic. I guess I am able to feel the numen of the place again. It occurs to me that I should take a stone from here and when I look down, there is one – a small, flat stone the size of a matchbox on a bare patch of grass on the top of the mound. Intrigued, I walk all the way round the top of the mound again looking for another stone, but the grass is continuous. You would need a spade to find another stone. Now, I am not saying anything. It is just a bit odd that there was a stone at my feet when I first thought of it. That is all.

Cú Chulainn was the son of the god Lugh (as in Lughnasa), by a temporal maiden, Dectera. It is appropriate that I am finding out about him, and his dad, now since the Lughnasa quarter day has just passed and I am on my way back across Ireland, deep into County Leitrim, for one more seasonal gathering to celebrate Lugh.

Leitrim is a quiet county of Ireland, full of rolling green hills and rural sounds. Not that I can hear the rural sounds since I am bombing along in a hire car. A Ford Focus is, whichever way you look at it, a poor way for a poet to get around, but I have pressing needs. True to form, all the Celtic countries have some sort of festival around the time of Lughnasa – it is strange how these dates hover in our consciousness – and in order to get to as many as possible I have decided to limit my exposure to the equally unreliable means of hitching and public transport. I am going to a small Lughnasa festival here in Leitrim, and then I have an all-night drive to Rosslare to catch a ferry across the misnamed St George's Channel to Fishguard. I then have three days at the Welsh National Eisteddfod in St David's. Then to London for a night, to show my wife my distended stomach and my furry tongue and from there to Lorient for the last three days of the Festival Inter-Celtique. It amounts to a rare and rude blast of all things Celtic, but I am ready for it.

I have come to Leitrim to visit the Grove of Sinaan, a small commune of New Age pagans that Kieron, who I met on top of Mount Brandon, told me about: 'Dey tark a lot uv bullshit,' he said, 'but yer shud check it out, see what dem pagans air rattlin un about.'

When I telephoned to see if it was all right to drop in, Chris, a Londoner guessing by her accent, said, 'Sure. You're welcome. Come on Sunday. It's the Lughnacy Games.' This, I thought, I cannot miss.

I have spent enough time wandering and bicycling around the heavily fenced, 'get off my land' English countryside to feel uncomfortable when I arrive at a deserted rural property. My immediate thought is 'trap'. Then I wonder if there has been a mass family suicide and I shall be the first to discover the bodies. At the gate of the Grove there is a sign with a leaping salmon which Chris told me to look out for. So I know I am in the right place and I drive down the track to a farmhouse tucked in a dip between round hills. It is very quiet and I hover around for a few

minutes, walking on the balls of my feet, whistling. I keep trying
to tell myself that the Grove of Sinaan is as near to a hippy commune as you will find east of Big Sur and I will not get salt shot up
my backside for trespassing.

In the barn there are leaflets about the work of Teach Sinanna.
I grab a few and wander along a path away from the house, up
the hill. It is a sunny evening, but the air remains heavy. From the
leaflets, it is not very clear what does happen at the Grove. There
is a sort of theatre company that does drama lessons for schools
or community groups, as well as magic and fire shows for festivals and parties. Much of this incorporates the ancient Celtic
myths and legends that I have been reading. At the Grove itself,
one can undertake workshops to 'regenerate empowerment . . .
and deepen contact with the spirit of the land' or 'explore creativity and self development through the framework of Celtic
stories . . . drawing inspiration from the "story lines" of the
land.' Umm. This is what Kieron struggled with: the borrowing
of powerful ancient stories for, as he put it, 'New-fengled,
mumboh-jomboh, self-improvement rubbish, erl in a sympa-
thetic, low impect un sustainable settin, wit a lot of fuckin tea
being drunk.'

He is right about the setting. Wandering around I come across
the tree circle, the turf-cut labyrinth which is a bit overgrown at
the moment and the well, which have all been created in tribute to
aspects of pagan spirituality. Beyond the property is Sheebeg, the
Little Fairy Hill in legend, the resting place of Finn MacCool, the
giant who created the Isle of Man by tearing out a chunk of
Ireland and hurling it into the Irish Sea. Further away is Sheemore,
the Big Fairy Hill, and Sliabh an Iarann, the Iron Mountain where,
as legend tells, the Tuatha De Dannan (the People of Dana), the
earliest and most important mythical invaders of Ireland, the
people of the shifting mist, landed in their cloud ships.

When I get back to the farmhouse, it is getting dark and lights
are on. The first person I meet is Bee, an English girl in a paisley

dress and Doc Martens with a face full of jewellery. She has the pale complexion of a committed vegan who dwells inside a damp cardboard box in Ireland in perpetual winter. This is how I imagine people looked after rationing and air-raids.

'Yeh, right. You must av spoken to Chris on the phone, yeah? She's not back yet. Put your tent up where you like, but not in the tree circle, right? That's the space for tomorrow, yeah? There's food on if yer hungry, yeah?'

There are a few other people mingling around. We all just nod and smile. When I am putting my tent up, an American voice behind me says, 'Ooh, nice tent, man.' I turn around and there is a great bear of a fellow with long blond hair tied in a ponytail and a straggly beard.

'Lovely soft bed here,' he continues, looking up at the darkening sky where the first stars are appearing, 'and I'd say rain'll stay off too.'

'Great. American?'

'Californian, actually.'

'I'm Ned. Good to meet you.'

He stretches out a hand the size of a tennis racket. 'Bjorn. Good to meet you, Ned.'

'Bjorn. I thought with a name like that, you would be from Michigan, or Wisconsin or Lake Woebegone.'

His eyes screw up as he looks at me. 'Bjorn-duh.'

'Right . . . as in Borg.'

'No, Bjorn-duh. As in B-E-Y-O-N-D. Beyond.'

'Beyond?'

'You got it now, Ned. Beyond.'

'But beyond is . . . er . . .'

'My name.' He says this with the sort of heavy calmness that suggests he has always moved in circles where his name is accepted implicitly and without childish sniggers.

'I see.' I take a moment just to make sure that this conversation is happening. I assure myself that it is.

'Beyond what?' I ask, easing tent pegs into the damp ground. 'Beyond reasonable doubt? Beyond the Pale? Beyond the Fringe?'

'Beyond Joy,' Beyond says.

'Beyond Joy. Ah, yes. Beyond . . . joy.'

'That's my name. My surname is Joy. My first name is Beyond. Beyond Joy.'

Beyond Joy! I want to say, 'Now, look here. You look like Conan the Barbarian and you talk like Timothy Leary. I know plenty of people who are one sandwich short, but to be perfectly frank with you, Beyond Joy, there is little evidence of there being any bread whatsoever in your picnic.' Beyond walks to the hedge and inspects a blackberry bush.

'You weren't by any chance born in the sixties, were you?' I ask.

'You got it,' he shouts over his shoulder.

'And, er, what is Beyond Joy then?'

He boots a tuft of cut grass away from the back of my tent from which a tiny thermal of air rises and he walks round to me with an outstretched palm full of blackberries. When I take one, he says, 'Me.'

In the morning I meet the rest of the team who live at the Grove. Chris, who is in charge, is a statuesque lady with a resonant voice. She is originally from London but she has been in Leitrim for over a decade. Dressed in a rainbow shift, she stalks about like a character from one of her dramas. She cannot remember speaking to me on the phone, but I am welcome anyway. Christophe, her partner, is another mad-looking fellow. He is as thin as a racing-snake with the curvaceous moustache of a First World War fighter ace. In a white shirt and black dinner trousers – this seems to be his gardening outfit – he looks like an off-duty waiter at a Parisian brasserie.

Bee and Emma, who has travelled up from Galway with her baby daughter Rowan, are talking about how to get paganism taught in schools in Ireland, as part of the religious studies curriculum, when I wander into the barn for a cup of tea. It is not a subject I have much of an opinion on, but that is fine because Emma has the verbals anyway. Three or four times, she offers me rhetorical questions and then answers them herself. On the one occasion I do say something, she just speaks louder, over me.

The entire morning passes and nothing happens. I go for a walk and move a few wheelbarrows of grass with Christophe to clear out the tree circle. In a rather un-Celtic way, no one seems interested in what I am doing here, or even in how I heard about the Grove of Sinaan. I guess they get a lot of travellers through here, people drifting round Ireland looking for some sort of Celtic spiritual epiphany. I am just one more vagrant, albeit one driving a burgundy Ford Focus.

It is a hot and humid day. I am lying by my tent when I hear Beyond calling me. 'Hey, Ned. It is the time. The Lughnacy Games are about to begin. Like your kilt. *Touché.*'

Beyond is walking down towards the tree circle. He is wearing combat boots, a black mini-kilt, a purple shirt and a velvet hat that Oscar Wilde might have donned to visit opium dens.

When things start to happen, it is Isolde who whips us in. She lives here in a caravan. She looks like a Greenham Common veteran, with a shaved head, comfortable shoes and the physique of a hod-carrier. Out of everyone, Isolde looks most like a real pikey, but it is an appearance that fits oddly with the fact that she is studying for a master's degree in early Irish language and culture. I shrink a bit when she tells me this.

The tree circle is made up of indigenous Irish species, Beyond tells me when we sit down inside it. He used to live here, though he is just visiting from the States where he is back at university. He helps me identify rowan, hawthorn, ash, oak, apple and blackthorn. Beyond confirms that the latter is associated with poets and I mention that I am keen to get hold of a stick of blackthorn.

There are about twenty of us sitting on benches and lying on the grass when Chris introduces the Lughnacy Games. I have absolutely no idea what is coming next. All I know of the Grove is what

Kieron told me in ten minutes and right now I am not put at ease recalling some of his words: 'Nudity. Lots and lots of nudity.'

Chris tells the mythical story of Lugh coming to Tara, the seat of the high kings of Ireland: Lugh fails to gain entrance to the royal palace as a carpenter, as the king already has one. So Lugh tries again as a smith, a warrior, a poet, a harpist, a physician and so on, but the king already has a master of all of these crafts in his service and so Lugh is rejected. Lugh then asks if there is any man who is accomplished in every one of these arts. There is no one and Lugh is admitted and the surname Ildanach (The All-Craftsman) is conferred upon him.

'So,' Chris continues, 'contests of some sort have been part of Lughnasa celebrations in Ireland for centuries and here we have our very own. Let the Lughnacy Games begin,' she finishes with a swirl.

'There are,' Isolde explains, 'feats of strength, feats of skill and feats of endurance, of courage and of bardship to be completed. You are competing, as most of you know, for the honour of being called the Ildanach, the winner of the games, and the person who lights the Lughnasa fire this evening.' There are rowdy cheers. 'I think we should start,' Isolde goes on, 'with a mighty slurp of this fine uplifting drink, in honour of Lugh, our sun god who is shining on us today.' At this point, Bee starts singing 'You are my sun god, my only sun god,' to the tune of 'You are my sunshine' and everyone joins in, 'You make me happy when skies are grey / Lu-uu-ugh, how we love you / Please don't take our sunshine away.'

This is not exactly turning out as I expected. I thought it would be some sort of high-pagan ritual celebration devoted to Lugh. It looks like it is going to be more of a cross between *It's a Knockout*, a village fête and trying to buy a drink at Glastonbury. The feat of bardship is to think of as many song titles on a given theme and sing them: can't think of one, lose a life, have a drink. The feat of strength is a game called Winkum where we sit cross-legged in a circle on the floor with our partner behind us. The person who is 'it' winks at someone who then has to crawl on all fours over and kiss the winker, whilst the partner has to grapple them back to the corner: in effect wrestling with a few more rules. My partner is Beyond, which makes the game like going six rounds with Giant Haystacks in his heyday. The feat of skill is the Chalicebearing Contest, whereby we have to run round a cricket stump thirteen times with our foreheads pressed against it, then dash across the circle, collect the replete chalice and return with it. We look like a crowd of navvies who just got paid, drunk and dancing on the deck of a ship in a gale. My valiant attempt sees both the chalice and me upended on a bench that swings erratically into my path. The contents of the chalice hit the sacred turf inside the circle and the gathering get an eyeful of my pale buttocks. There is a kind of grandmother's footsteps to music next, though I can't be sure what this was a feat of.

The one game that we are not allowed to play this year, Chris insists, is the Druid Stance, the prize for which goes to the person who can stand on one leg with one arm raised and one eye covered for the longest. Interference from people around you is allowed. Remarkably, Beyond did this for over an hour last year. An hour.

We drink a few more cocktails from the chalice and a few cans of Druids' Celtic Cider as the afternoon drifts on. When the games are finished, Beyond and I drift up the hill to what was once the 'air centre'. It is looking a bit knackered now. We are purportedly looking for logs for the bonfire but the fields are soaked and what fallen wood there was has been sucked into the dank earth.

As we walk through a wood of recently planted oak and ash, I ask Beyond why he has come back for Lughnasa.

'It is a special time. The ever-living ones are abroad,' he says, flicking me an arched eyebrow look.

'The ever-living ones? You mean the fairies?'

'If you want to call them that. They are strong here.'

'You have seen them?'

'I sense them . . . in the strange shapes of old trees, in the wind-blown mist, in the babble of the stream, in the strange turning of a stone at your feet.'

I tell Beyond about finding the stone on top of Emain Macha. He looks at me seriously for a moment, and nods with pursed lips.

'The games and the fun are a part of it, but Lughnasa is a time of assessment,' he goes on. 'The wheel has turned again towards winter. You know it is the festival of first fruits?'

I do know this. Like Beltane, like the whole Celtic calendar, Lughnasa is set in response to occurrences in nature and it is the time when the first berries appear on the trees. It seems odd that a harvest festival should take place before the harvest, but this is just it: it is time to assess how the harvest will be, time to assess how the 'seeds of potential' as Chris called them, that were planted in spring, have fared.

So how has Ned Clague fared? There is an old string hammock hanging from the wooden remains of the air centre and I carefully ease my way into it as Beyond disappears over the hill into another wood. Yes, how has Ned Clague fared? As a poet: average. Average poems, average performances, but nobody has accused me of being a fake, which is something of a success if the profound love of and respect for poetry among the Celtic peoples is to be believed. And I am definitely getting the hang of it. My poems are better. The performances are stronger. I am beginning to enjoy this bardic lark.

And as a Celt? Ned Clague is a full-throttle Celt, always has been. But Rob Penn started as something of a Celto-sceptic, and he is shifting. What seeds are then growing? Seeds of doubt about the veracity of English history; seeds of understanding of the linguistic, cultural, historical and political affinity that the Atlantic Celts have; seeds of desire to belong: they are all growing, at about the same, even rate as my stomach which means I could end up at Samhain as a great Celtic poetic genius weighing over twenty stones.

If the awful creaks that the screws supporting the hammock are anything to go by, then I am well on my way to the big two-zero stones already. Each idle swing prompts the sound of a Marlboro-smoking seagull with chronic bronchitis. Otherwise, the world is silent and still. The sounds of revelry from the farmhouse are swallowed by the wood and the crunches of Beyond's great feet have disappeared. The damp heat is finally going out of the day.

It is a good time to call Vicky. With expectation rather than intent, I turn my phone on. Crap mobile phone reception is a modern feature of the Celtic Fringe. If I had a pound, or even a euro, for every time I have stood outside a pub and turned on my phone during this journey, only to have the damn thing joyously flick up 'No Service' or 'Emergency Only', then I could have bought a mobile phone company and sorted out the network problems myself.

Convincing my wife that I am actually engaged in a job of work, rather than having a stab at the world record for pub crawling while she endures daily combat with my son and bears child number two in her tummy, is proving to be rather tricky. We did talk through every detail of my journey to the bottom of the Celtic Fringe well in advance and we tried to foresee the difficulties that my extended absences might throw up, but being apart is always more complicated than you think. A daily telephone call is one of the few things that I can actually do to make up for my absence.

Crucially, if my fortunes are to advance in this intricate game of snakes and ladders that we call marriage, I have to call when I am sober. Call sober: advance one square. Call sober and remember to say 'I love you': go up a small ladder. Call drunk: go down a ladder. Call past midnight, ten pints down, kilt up and singing 'Sweet Molly Malone': go back to the beginning of the game and spend a lot of cash at Interflora.

Six p.m. is a good time to call. I am usually sober. Lucas is clamped in his chair having tea. Vicky is relaxed, knowing that another day is nearly over. And this is when it always happens: 'No Service'; 'Emergency Only'. This is a fucking emergency! What happens next, of course, depends on where you are, but if I can just draw a few themes together from my most recent experiences in Ireland . . . what happens next usually goes something like this: I am in a pub staring at the screen on my phone when an old fellow with a face like a bleached walnut, who I am certain has never used a mobile phone, who most probably has only used a terrestrial phone twice, to break the news of the death of his parents to his brother in Australia, steps forward: 'Her yer hevin a bit a bather wit yer mawbeel cohm-humincator thar?'

'I am actually. There is no reception.'

'Well, I wud sea thut yer wud be hobtainin a reception hun tap a Slieve Hell, da moontin behoind the poob thar. Tis foive munites oop, un see when yer reach de tap, thar us a view a de east, un I wud sea thut thar will be sumting af a glorious reception waitin far ya in de east.'

'Very good. Thanks very much.' I pay for my pint, check that the nearest pay phone is in fact further away than the top of Slieve Hell, put my raincoat back on and head out into the swirling mist to find the footpath up the mountain. Only at the very top, after forty minutes of climbing in the rain, do I get one bar. I call: 'Hello, my . . .' It cuts out. Vicky and I then have ten conversations all consisting of eight or fewer words. Finally, when she picks up again, I gabble 'I love you, I love you, I love you' before the line goes dead again. My tone is too effusive, desperate, perhaps even intimating guilt. Do not advance one square. Shit.

County Leitrim is so far from anywhere that I hold out little hope of getting through today. After several minutes of forlorn searching, my phone aborts the attempt and flashes up 'No Service' just when I hear someone calling my name.

'Ned, Ned, Ned! Air yuh up der now?' It is Ritchie, another member of the Grove team, and a great lumbering, lovely giant of an Irishman who in his coarse linen *léine* or smock looks as if he might have been lifted straight out of a tale of Cú Chulainn. 'C'mun now,' he says. 'Tis toime ta loight da fire.'

I have had a nagging thought that I recognise Ritchie all day. I cannot pinpoint when or where we might have met, but I have a stab at it now as we walk back to the house.

'Were you ever at Glastonbury, Ritchie?'

'Y'are not wrong. Oi worked der for many years.'

'And did you ever have a beard?'

Well, yes, ther wuz a toime when I did sprout some hair an moi chinigan.'

'And did you ever own a purple jelaba?'

'Neow, what de fucks a jelaba?'

'A sort of hooded coat that goes on over the head. North African . . . Moroccan affair.'

'Ah roit. Purple did ya say?'

'Yes.'

'Naw.'

'No?'

'Naw. Oi never hed a purple jelaba. Un whoi is it yer askin?'

I tell Ritchie about an experience I had at the Glastonbury festival a few years back. I arrived on the Friday night with Jim, a friend, who had managed to get his hands on two press passes which was a hell of a blessing because it had been raining all week and Mr Eavis's farm looked like a plain in Flanders during the Battle of the Somme. The main public areas made a cow midden look like the Augusta National golf course. Behind the main stage, where only press and crew were allowed, the mud only came up to our shins. The media bar was carnage. Soho had come to the country and it was not dealing with it very well. New Hunter wellies, bin liners over the top of Ted Baker and steamed-up frameless glasses were de rigueur. Jim and I got pints and we slipped into a couple of chairs in the corner of the marquee.

Next to us, slumped in a plastic chair, was a lad with the look of a rock star who hadn't quite made it yet. He had a Beatles haircut, heavy black eyeliner, fitted leather trousers and a leather jacket with a Nehru collar. He was a bit of a dandy. Either the excitement of the day had been too much for him or, more likely, a cocktail of barbiturates, tequila, LSD and ketamine had finally cracked him and he was unconscious. Every now and then his head rolled back and forth and occasionally we checked his breathing.

We had almost forgotten about him an hour later when we saw this great red-bearded fellow wearing a purple jelaba and no shoes – straight out of the *Book of Invasions* – lean over him, sniffing. Sniffing avidly, like he was sniffing the first honeysuckle of the year, like a Staffordshire bull terrier who knows where the cat is hiding. He sniffed the rock star's neck and head, again and again. He starts muttering to himself, like Gollum, which is how I knew he was Irish. Then he stood up and had a quick look around. No one was watching, so he pulled up the front of his jelaba, carefully thumbed his penis inside the collar of the wannabe pop star and with one hand on his hip and the other running through his hair, he hosed the man down with several pints of his own steaming Irish urine.

'Jesus, mun,' Ritchie exclaims, 'un yew tort dat was me? Well, Oi daunt gnaw if Oi should be rejoicing er disgusted. Tell me, wuz da fella dat was behervin loike he wuz a urinal, wuz dat fella English now?'

In the middle of the tree circle there is a figure made out of bound sheaves of corn on a bed of hay and wood. We all gather round it. A few more people have turned up and there are kids tearing around with fake swords and poles. Isolde speaks solemnly for a moment, about Lughnasa and the relevance of today to the year ahead. It strikes me that most of the people here are pagans, practising ones, and the Lughnasa quarter day will be important to them.

No one has asked or mentioned all day about my being from the Isle of Man. I haven't had a single conversation about my being a poet. In a way this is quite refreshing, and it is not so surprising. There are Irish, English, French, American, Spanish, German and

Basque people here now, who all live nearby. They have all ended up in County Leitrim on a journey to take them away from 'modernity' – that is a horrible word, but I cannot think of a better term right now. They have found some sort of sanctity in the hotchpotch of New Age philosophies and Celtic paganism along the way. But mad and entertaining as they are, they are not the modern Celts I am looking for.

'Un de winner ar the title Ildanach,' Isolde trumpets, 'the winner ar the games, the moast accumplished person in all atha feats un contests, the person who shored the greatest skill, strength, speed, persistence, and above erl, the person who gave us the greatest number of laughs is . . . actually it's two people, are ya ready? Emma and Ned. Hooray!'

There are whoops and howls from the crowd who are beginning to cut loose on the cider now. Emma and I get a big swig of the cocktail chalice and a burning stick each with which we spark the corn dolly. It all feels momentarily like a scene from a movie about human sacrifice, as the golden flames leap off the burning figure and light up the cackling faces. Then, in a moment of supreme pathos, we start singing a song, 'Thirteen days of Lughnasa', to the tune of 'Twelve days of Christmas' and I know that I am not going to get barbecued tonight.

9

All Over the Irish Sea

I am not sure who looks more grim, unwashed, unkempt, filthy, grey, low-down and dirty on this uninspiring August morning: the port of Rosslare or me. It is a close-run thing. I have only been living in a tent for five nights, but it is as long since I have seen a bath, washed my hair or changed my socks. I feel like I have just got off the plane after a six-month backpacking trip round India. That I am fat and ruddy rather than gaunt and brown means that I actually look more like a young farmer heading home after an Easter rugby tour with empty pockets and a selection of rare sexually transmitted diseases.

I know I look something like this because when I drop the car hire keys off, the girl leaves her desk and runs, and I mean runs, across the ferry terminal and out into the car park to inspect the car. As it happens, I gave up trashing hire cars for sport years ago. I don't even do handbrake turns very much any more. But my protestations were for nothing. I look like a prop forward with VD, ergo the car must be a write-off.

It is a stroke of good fortune that she does inspect the car because she finds a stick in the boot that I didn't even know was there. It takes me a moment to work out what it is – a blackthorn staff. It has been roughly planed and cut to my height. Beyond? Beyond must have slipped it into the car before I left the Grove late last night. Either that or the fairies put it there. It is about nipple height, quite light and there is a fine bulbous head to clasp. It needs to season and I should varnish it, but I am immediately attached to it. This is the final piece of the jigsaw. It completes the costume of Ned Clague and it is sure to become a trusted friend.

At the ferry ticket desk, I ask a young man who is eyeing me suspiciously if there are any showers in the building. 'Naw, but der her sum fur da truck droivers across da rohd un I daunt think they'd moind, seein as the state yer in an all,' he says. 'What oi mean is, if tis hempty, twill be aw roight.'

The shower is a joke. The volume of water dispensed is what you would get from the vigorous use of a pipette. My own bar of soap has been in a tangle with a cheese sandwich at the bottom of my rucksack so I have to pick the shavings of cheddar out. I have lost my towel and my razor is as blunt as Donald Rumsfeld. I dry myself with the filthy T-shirt I have just taken off. Feeling only marginally dirtier than before my shower, I head for the ferry.

This state of personal hygiene is reminiscent of being a student again. I have to say I do not mind it too much and besides, smelling like a bison somehow makes up for driving a Ford Focus. A measure of physical disrepair goes with the territory. I can't be sure why, and it may be something of a cliché, but when I take my boots off and the inflammable armpit odour of an Algerian middle-distance runner invades my nostrils, I grin. My poetry may still be crap, but at least I do now smell like a bard of old.

I love ferry journeys over the Irish Sea. No doubt it is because of sweet childhood memories, but I am flush with a lightning strike of happiness when the horn booms, the ropes are cast off and the propellers churn the murky harbour water. We are off.

One of the great things about ferry journeys is that, if you do not play fruit machines, there is absolutely nothing to do except have a couple of pints and watch the boat's wake drift into the distance. This is precisely what I do (even though a pint at 8 a.m. may seem excessive). It is a good opportunity – in the middle of my journey, in the middle of the Irish Sea – to ruminate on where I am at with my Celticity.

The term Celtic (or something very like it) was first used by classical historians in the sixth century BC – and it remained in use for several centuries – to describe communities living across temperate Europe; communities that these observers viewed as different (basically, more barbaric) from their own people but of sufficient homogeneity to allow the application of the one term: Celtic. Today there are academics who get their knickers in a right twist about the validity of the term. They denounce its use saying that it imposes a misleading likeness on a great number of diverse Iron Age cultures, from Ireland to Hungary. Me? I cannot get worked up about this.

A more important question is: what, if any, relationship is there between these ancient, pan-European peoples and the modern inhabitants of the Atlantic periphery? Take bloodstock, for example. Genetic testing today reveals just how extraordinarily mixed our bloodstock is across the British Isles. I would like to think that somewhere deep up a Manx glen or on a remote Hebridean strand or high in the mountains of Snowdonia, there is a family who have never bred outside the Celtic strain and whose blood remains unadulterated. It seems doubtful, but if there is they will be humming mad with club feet, too many fingers and dozens of cross-dressing children. Imagine *Deliverance* set in the Highlands. The mere thought of it could set tourism in Scotland back by twenty years.

Our blood, our ethnicity, our origins – they are all mixed, which means a Hebridean crofter of today has, in strictly biological terms, as much or as little to do with a fifth-century BC druid from Lewis as an accountant from Sevenoaks has. We are all mongrels, a colossal hotchpotch of all the invaders, settlers, marauders, troubadours, sailors, itinerant barbers and travelling salesmen that have criss-crossed these islands over the centuries. Many modern Celts like to believe otherwise, but I fear they talk nonsense. Take me, as an example of all the people who speciously believe their bloodstock to be pure Celt: my dad is English, from Warwickshire, though the name Penn is from Somerset and some of his ancestors were from Portugal. My mum is Manx, very Manx and from an old Manx family. Yet her mother came from Lancashire, and on it goes. Who knows what else there is further back?

So the ancient Celts and the people who inhabit the Atlantic Fringe today are, effectively, biologically indistinct, which means the debate about 'Who were the ancient Celts?' begs another question, 'Who cares?' Sure, the term may be misleading but I don't think that matters much. What does actually matter is that 'Celtic' self-identification is real for millions of people who live today on the western periphery of Europe. Why is it real? Because of the accumulated effects of all their histories, because they share languages, culture, landscape, weather, political experiences and perspectives, sports, spirit – pretty much everything but the biological ancestry of the ancient Celts.

There are gulls floating along behind the boat, waiting to be fed. It is a lovely morning. Tucking into pint number two, I get my notebook out and I start a poem on an A to Z of things that the modern Celts from the six countries share. I hit rocky ground fairly early on with my rhymes, so I just start jotting down a simple list.

A has to be for the Atlantic. It still just about defines the modern Celts. I have already mentioned how it sculpts the geography and delivers most of the weather in this part of the world. Weather affects behaviour, which determines character. The Atlantic was also the highway for most Celtic communities for 2,500 years. For the people who live in the remotest seaward areas, this situation has only really changed in the last fifty years, yet we have managed to lose sight of it quickly. The seafaring tradition may be fading fast now, but all the countries of the Celtic Fringe were renowned for their skilled sailors and they shared a common culture of the sea, which is like sharing a language.

Less obviously, the Atlantic is a way of escape, a place to elude the frustrations of being little people from what Lloyd George called 'five-foot nations'. The sea is not the end, but the beginning.

B is for bagpipes. The 'skirl', as the high-pitched wailing of the pipes is known, is the most oft-heard and defining sound of the Celtic Fringe. This is partly because you can be two glens away in a soundproofed anti-nuclear underground bunker listening to Motorhead on a Walkman and still hear the bagpiper giving it what for up on his hill, and partly because there are pipers everywhere. All six countries have proud piping traditions, though they are most commonly associated with the glory of the Highlands of Scotland.

Pipers, like poets, were often seen as subversives, probably because of their ability to alert, rouse and, when they were novices, scare the life out of people. When Cromwell invaded Ireland, he had all the local pipers summarily hanged.

C is for colonialism. The Celtic countries were the first English colonies and they are the last to go too. As Renton puts it in *Trainspotting*: 'Some people hate the English, but I don't. They're just wankers. We, on the other hand, are colonised by wankers. We can't even pick a decent culture to be colonised by. We are ruled by effete arseholes. It's a shite state of affairs and all the fresh air in the world will not make any fucking difference.'

D is for the deadly Drink. The Celts are notoriously fond of strong hooch (though historical evidence suggests the English match them in this passion). My Celtic credentials shine here. I don't mind a drop myself. It is said that 0.7 per cent of the world's population is drunk at any one time. It is safe to assume that at least half of that number are Irishmen who have popped out for a pint of milk and inadvertently got totally lashed on the way home. Who else but the Irish see a funeral as a good opportunity to nail a bottle or two?

The reputations of the Welsh, the Manx and the Highlanders took something of a knock under the frowning face of radical Protestantism in the eighteenth and nineteenth centuries. The alehouses of Wales were barred up when the tumescent self-restraint of the chapel movement reached its peak, but this is really no more than a temporary blip which procured for the Welsh an unfair veneer of temperance: the 'land of the white gloves' it used to be called. Before the do-gooders associated the drink with the devil, the Welsh were just as fond of a session on bootleg whisky as the Irish. Go to Wales now (licensing laws were only changed to allow pubs to open on Sundays in 1982 but the grim Welsh Sabbath is almost forgotten) and you will find that pubs are the main social mustering centres once again. There you will find the Welsh having a good go at making up for a century and a half of self-imposed abstinence. As for the rest of them – the Irish, the Cornish and the Bretons – well, the Romans commented on the Celtic predilection for a drop of the hard stuff and these peoples have hardly looked back since. 'Time, please, gentlemen!' I don't think so.

E is for emigration. From the late eighteenth to the middle of the twentieth century, huge populations from all the Celtic countries left for the New World, like rays diverging from a prism. Wherever they went, they had a massive influence on the development of new national identities, an influence out of all proportion to their actual numbers. Many other European countries also saw huge emigration over this period, including England, of course. The difference, however, and the reason that emigration remains relevant to the modern Celtic Fringe, is that nobody misses home quite like the Celts do.

The Welsh actually have a word for this: *hiraeth*. It is a lovely word. It means something like 'longing' or 'yearning'. It is homesickness to the power of three and all the Celts suffer from it. The Celtic diaspora manifest their longing today in literally thousands of Celtic cultural festivals that take place across the New World every year. Most of them are without any sort of authenticity whatsoever, but nobody cares. The diaspora also finance whole industries back home (the manufacture of tartan, the genealogy business) as they clutch at straws of identification that tell them who they once were. They visit their homelands as often as they can and, of course, they pour money back in (think of NORAID).

F is, then, for famine, which increased emigration in a big way. There was famine in Cornwall in the 1840s, in Scotland in the 1860s and in Brittany after the First World War, but it is the Great Hunger in Ireland that can never be forgotten. One million Irish people died of starvation or related diseases when the potato crop failed in the 1840s. No one put the blight on the potatoes, of course, but it was the perceived haughtiness with which the English administration looked upon the disaster that has coloured the relationship between the two countries ever since. The Irish drive towards nationalism did much to mould the notion of pan-Celticism as we know it today, and thus famine via the Anglo-Irish relationship has affected all of the Celtic countries, even Brittany.

It is important to know that English peasants died from starvation during the 1840s too, but no one was reliant on the potato as a staple to the extent the Irish were. I may be reading too much into this, but I do sometimes sense the last vestiges of the collective memory of the Great Hunger in the undue reverence that graces a dish of flaky, white potatoes when it is placed on a farmhouse kitchen table in Ireland today.

G is for genealogy. With a Celt, you need a few hundred years of family history before you can presume to talk sensibly about the present. To a degree, I think it is good to carry your past. I never really have, though I am finding out more about my mum's family now. But that degree is crucial: the Scots, the Welsh and, most obviously, the people of Northern Ireland can all too often appear to be bowed under the great weight of their history.

H is for harp, the instrument that is part of the Celtic condition. The Celtic harp is still extant and it provides a musical continuity between the ancient and the modern Celts, between the Court of Conchobar macNessa and the lounge of Matt Molloy's Bar in Westport on a Friday night. Harpists have traditionally been given great respect and often unique privileges. Even today, a special reverence is reserved for them. A harp is famously the emblem of Guinness and with this illuminating fact I rest my case.

I is for immigration: a new phenomenon that the modern Celts are only now having to confront. After 250 years of continuous emigration, it may take some getting used to.

J is for Jeremiahs, as in the Old Testament 'Lamentations of Jeremiah'. The Celts are as partial to a good lament as they are to a pint. In fact, the two go rather well together. This is not whingeing or whining. It is far deeper and more expressive than that. It is the swelling of a profoundly mournful, self-obsessing pity. It is the flip-side of the coin that makes the Celts so convivial and hospitable, and which distinguishes them so keenly from the English and the French. If you really want to hear a lament, listen to the Welsh on the state of their national rugby team, the Irish on the Catholic Church, the Cornish on emmets, the Scots on, well, on all sorts of things, though they specialise on their football team, and the Manx on pretty much anything you care to mention. One of the familiar responses in Manx Gaelic to 'How are you?' is '*Goll as gaccan*'. It means 'going and grumbling'.

So many of the great and popular songs and poems of the Celts are laments: laments on having to leave home and on staying behind, on unfair treatment by the English, on penury, on hunger, on failed rebellions, on always being treated as a lesser people. This predilection for a good lament may well be something to do with the perpetual yearning that all the Celtic peoples feel for a more glorious past.

K is for kilt. The Manx hunting tartan has done me proud so far.

L is for landscape, which I have banged on about enough, but there is one more important point which my journey has made me aware of: the nature of the use of the landscape has changed dramatically in the last fifty years. Extensive parts of the Celtic Fringe – the Highlands, Pembrokeshire, Cork, Connemara, Cornwall, and large parts of Brittany – are no longer what you could call 'working countryside'. These regions are increasingly nothing more than beautiful landscapes for tourists. The whitewashed cottages are owned not by crofters or smallholders, but by middle-class people from faraway cities. The fishing boats now take visitors out to spot basking sharks and seals, instead of fishing for pilchards. The mines are museums. Nobody digs peat for fuel any more. I am not going to spill some tear-jerking story about the purity of peasant life (for most people who lived this way, it was gruelling and hellish). I am just making the point that the way the landscape is put to use has changed.

M is for magic – it has always gripped the Celtic character. The ancient Celts assumed the existence of supernatural forces and they have consistently featured in the literature and poetry ever since.

N is for New Age Celts. I think we have been there, done that and got the fuchsia tie-dye T-shirt with the dubious Celtic motif on.

O is for the oral tradition, which is still very much alive among the modern Celts. It is there in the loquaciousness of the Irish, in the Scottish love of political debate, in Welsh singing and in the often-experienced intensity in the way the Welsh speak, in Cornish storytelling and in Breton songwriting, but, above all, it is there in the poetry.

P and Q are for the two Celtic language groups: P-Celtic and Q-Celtic. Manx is Q-Celtic. I am really struggling to learn it.

R is for rain. You get a lot of it along the Celtic Fringe. The lexicon for describing it in any of the Celtic languages is as rich as the Inuit vocabulary for snow. This will surprise no one who has stood around being lashed by it as frequently as I have in the last three months.

S is for superstition, a collective passion of the people of all the Celtic nations and something that they have married easily with Christianity. The whole web of fairy people who inhabit all the Celtic countries is testament to this deep superstition. Plenty of Irish people still surreptitiously leave the dregs of their drinks for the leprechauns when they retire to bed, to ward off bad luck.

And why not? I say you have to give yourself every chance you can get.

T is for tourism, the *ignis fatuus* of the Celtic Fringe. With the exception of the Isle of Man and possibly Ireland now, all the countries of the Celtic Fringe are economically reliant upon it.

U is for Union, or rather Acts of Union. Acts of Union were passed between on the one hand England and on the other: Wales (1536, 1542/3), Scotland (1707) and Ireland (1801). The Bretons got it in 1532 when the Act of Union with France was passed. These Acts basically snuffed out political independence in the Celtic countries. As the Act dealing with Wales declared, the country was 'incorporated, united and annexed' to England. Scotland and Ireland were dealt something similar and the intention was always the same: to make governing easier for the English, to guarantee the succession of a French-speaking German monarch and to secure England's borders. I mention this because modern nationalism along the Celtic Fringe is focused on getting these Acts repealed.

V means vibes, mystical vibes: they are transcendent and powerful the length of the Celtic Fringe and you don't have to live in a tepee to feel them (though it helps, of course).

W is for warlike, a prominent characteristic of the Celts, noted by the Romans and pretty much everyone who has had the misfortune to cross them ever since.

X is for xenophobia. The English hate the Celts and the Celts hate the English. Enough said.

Y is for Yeats, W.B. Yeats. He is not my favourite, but no other poet has had such a great influence on the Celtic cause. His nationalist poetry elevated the myth of Ireland as a spiritual entity with its roots in a Celtic golden age, all in the cause of creating a single Irish community against English colonialism, even though he was a Protestant toff and the people he was rousing were mostly Catholic peasants. His poems were consciously designed to contribute to the process of a collective definition. He used the Irish sagas and legends and folklore for symbols and themes, to create a literature that was recognisably Irish, deriving directly from the country's Celtic past. His influence across the Celtic Fringe was enormous. Among the more romantically inclined, it still is.

Z is for . . . don't be ridiculous, I don't have a 'Z', but my pint is finished and I can see Fishguard if I lean over the side of the ferry now. Welcome to Wales.

10

Aigh Vie at the Eisteddfod

The Romantic Movement of the late eighteenth century did a lot of lasting damage to the image of the Celts. Almost as much damage as the New Romantics did to the credibility of the British pop industry in the late twentieth century. Both are testament to the fact that, though the prominence of intellectual ideas may fade with time, no one ever forgets a bad haircut.

The original Romantics, no doubt aided by some heavy narcotics, inspired the Celts to reinterpret their past with lofty embellishments. The displacement of reason with imagination – a central tenet of Romanticism – as the faculty by which the truth is apprehended was nothing if not a licence for Celtic revivalists to create specious genealogies, mock organisations, daft ceremonies and some very silly costumes. And all of this, the Welsh did in spades.

The Welsh Eisteddfod is something of an identity parade for sartorial suspects. I am sitting high up on a row of seats in an enormous marquee on an airfield outside the Pembrokeshire village of St David's, waiting for one of the key ceremonies of the Welsh Eisteddfod to begin. Standing on the gantry below me, ready to take the stage in a grand procession, are a few dozen druids – senior and influential Welsh men and women dressed like walk-on parts in a low-budget nativity play. They are draped from neck to ankle in white or blue bed-sheets, which are hardly flattering, but it is the headgear that really offends. An off-cut of sheet is clamped about the forehead with an Alice band and thrown over the back of the head, resembling an unstarched wimple. It is a piece of apparel – I am not sure you can call it a hat – reminiscent of a matron in a Crimean War hospital having a bad hair day, or possibly John Belushi near the end of a week-long bender. Yet this is the dress of the esteemed members of the Welsh Gorsedd of Bards, Ovates and Druids.

Gorsedd Beirdd Ynys Prydain or the Assembly of Bards of the Isle of Britain, as the official title goes, is an association of people who have made a distinguished contribution to the Welsh nation. It is the Welsh equivalent of being knighted for services to your country. Honoured members include writers, poets and singers as well as rugby players, politicians and TV stars. Members are known as druids, which is a most unfortunate term as it makes one think of goat-footed nutters frolicking around Stonehenge on the winter solstice. The Gorsedd is desperately keen to disassociate itself from 'druidism' as a religion – something that is not always easy to do.

The Gorsedd is the invention of one seriously odd man; so odd, in fact, that he stands head and shoulders above the rest of the loonies in the history of pan-Celticism. Almost single-handedly, Edward Williams, or Iolo Morgannwg as his bardic name went, created the Gorsedd and its entire historical fiction.

His intention was basically legitimate: to connect the modern Welsh with their Celtic heritage. His methods were more suspect. No doubt with the help of near-lethal doses of laudanum, he invented practices which had little or no historical basis. He conjured up a 'pedigree' of Celtic Welsh bardism which he spanned from his age back to pre-Roman times, forging legends, poems and chronicles – basically anything he needed to make real his claims – along the way. You could argue in Iolo's defence that the whole history of the ancient Celts is so tangled in fiction and folklore and doubt that he was merely icing a well-baked cake, and it is worth mentioning that his forgeries were outstanding. He was clearly something of a literary genius in his own right.

The first meeting of Iolo's Gorsedd and the druidic ceremony that attended the event took place in 1792 in the rather less than

Celtic surroundings of Primrose Hill in north London. By the time
the Gorsedd first appeared at the Carmarthen Eisteddfod in 1819,
the ceremony had been perfected to the point where Iolo had over-
come the problem of there not being a druidic circle everywhere
he wanted one: he carried his own in his pocket (this is not, inci-
dentally, the inspiration for my pouch of stones and crystal), and
in the beer garden of the Ivy Bush Hotel in Carmarthen, he laid it
out. Wearing hospital bed-sheets, they danced round these peb-
bles on the lawn. It is all very *Monty Python*-esque and, quite
frankly, worrying. The Gorsedd – have stone circle, will travel –
has been an integral part of the Eisteddfod ever since. Today the
stone circle is no longer pocket size, but it is still mini and move-
able. I saw the one erected at this site on my way into the marquee.
This morning – I missed the ceremony as I was still on the bus
from Fishguard – Dr Rowan Williams, the next Archbishop of
Canterbury, was inducted into the Gorsedd as an honorary white
druid, within these stones. The flak about 'druidism' will surely
be all over the English newspapers tomorrow in a timeless replay
of the half-amused irritation with which the English most familiarly view the Welsh, and which really pisses the Welsh off. Today
an Eisteddfod without the Gorsedd is unthinkable. Iolo's legacy
lingers like serious halitosis.

There are three main Gorsedd ceremonies at the Eisteddfod: the
Chairing of the Bard, the awarding of the Prose Medal and the one
that is about to begin right now, the Crowning of the Bard. I can't
wait.

As the entire ceremony is conducted in Welsh, I am wearing a
headset and listening to a very chatty translator. It is a full house:
all 3,500 seats are taken, which says something about how the
Welsh love these ceremonies. As it is a sunny afternoon, it is also
a hot house. The lights go down on the empty stage, the doors shut
and then there is a great trumpet call. With that, the druids are off,
proceeding at a slow march on to the stage where 200 or more –
all in white, green or blue bed sheets – finally take their places.

Quite honestly, it could be a line-up waiting for screen tests for the next *Carry On* film. *Carry on Barding?* Appropriately, the next thing to come out is the Horn of Plenty. I feel Sid James and Barbara Windsor would have made light work of getting a gag out of this prop. It is presented to the archdruid by a young matron from the local community who urges him to 'drink of the wine of our welcome', the translator informs me.

Next up on stage is a troupe of maidens in green mini-dresses with floral wreaths and mistletoe. In other circumstances, they would be too young to avoid the smear of suspicion and I am struggling to dispel the image of the sacrificial woods. I think of the film *The Wicker Man*. In one marvellous scene at the castle, there are naked nymphs cavorting round the garden and Lord Summerisle (played by Christopher Lee) asks the Calvinist copper (Edward Woodward), 'I trust the sight of young people refreshes you?' 'It does not refresh me,' Sergeant Howie replies. 'Oh, I'm sorry,' Lord Summerisle goes on, 'one should always be open to regenerating influences.'

The archdruid has the funkiest costume of them all – a sort of part bishop, part Harlem Street-funk, part Egyptian sun-god ensemble. He has now got his hands on a great sword, which he half unsheathes, shouting, 'Who has a headache?' 'Headache,' 3,500 people reply. I am beginning to wonder if this has something to do with the raucous noise the trumpeters make, when the translator pipes up: '*Oes heddwch?*' means 'Is there peace?' '*Heddwch*' or 'Peace' we all shout back. This happens three times.

The representatives from the other five Celtic countries are then welcomed on stage. They all make speeches in their own languages saying something about how lovely it is to be here, how kind the weather has been, how embarrassing it is to share a stage with Wales's answer to *The Muppet Show*. Actually, I have no idea what they are saying as neither the translator nor I can understand a word any of them deliver. The biggest round of applause is, curiously, reserved for the delegates from the Welsh colony in

Patagonia. The trumpeters, in costumes that suggest they have just sprung straight from the court of Llewelyn, the last independent Prince of Wales, sound off again and we all stand for a prayer.

Finally, we are in business: it is the Crowning Ceremony. Poets from all over Wales have submitted anonymous entries of poems or sequences of poems of less than 200 lines, in Welsh, of course. The anonymity is interesting as it pits builders and farmers with professors and doctors, on a level playing field, displaying a truly Celtic trait that predates modern political socialism by thousands of years. Among the Celts, everyone is equal, which may be the reason why the Welsh have never tolerated an indigenous aristocracy.

The adjudicator takes the mic and presents his analysis of the entries rather like a schoolmaster about to hand back homework. He talks of loose adjectives and overly decorative imagery, superficial subjects and stereotypical phrasing. The work of five entrants is singled out, but strangely we do not get to hear any of the poems. I have read that classical Welsh poetry is essentially an aural pleasure and I am keen to hear it.

Then the lights are dimmed and the audience hushed, ready for the announcement. The pseudonym of the winner will be revealed and he or she will then rise. 'Don't stand up if you're not the winner,' the translator commands in my ear. There is a dramatic trumpet call.

'And the winner is . . . Alfred Bored Venison.'

What?

The old boy in the seat next to me jumps up. Clearly my look is one of incredulity as he says, 'Naw. Naw. I jus leavin, boy. Too hot, see.'

A spotlight searches the marquee, and there he is, Alfred Bored Venison, standing like a rabbit in headlights. Bards rush down from the stage to garb him in a great purple and gold cloak and he is led in a small procession back to the stage. The archdruid heaves what looks from the way it is being handled like several pounds of iron and stone crown on to the fellow's head and he visibly shrinks under it. That will be a trip to the chiropractor then. We are treated to the winner's biography, which is tedious. Still we do not hear the poem.

A chap in a green toga sings a beautiful song, accompanied by a harpist, and there is more floral dancing, the national anthem and a final funeral procession to come. But it is now hot like a tandoori oven and I have lost interest in the pageantry. I drift outside.

In a way, it is great to see poetry celebrated. I wonder if there is any other country on the planet that puts on such a show to honour the humble composer of verses? I doubt it. I have read that Wales has more practising poets today than anywhere else and many of them, I am told, write using the extremely complex metres of a poetic tradition called *cynghanedd*. I am not sure how you do a survey like this, but it is illuminating nonetheless. When you see where we have got to with free verse thanks to Ezra Pound and the like, choosing to use these ancient poetical devices is odd. It makes life very, very hard for a poet. I liken it to playing Brazil at football and tying the bootlaces of all your players together and then selecting an armless man to keep goal.

The Welsh bardic tradition has the same sort of longevity as the Irish one. It kicks off with the epic verses of Taliesin and Aneurin – two great names of world poetry and two great names for poets – whose sixth-century AD verses are among the most ancient products of Welsh culture. Dafyd ap Gwilym was the famous poet who carried the tradition through the medieval period. The poetic tradition may well be more alive today than at any time since the Middle Ages and it remains a keystone of Welsh culture, just as it has been for centuries. So it is right that it should be celebrated, but all this pomp, all these costumes and prancing maidens? Is this really necessary?

The rest of the Eisteddfod site is, by contrast, pleasingly ascetic. Thus it is more Welsh and more authentically Celtic. Despite their love of flashy eloquence, the Celts are not naturally a showy people. There are rows and rows of white marquees occupied by a wide range of organisations: government agencies, political parties, universities, craft groups, global corporations trying hard to look Welsh, NGOs, colleges, cultural bodies and shops selling junk from India. There are also bookshops as well as galleries with some fine paintings and harps for sale. It is not a familiar 'festival village' by any means, probably because the Eisteddfod is so many things rolled into one: Glastonbury, the Edinburgh festival, Mecca and a thousand village fêtes. There is, though, not much you can't buy here, except a pint: the old Welsh temperance reigns within the boundaries of the Eisteddfod, though I am sure there will be the happy sound of popping corks in the caravan park next door and the pubs in the village will be coining it like they have never known.

As I walk round, it is impossible not to experience the alienation that the language creates. The Eisteddfod is 'Welsh Only', as it has been since 1937. Every single word on every single banner, poster and information leaflet is in Welsh. Everyone speaks Welsh. Everyone except me, it seems. Of course, everyone speaks English as well, but the assumption is if you are here, then you speak Welsh, which leads to a number of mildly embarrassing situations for me.

When I stop to buy an ice cream, the lady looks kindly at me and says, 'Llanfairpwllgwyngyllgogerychwyrndrobwllllantysiliogogogoch.' Actually she doesn't say this. This is, in fact, the longest place name in Wales, but what she does say sounds similar enough, and it leads to the same conversational impasse. I can now do one of two things: pretend I am shopping in a bazaar in Damascus, ignore what she said and go straight in with pointy-pointy language. One finger on a cone and one finger on the raspberry ripple, a lick of the hand and a final flourish with a fiver in the air ought to do it. Alternatively, I can stand here and look stupid until she realises what is going on and repeats what she said in English. I go for the latter and after a squirmingly indecent length of time she says, loaded with reproach, 'Ice cream is it, young man?' – the 'young man' leaving a small window of opportunity for me both to grow up and learn to speak Welsh.

Lots of people criticise the Eisteddfod for being 'Welsh Only'. Four out of five people in Wales cannot speak Welsh, they say, so it is unnecessarily exclusive. Personally, I think it is fine. I feel like I am on holiday. Much more importantly though, it is an annual flourish for the language which is the greatest tradition that Wales has. As many have noted, the history of Wales is the history of its language. That it has survived at all is nothing short of a linguistic miracle and who would begrudge a miracle its week-long flourish at the beginning of August every year?

I remember the first time I heard Welsh spoken: I was appalled. I was a kid and we were driving in the family Fiat across mid-Wales on holiday, probably the same holiday that had me sulking my way up Cader Idris. Someone was tuning the radio and we hit this extraordinary cacophony – the sound of a man who had swallowed a mouthful of hydrochloric acid and was emitting what was surely his strangled, painful and terminal breath. We were going to hear a man die on the radio. It was a public suicide. It was shocking. But he didn't die and eventually we worked out what we were listening to: someone commentating on a horse race in Welsh. This was an alarming introduction, but in fact you do not have to listen to the language for long before you tune in, before it becomes gentle and melodious to listen to. It is rich and 'rhythmic like the landscape' as Gerard Manley Hopkins noted.

The English have never really got on with Welsh. It has always been a crude tongue to them as well as a badge of that 'apartness'. One of the few Englishmen who did fall for its charms was J.R.R. Tolkien, who actually tried to learn it. Apparently the language that Legolas and the elves speak in *The Lord of the Rings* actually echoes the sounds of Welsh, but I don't speak Elvish either, so I wouldn't know. This makes sense when I think about it. *The Lord of the Rings* and all of Tolkien's fantastical adventures are loaded with Celtic imagery, tinged with Celtic myth and set in a Celtic landscape. I do not wish to disserve New Zealand, but filming the trilogy there was a great mistake. To have filmed them in Wales and Scotland would have added a richer dimension to the movies.

When I do eventually hear English being spoken for the first time this afternoon, it is rather like being in a restaurant in southern Spain or a bar in the Dordogne, inasmuch as I recoil with embarrassment. There is a lady in a stall which is selling T-shirts, complaining about a cartoon on a poster. The cartoon is a not entirely kind pastiche of a Colonel Blimp-type character. The writing is in Welsh, so the lady and I have no idea what it is on about, but she is blurting 'racist stereotyping' . . . 'offensive to me as an Englishwoman' . . . 'most unwelcoming'. The woman behind the counter is graciously saying she will take the poster down, though I can see that her eyes are saying, 'Hey lady, why don't you go and do some yoga on the M4.'

The T-shirts this woman is selling are unlike anything I have seen before. They are well-cut clubbing T-shirts with trendy types and imagery, all bearing pro-Welsh or pro-Celtic logos, and there are no swirly patterns in sight. Being Welsh is not as unfashionable as it once was, and now you can get the T-shirt to prove it. They say things like: 'Vorsprung durch Celtique', 'Foreign Interference', 'non sono inglese, io sono gallese' amongst other nationalistic soundbites. They are selling fast. I pick one out that says 'CELT' and in much smaller type beneath it, 'Alba • Breizh • Cymru • Eire • Kernow • Mannin'. While I am queuing, I cannot help reflect that there is no way I would have bought a T-shirt like this three and a half months ago, before Beltane. And now I am looking forward to wearing it proudly. I could sweep this aside and say I am buying it for Ned Clague, but I am not. I know I am not. The truth is I am falling for this 'being Celtic' lark faster than the devil stings the hides of the shrieking damned.

'Llanfairpwllgwyngyllgogerychwyrndrobwllllantysiliogogogoch.' It is the T-shirt woman and she is speaking to me. She is attractive in an older, sexy way. Suddenly I hate the 'Welsh Only' policy. So we go through the rigmarole: Rob plays at being dumb, in every sense of the word. Sexy older woman thinks Rob is a jerk. Sexy older woman knows Rob can't speak Welsh (ergo he's English – double jerk) and decides to let him sweat. Sexy older woman puts her hands on her hips and tilts her head to one side as if to say, 'What is it, fuckwit? Need your nappy changing?' In truth, it is no way to sell T-shirts, but sexy older woman doesn't care. Rob wants to shout, 'I'm Manx, I'm Manx, I'm Manx,' but knows such a public display of ardent Celticness would make things worse. Rob finally blurts, 'Got this in green?' and sexy older woman goes off to rummage for it.

While she is out the back of the stall, I spot what is undoubtedly the finest T-shirt of them all on the wall above me. It is red. Across the front in tight black lettering is printed: 'Fuck off. I'm Welsh'. How brilliant is that? It says it all. A four-word summation of the Welsh condition, a pithy abridgement of the perpetual protest that is instinctive in these people. This T-shirt represents both the pride and the sense of humour that the Welsh have about their own identity – the two things that have ensured that no one, least of all the English, has ever been able to patronise them. When she comes back, I jab a thumb at this T-shirt and mustering my best effort at a conspiratorial smile, I ask, 'What's the inspiration for that one?'

She looks at me with cool, green eyes and says, 'How about seven hundred years of subjugation?'

It is a golden evening as I wander towards the exit of the main Eisteddfod site. Music and hymns are still coming out of some of the cultural tents and despite the absence of an amiable cocktail or two at this hour, everyone looks very cheery. I stop to be nosy when I see a TV crew fiddling with equipment, but they are packing up, having interviewed the man who just claimed the 'crown' for his poem, Alfred Bored Venison himself.

'Bored Venison,' I say, approaching him, 'congratulations!' I think we ought to have a chat, poet to poet as it were. He gives me a big but tired grin.

'Are you walking this way?' he says, shifting his great crown from arm to arm. 'Let me join you.'

'Obviously you speak both Welsh and English fluently. Which language do you prefer to write poetry in?' I ask. It is a question I suspect I know the answer to, but I want to hear it from the mouth of the man of the moment.

'Oh, Welsh, by a mile. Thas noo competition. Ituss truuly ah pooh-etic language, so rich in idiom. After right-ting poor-try in Welsh, to try in English would be like paint-ting with only half the colours otha rainbow. It is said tha yew speak Welsh when yew ur in love, and tha yew keep the English for counting. Now, if yuwll excuse me, I must . . .'

'I am a poet from the Isle of Man actually,' I interject. I have a sudden urge to try my verses on the champion, but he sees this coming and steers a course for clear water. 'I would love . . .' I try to go on, but he is having none of it.

'Oh, I'd luv to hear your poo-hms some time, I wud, but now I must just go and talk with . . .' and he is off, pressing flesh with someone more important, leaving me to wonder exactly what language he speaks when he is counting all the sheep he is in love with.

I am lingering by the main gate to the site wondering what to do next when I get talking to an ageing security guard. I ask him about places to camp and he suggests two: beyond the caravan site with the oldies, or on the far side of the airfield at Maes B. 'All-night parties, bonfires, rock un roll. Iz where all the young guns ur. But you'll noh sleep a wink dawn there.'

'Perfect,' I say. 'Thanks very much.'

Just ten years ago, the Eisteddfod was only attended by the worthy Welsh: farmers and their wives, academics, nationalists and a few reluctant politicians, the average age of whom would have been nudging fifty. To address this problem, the 'Youth Field' was instituted in 1997. When I climb a sod bank halfway across the airfield to look where I am going, a sea of Eurohike tents opens out before me. Maes B has been a runaway success for the Eisteddfod organisers. Yet the fact that the Welsh national cultural festival can attract 50,000 people under the age of twenty-five is illustrative of something more than a well-organised event. Like the T-shirts, it smacks of a bolstered belief that the Welsh youth have in how cool it is to be Welsh.

'Ut will be full as far as tha eye can see buh Thursday, it will. See tha hedge oar tha, thas the boundary. Pit'you can't stay for tha weekend, like. Right crack, it is,' Gwilym says. He is one of a team of young security guards who are punting a rugby ball about in the evening sunshine when I arrive at the gate of Maes B.

'Baah's oer thar. Tonight thas loads a bands on un stuff. Showers, toilets thar. Best spot fur campin thar. Any probs, you come un see me. Arl help you out. Very good to have a Manxman here, it is.'

I can see the rough tors of the Preseli Mountains – whence came the blue stone of Stonehenge – as I weave between the tents, snagging my boots on guy ropes. Young people are lolling around on the grass, drinking, chatting and getting high. Tinny beat boxes are playing music I have never heard (or even heard of), people are wrestling with their tents to get them up, bathers are returning from the showers, others are blowing up floor mats and making pot noodles. It is a good scene. Almost everyone seems to be speaking Welsh, but they readily drop into English when I say 'Hello'. They are very young. Half of them cannot even be university age yet. Or rather, I am very old. The guys at the gate were remarkably courteous towards me and I thought this was just because I am from the Isle of Man; the Welsh are well known for their hospitality. But in fact they were being overly polite because I am old enough to be their dad.

When I have my tent up, one of the guys from the little encampment next door whistles through his teeth and waves me over.

There are three lads: Brysor (pronounced 'Breesor'), Gwion and Rhondrey. The first two names I have never heard of before and as with Gwilym on the gate, it takes me an embarrassingly long time to master them. They are all from north Wales, near Betws-y-coed, in the very heart of the kingdom of Welshness. Up there, Christian names were never anglicised as they were across the south.

Getting a handle on Welsh Christian names and place names is a perennial problem for the English. Anyone who has ever been a tourist in Wales and in need of directions to Dinas-Mawddwy or Tre'r Ceiri, Bryngwyn Tygwydd, or Dwygyfylchi or pretty much any place you care to think of, will know how far from the correct pronunciation you can stray. Apparently, this is quite a problem in the emergency services. English tourists or recently arrived immigrants dial 999 because their cottage is on fire, but no one can work out where they are calling from. I can well imagine it:

'Whuss tha nehm a tha village then, bach?'

'Llanfairpwllgwyngyllgogerychwyrndrobwllllantysiliogogogoch.'

'What d'yiow mean, "Nan's coming for tea on Tuesday"? Noh, I want the name a tha village.'

'That's it!'

'Look, you'll have toe spell-it, see.'

'By which time this bloody house will be burnt down!'

Brysor has to correct me on how to pronounce his name a dozen times, but he remains very relaxed about this. I ask if I might call the three of them 'Knee-sore', 'Get-on' and 'Fondle-me' which does help me get my mind and my tongue in gear.

There is something about the way they speak English that suggests it is an acquired or second language and Gwion tells me that he only started to learn English when he went to primary school. As with so many Celtic language speakers that I have met on this journey, these lads speak English in a cautious way. It is as if they are anticipating an electric shock at each slurred word or phonetic mistake. Listening to them, I can only wonder if this is some horrible legacy of the way that English was taught in Wales not so very long ago. In Victorian times, when the policy to suppress the Welsh language in schools was at its most ardent, school children caught speaking Welsh had to wear a placard round their neck which read 'Welsh Not'. The next person to speak in Welsh took over the placard and the pupil bearing it at the end of the day felt the *cribban* or cane across his youthful flesh, no doubt applied with vigour by some jelly-bottomed English teacher. I guess the 'Welsh Only' policy at the Eisteddfod has its origins in these unpleasant memories.

Two girls join us. They barely look old enough to be allowed bubble-gum, but the homemade bong is stoked up and it does the rounds. Feeling my age, and remembering the story of the man who passed out in front of his daughter in a vegan soup kitchen, I decline my hit.

The girls are from Caernarfon, which I have visited on a number of occasions over the years. 'Tis the most Welsh town on earth,' Myfannwy says proudly, which must be the greatest irony in the entire history of Wales. Edward I began Caernarfon Castle during his conquest of Wales in 1283. It is an exceptional piece of military architecture, built at colossal expense using the finest architects and craftsmen in Europe. It was probably the most advanced military fortress in the medieval world and it was almost alone in the English garrisons that held out during the rebellion of Owain Glyndwr. It was constructed as part of a ring of fortresses that Edward conceived to encircle and subdue the seditious Welsh. The fortified 'bastide' town built around the castle became a little English colony since no Welsh were allowed to live in it. The whole fortress was a grandiose, granite badge of subjection for several centuries. Though the castle remains almost entirely intact, a gentle process has seen it turn into the heartland of the Cymru Cymraeg – the Welsh-speaking community of nearly 800,000 – and if you want to hear Welsh spoken today, there is no better place to head for.

Whenever I think about what has happened in Caernarfon, it amazes me. Since the time of Edward I, the English have gone on to create the greatest empire the world has ever known. They have affected the political systems, judiciary, armies, sporting activities and manners of half the world. The English language has risen to be the dominant language of the twenty-first century, the language of science, technology, global communications and the future; a quarter of the world's population have some command of it. Yet this north-west corner of Wales has quietly slipped away, almost unnoticed, and returned to being completely and utterly Welsh. The English still laugh at the idea of a 'Welsh way of life', but a trip to Caernarfon on a damp autumn day will predictably confirm what they have perhaps never wanted to know. Wales is alive and well and showing greater self-confidence than it has for centuries, possibly since the thirteenth century and the time of Llwelyn Ap Gruffydd, the last native Prince of Wales.

More happy campers, all young enough to be my offspring, drift in and out of the tents around us. They nod at me and then speak Welsh to Rhondrey or Gwion, no doubt asking, 'Who's the old fella in the skirt?' But Rhondrey seems proud of his avuncular friend and he replies in English, 'This is Ned, a por-ht from the Isle of Man.'

The music they are playing is terrible. Brysor keeps changing tapes but it never improves. Between post-bong paroxysms of heart-stopping laughter, he jabs me in the arm and says, 'Now, this is a greet bund, mun. Listen. This is . . .' But I am not listening. The type of music is 'New Metal' or 'Hot Metal' or 'Metal Fatigue'. I forget. It all gives me head fatigue, which is a sure sign that I am a parent. The bands are called Sudden Cot Death or Squashed Dog Faeces or Lung Cancer or some other equally engaging name.

'Eh, Ned, listen ah this wun, mun,' Brysor enthuses again.

'I think it sounds like a recording of an anthrax attack on a Kurdish village in northern Iraq,' I suggest.

'Yeh, right, mun,' he says, passing me the bong again. 'Fuckin brilliant, eh?'

When they all head off for the marquee where the bands are playing this evening, I find a bus into St David's where lots of Eisteddfod fringe events are being staged. I am looking for the poetry recital or 'slam' at the rugby club. When I get there I find that it is not on, which is a bit of a blow as I was hoping to pick up some performance tips from these hot-blooded Welsh. Either I have got the wrong night (quite possible as my programme is in Welsh) or the schedule has been changed but no one seems to know which.

I will catch some poetry somewhere else though: the schedule is packed with poetry events. Not only are the most important awards that the Gorsedd makes for poetry, but there are also daily competitions for sparring poets in the Pabell Lên (the Literature Pavilion) and a couple of evening slams at the rugby club. Tonight turns out to be comedy night. I have to say listening to comedy in Welsh proves to be about as much fun as reading a macroeconomics textbook in Urdu. For reasons I cannot fathom, I stay for half an hour. Assuming that an Englishman as mad as me will need every penny he has, the guy on the door gives me my £3 entrance charge back when I step out.

I do a few pubs in the village, all busy with Welshmen getting drunk, before finding a bus going back to the campground. It is a shuttle bus running from St David's to the airfield, so the driver waits a few minutes for the seats to fill up. As we are about to depart, there is a clamour on the pavement and a hand slaps against the window. On steps an old boy with a face flushed crimson with drink and bonhomie. He is wearing a club tie and a maroon, lime and brown striped blazer. Standing at the front of the bus, he buttons up the blazer and, throwing both his hands out like a man releasing a pigeon, he starts to sing. There are heckles from the back of the bus, in Welsh, and the only word I gather is

'Joseph', which must be in reference to his egregious coat. When the bus swings round the first corner, he is flung with great force into my kilted lap, where I half catch him and he half grabs me.

I wedge him into the seat next to me. Slapping his hand down on my bare knee, he asks me something in Welsh and I do my, by now, well-practised imitation of a man who has recently had a disabling stroke.

'A Scotsman, is it?' he shouts with his face inches away from mine.

'Manx, actually.' The back of my head is pressed against the window.

'Bugger me, a Manxman,' he says melodramatically. 'A real live Manxman? So you have to tell me now, what is a Manxman doing here?'

I shrug my shoulders. I am not going to tell my story here and now. I could get stuck with Joseph all night. 'Well, I just wanted to come and have a look, to find out what the Eisteddfod is all about.'

He smiles a smile of unabashed delight and his eyes go watery. I have never seen anyone so obviously moved by Celtic solidarity. I don't know what to say. He grips both sides of my head in his hands. As he hauls me towards him to kiss my cheek, the bus lurches round another corner. We go lip to lip.

'Here to suppawt yer Welsh brothers? Well, you ur welcome here. Verrry, verrry welcome here and . . . and . . .' – he looks round the bus as if the inspiration for what he wants to say is written somewhere, then he fixes me again with a hard stare – 'and fuck the English!'

'Maes B!' the driver shouts and I spring for the door.

On my journey from Cader Idris to here, I have been seduced by so much of what I think it means to be a Celt today – the music, the poetry, the sense of belonging, the historical perspective, the imagination, the mystical allure of the landscapes, the different ways, the drinking, the resoluteness, the lack of deference, the fact that everyone is the same height as me. Yet I still can't cross the Rubicon. I cannot hate the English. I am bloody English!

If you ask me, the Welsh have wasted too much time hating the English. So have all the Celts (and that goes for the Bretons hating the French too). With up to a millennium of resentment to draw on, the Atlantic Celts, the losers time and time again in the history of these isles, have spent far too much energy in defining themselves as un- or anti-English or French. It is a reductive response to a complex problem and it has never got the Celts anywhere. It is like using painkillers to treat cancer: it may make things momentarily better, but the problem will return. Yet it is impossible to try and define the modern Celts without coming up against the feeling that, for most of them, hating the English remains a defining feature of their identity.

To a great extent, it is a hatred that is still reciprocated. Certainly the English media seldom disguise their distaste for anything Welsh. 'Taffy' remains a pejorative term and 'to welsh' is an extant slang term that means to swindle someone out of money laid as a bet. One Englishman whose name you do not wittingly mention in Wales is A.A. Gill, whose excoriating description of the Welsh as 'stunted, bigoted, dark, ugly, pugnacious little trolls' did not, funnily enough, place him high in the running to be made an honorary member of the Gorsedd for his distinguished contribution to the Welsh nation.

Hatred of the English remains, then, one of the clarion calls that throws these diverse Celtic peoples into each other's tight embraces. How tight I can let those embraces wrap me, I just do not know. It is at times like this – snogging the old boy on the bus – when I feel most vulnerable and exposed, when the central ambivalence of my journey is most obvious. This is precisely the time I am likely to trip on my tightrope.

Fortunately, this anti-English breast-beating is far less prevalent among the young, and it is some relief to get to the bar in the Maes B marquee. Rhondrey, Brysor and Gwion are there. Like all good students, they are avoiding the hefty bar prices and drinking the booze they have smuggled in. When that runs out, they start 'minesweeping', which is a euphemism for pinching other people's drinks.

A dozen Welsh rock and pop bands are each having their turn on the stage. In a drunken moment of exasperating boldness that completely surprises me, I ask the technician behind the mixing desk if I can get up on stage to read a poem between bands. To my incredulity, he thinks this is a great idea and he goes off to check with the boss. Five minutes later, I am backstage with the director of the entire Maes B entertainment programme. He is taking me seriously. He too thinks it is a good idea to have a Manx poet on stage, and suddenly I am facing the prospect of getting up before 500 people. After some talk, the logistics of achieving this prevail and I am told it can't be done, not tonight, and I am invited back for Friday night.

'I have to leave on Wednesday,' I say, 'I am heading to Brittany for the Lorient festival,' which fetches me a veneer of authenticity. It also makes my blood run cold. I might actually be on stage in front of hundreds of people in a week's time.

Bryn Fôn, a legend amongst the Welsh-speaking youth, fronts the last band on stage. I have never heard of him. I am standing with Gwion when the first song starts and he knows all the words. I wander through the crowd who are thrashing around in front of the stage. They are all singing along, to every song.

'He's big,' Gwion says when I get back to him. 'Big like Robbie Williams . . . only he's Welsh.'

I am leaning against a steel post at the side of the pavilion when a man comes and stands with his hands thrust deep in his pockets, between the stage and me. He is facing me, but he has the frame of a nightclub bouncer, so I smile politely. He tries to say something but Bryn Fôn drowns his words out. I point to the bar and walk over but he does not follow. Five minutes later, when I am buying a pint, he is beside me again.

'Llanfairpwllgwyngyllgogerychwyrndrobwllllantysiliogogogoch,' he says, rolling forward on the balls of his feet as if he is about to lose his balance. I guess he has been on the sauce all evening.

'I don't speak Welsh, I am afraid,' I say. He just breathes deeply, exhaling through his nose, and stares down at me. There is a flame in the stare that makes me wonder if I am too close to the fire.

'Scotsman?' he eventually says.

'No. A Manxman, actually. My name's Ned,' I say, still trying the friendly approach and offering a hand that is not met. The attention this overbearing drunk is giving me makes me feel uneasy.

'The Manx don't wear kilts,' he says emphatically.

'Well, they do actually. What's your name?'

'Boarlacks!' Such is his enthusiasm for this word that he expectorates heavily on my face as he exclaims it. 'Boarlacks the Manx wear kilts.'

'Well, I am from the Isle of Man. And as you have so astutely observed, I am wearing a kilt. QED the Manx wear kilts, I think you'll find, Mr Bollocks.' I must say we have not got off to a good start, the two of us. Right now, I cannot see this conversation ending in the exchange of telephone numbers and sorrowful expressions of reluctant parting.

'Thasa blud-dee strange axhunt fur a Manxman, you ave.' We are steering into troubled water here. 'You daunt sound like noh Manxman to me.' He changes his gait purposefully.

It is well known that people who express themselves orally, who maintain an oral tradition central to their culture, are very sensitive to language and speech. Not only are they heedful of it, but they also have an advanced aural perception of speech. I am not making this up. I have read about it. In short, the Celts can hear like dogs. When English people meet, there is a great analysis and processing of information extracted from the first few words exchanged: assumptions about class, status, wealth and origin are made. People are often critical of the English for doing this, but I think it is pretty impressive detective work. Yet it is nothing compared to what a Celt can extract from the same short conversation. Like a CIA agent who can know when a man is lying just from the way his nostrils inflate, a Celt can plumb the depths of your character from the shallowest nuances of your voice.

Mr B has detected something wrong with my accent and he does not like it. The Manx accent is singular and rarely heard. I don't think he would be familiar with it. What he has detected is that my accent is largely nondescript and metropolitan, which means that it is hiding something. And, of course, he is right – I don't sound like a Manxman. I am stumbling a bit here.

'*Ta mee cummal anys Rhumsee, ayns Mannin,*' I say. '*Cre ass t'ou?*' This means 'I am from Ramsey in the Isle of Man. Where are you from?' My thinking is that speaking a little Manx Gaelic may reassure him, and throw him off the scent, but to my astonishment, he replies in Gaelic. I am only able to understand the first few words and when he realises this, he carries on burbling and spitting. I think it is Irish Gaelic, but I can't even be sure of that. He pokes a finger into my chest. His face is turning red hot with excitement.

'I only have a few words of Manx,' I try to explain. 'I have recently started to learn it.' Mr B just carries on jabbering and occasionally shouting. He regains a little civility when I ask how it is that he speaks Gaelic. He learnt it at university and lived in a Gaeltacht in Ireland for a time. You could say that it is my bad luck meeting a Welshman who speaks Gaelic, but actually it has little to do with luck. It is the kilt, now embellished by the blackthorn stick, which draws people in like bees to a honey-pot. I suppose that I should not be surprised that a Welshman is picking an argument with me. After all, as the saying goes, you only need two Welshmen to form a debating society. What I am worried about is how many Welshmen you need to start a boxing club. I suspect that it is one.

We are back on my Manxness and he does not buy it one little bit. He is frothing and spitting now like a man who has been dunked in a bath of custard. He is drunk and angry and he is sure that he has sniffed me out. Fee fi fo fum, this fat fella smells the blood of an Englishman . . . an Englishman who is holding himself out as a Celt. I turn away from him, but he catches my shoulder with his arm.

'See, if you hadn't said you was Manx, I'd ah had you fur a bloody Sais, an FEB. Know wha thar is?'

I know what a 'Sais' is – a Saxon. It is not a kissy, cuddly, love-you-madly term of endearment. Something tells me I don't want to know what an 'FEB' is.

'Thasa fucking English basturd,' he exclaims. These three words roll off his tongue with well-rehearsed ease. His eyes narrow to look through mine. It is decision time. I have worked myself into a corner here. What a mess. I have two options. Stay in my corner and receive further verbal and quite possibly physical abuse, or come out guns blazing.

'And you, my friend, are an FWC. Know what that means? Fat . . . Welsh . . . cunt.'

He blows. Fortunately for my jaw, he is at the end of a long day at the bar. The punch he unleashes in my direction is less like a hawk dropping out of the sky on a field mouse, and more like a balloon being propelled through treacle. I could learn Welsh in the time it takes to reach me.

The predilection of the Celts for a fight is well known. Julius Caesar himself noted how eager his foes in western Europe were to get their shirts off and square up. In more modern times, the police reports on any given Saturday night in Limerick tell the same story. Should you study the history of pretty much any European war in between, you will find Celtic soldiers involved somehow. The Celts are a profoundly pugnacious people, evidenced in recent centuries by the gallery of outstanding boxers the Celtic countries have produced: Tommy Carr, Rinty Monaghan, Jack Dempsey, Jimmy Wilde, 'Peerless' Jim Driscoll, Steve Collins,

Dave 'Boy' McAuley and Ken Buchanan. The list is long and distinguished. I got my first taste for boxing listening on the radio to Barry McGuigan outpoint Eusebio Pedroza on a heady June night in 1985. And if there is one Celtic characteristic that I do feel I share, it is this. I don't mind a fight myself.

So the punch comes in like a large meat pie and I nip under it. Then I am back up and straightening a right into a fleshy cheek. I think I land three punches before Rhondrey and Gwion have an arm each and they are hauling me across the dance floor. Mr B, bound by the arms of others, is bellowing at me in Welsh and I can be sure from the tone, if not from the words themselves, that these are not expressions of sweet Celtic kinship.

Another day of glorious sunshine – this good weather is long overdue. It seems that grey skies have loured over me relentlessly for the last two months. My skin has gone the colour of milk, which I suppose does give me the appearance of a genuine Celtic poet, a crepuscular creature who hides from the weather in pubs and composes verses all through the night.

I walk down to the village of Solva where there is a perfect little harbour to shelter boats from the Atlantic. It is very like Cornwall. It is deliciously twee, though the history of Solva is darker. I read in a guidebook that ships full of Welsh emigrants used to set sail from here for America in the nineteenth century. The excitement and fear that the emigrants experienced as they boarded the ships must have been the dominant human emotions then. Wondering if such latent but powerful feelings might still resonate in the harbour, I pick up a dappled stone from the beach and drop it into my pocket with the other stones.

I have never associated the Welsh with emigration, though it is in fact a historical phenomenon that affected all the Celtic countries. I have already written about the Cornish mining communities heading for Australia and the Highland Clearances. Irish emigration scarcely needs a mention. It is not so much a historical event, more a phenomenon – the dominant social and economic experience of the Irish people for the last 250 years.

In 1765, when smuggling was outlawed, the Manx hit economic hardship and emigrated in their thousands, starting a steady exodus that only really halted in the mid-1990s. My mum left when she was eighteen, never expecting to return, and so did I, I suppose. There are strong Breton communities still in Montreal and New York City (Jack Kerouac was of Breton stock). Welsh Quakers were the first to settle much of Pennsylvania. Henry and Sam Adams, and Thomas Jefferson were of Welsh descent. Eleven out of the first fifteen Presidents of the United States of America were straight-talking Ulster Scots. New Zealand, South Africa and Australia all had huge populations of Celts from the start. The story of the global distribution of the Celts goes on and on.

Perhaps the most peculiar story of Celtic emigration was the attempt in the 1880s to establish an independent Welsh-speaking state in Patagonia. Y Wladfa set out to be entirely Welsh, a sort of satellite community at the arse end of the planet where 'Welshness' could thrive, should it succumb to the steamrolling of 'Englishness' back home. Remarkably, this community has survived – representatives were at the Gorsedd ceremony yesterday – and hearing Welsh spoken by short, ruddy-faced men in the Chubut Valley, in what is now Argentina, continues to amuse travellers today.

Millions of Celts sailed away towards the new lands of opportunity, which is not surprising when you consider how difficult it was to scratch a living from the poor soil on the Atlantic seaboard, and how fine the margin for survival was for subsistence farmers. They left for predictable reasons: to escape enclosures, tyrannical landlords, high rents, religious persecution, famine and Englishmen, and because they were made to leave.

Today the harbour at Solva is full of dinghies and small yachts, chinking on the water that reflects the white heat of the sun like a mirror. I walk along the famous Pembrokeshire coastal footpath, striding out over the headland with my blackthorn stick. The colour of the sea, the lichen on the rocks, the coconut smell of the gorse and the vividness of the young heather are all strikingly familiar. What is also familiar is this niggling feeling I have, a feeling that reminds me that the business of poets is to write poems and I do not seem to have written many. It is the end of the first week in August; over three months since I stood on the top of Cader Idris, and what do I have to show for it? Three poems. It is a meagre collection. I can hardly say that poesy has gripped me. Whatever effect my nocturnal encounter with Prince Idris had, it has not resulted in my being prolific at churning out verses. Perhaps then the old adage *'poeta nascitur, non fit'* – poets are born, not made – the same sentiment that Calum expressed over a dram in the Royal British Legion club in Stornoway, has something in it.

I have been approaching writing poetry with the same unease with which I approach cats. That has to change. I could carry on waiting for inspiration to come to me. I could idle away more time waiting for the feminine archetype, the goddess of poetry, St Brigit, to assail me. That has not really worked so far. Perhaps I am not 'wooing' the muse well enough. No, I think this is like standing under an apple tree waiting for the fruit to drop into my hand. It could take all summer, all of the lighted half of the year. Time is no longer on my side. The alternative is to take a more pragmatic approach.

As I walk along the coast, Welsh poets are currently engaged in competitions at the Eisteddfod. These are dynamic challenges that require poets to pen verse in accordance with the immensely complex rules of classical Welsh poetic tradition, on the spot. It is like *Just a Minute* except what you say has to be in strict metre, and involve rhyme and alliteration. I would not stand a chance . . . and I call myself a bard?

The word 'Eisteddfod' means something like 'sitting' or 'chairing' and an Eisteddfod was originally a gathering of poets with precise rules and rather odd prizes – chairs. The first record of an Eisteddfod is from 1176, though they probably go back further. In Elizabethan times, these bardic competitions were used to sort out good from bad poets, the real ones from the cons, the winners receiving licences and patronage from noble families. Such festivals of poetry lost their place with the gradual Anglicisation of Wales in the seventeenth century, but they were back by 1860 and eisteddfodau have taken place regularly since. The modern festival has expanded to include competitions in drama, dancing, prose, music and singing. This, the National Eisteddfod, is the culmination of smaller competitions at regional eisteddfodau held all over Wales. Yet it is the poetry that remains central to it. The greatest award given – and the highest honour a poet in Wales can attain – is still a chair.

What I need to do is take this sort of creative professionalism, if that is the right word, and apply it to my own poetic vision. I have been re-reading the poems of T.E. Brown, the Isle of Man's greatest poet and one of its favourite sons. He was an Oxford scholar and the second master of an English public school, so he lived for many years off the Isle of Man, but the Manx remember him for his wonderful poems written in a Manx-English vernacular (through which he avoided both English and the strictures of Gaelic poetic techniques). The poems display all that is admirable about the Manx character, as well as the pride and the grievances. The rhythms and idioms of Brown's voice are very distinctive and it would be hopeless to try and copy them, but in these poems I have found plenty of encouragement, not least in the momentary benediction of common things that he chose as subjects. He is the antithesis of Yeats, in this respect.

What I need to do, I realise, is tell a simple story, only in verse. And with this conclusion, I sit myself down on a rock above the aquamarine sea. I stare at a piece of paper with '*Aigh Vie* Tommy Collister' written across the top, holding a sharpened pencil in my left hand. I am ready to go, and I am not leaving this spot until it is done, until I have a poem. Muse or no muse, it is going to happen.

It happens. It actually happens. By the time I leave the footpath and head back across the airfield towards my tent, I have a new poem and – here is the astonishing bit – I think it is halfway decent. Now I am not going to get all up myself here and suggest that they should start dusting down a square foot of Poets' Corner in Westminster Abbey in anticipation of creating a monument to Ned Clague. I am just saying that I think it is a halfway decent poem by my own pretty desperate standards.

I am lying on the grass, watching the sunlight play on the Preseli Mountains, trying to commit the poem to memory when Gwion walks over with a joint and a can of beer.

'Right, big Joe, the fightin poht?' he says. 'Joe' is Joe Calzaghe, Wales's current great white hope and a good heavyweight boxer. In the campground, people have been calling me 'Joe' all day, pretending to cower away from me and dropping to the ground when I come within ten feet of them. 'Yoo cumin to ah foam party, then?' Gwion continues. This is tonight's entertainment – a rave with gallons of soapsuds pumped into the marquee.

'Not if I am going to have to fight my way out of there, I'm not.'

'Naw, naw. We'll see you right, big Joe. The chicks will be hot, though.'

'Really?'

'Naw, nat really, you idhiot. Is ah jawk. This is Wales, noh Ebeetheur. We pick you up when w'er gawn awver.'

The foam party is, as Gwion said, like a rave in a big washing-up bowl. The foam is supposed to fill the whole room and glow iridescent with funky lighting. In this case, it is ankle deep and it ruins everyone's shoes. Not that anyone cares. They are all high on ecstasy or temazepam or diazepam or Pan's People or whatever it is the youth of today get nutted on, and having a great time. I

choose my usual path to enlightenment – ten pints and a few whiskies – and I just manage to maintain my enthusiasm.

My notoriety continues to spread, which I guess is inevitable if
you will wear a kilt and scrap in public. Two late teenage girls
come up to me at the bar, pretending to box. Bess and Angharad
are from south Wales, near Neath, but they speak Welsh.
'Wenglish' they call it jokingly. They force me to rehearse the few
Welsh words that I have learnt: '*Bore da*' is 'Good-day', '*Sut
rydach chi?*' is 'How are you?' They teach me a few more phrases
but they go in one ear and out of the other. My pronunciation is
dreadful. My dad once told me that if you say 'haemorrhoids'
often enough and with sufficient conviction, you are halfway to
speaking Welsh.

'Imagine you've a large mouthful a lasagne,' Bess says. 'Now
then, again – *Diolch* . . . *Os gwelwch yn dda*.'

'It's hopeless,' I say. 'Perhaps if I had a local anaesthetic in one
side of my mouth, that would do it.'

When Rhondrey and Brysor swagger over, the girls tease them
about coming from the north; 'nogland' they call it. The south-
erners take the mick out of the northerners for being backward,
inbred and doltish. As a whole though, I am astounded by how
friendly, confident and cool the Welsh youth are.

'Is this emerging Welsh confidence to do with having a Welsh
Assembly?' I ask Angharad, who is studying politics at university.

'I think thus an effect, noht a cause,' she says. 'Awnly a generation ago thu were a lot oh Brittish-Welsh in Wales, if you know
what I mean. Now, look around here, everyone is Welsh-Welsh. In
1979, four out oh five people vorted un a referendum for a Brittish-
Wales. Un 1997, tha same referendum went the other way and the
National Assembly is the result. I can't be shoer why but there as
been a big shift in how we think about ourselves. After seven hundred years, England failed to re-make Wales as an image aw itself
an it has finally stopped trying. We are, I guess, the first generation not to be bothered by this hugely complex relationship with

ah neighbours. Which is why this lot' – she waves her hand above the heaving morass on the flooded dance floor – 'are arving such a good time.'

Well, the drugs and the music might help, but essentially I agree with her. There is a new sense of ease about the Welsh youth, which is a pleasure to experience. Mr B did not have it, but then he was no teenager.

'Anyway,' Angharad says, 'why are we having this heavy conversation when we should be enjoying ourselves? And I've a question for you. Wha yoo wearin under tha kilt then?'

It is some relief to get back outside. The night has changed completely. Before we went in you could see every star in the firmament, but the mist has now rolled in. It is cold and thick, like mayonnaise. It is fresh off the sea and you can taste the salt in it. Back at the campsite, there are a hundred people in a big circle round a huge bonfire, in a dug-out pit the size of a badminton court. The flames from the fire are fifteen feet high and crackling noisily. A couple of guys are strumming lazily on guitars. Occasionally the rhythms turn into a tune and someone sings a song. I pass round the last of my whisky between Brysor and his friends.

'Eh, Ned, what about a poem,' Brysor says. 'We have noh heard wun.'

'I am not sure if now is the time . . .' I say but I don't have time to finish before Brysor runs up the shallow bank behind me. At the lip of the fire-pit he turns and, waving his denim jacket above his head, he starts shouting. It is all in Welsh but I have a sense of what he is saying. I am on.

'Shhh . . . shhh,' some of the other lads start saying, patting the air down with their arms.

'Silence, please,' Brysor finishes in English, with a flourish like he is introducing a heavyweight title fight, 'for, all the way from the Isle aw Man, the boxing poet . . . Ned . . . Clague!'

There are whistles and whoops and cheers. I get to the top edge of the pit. It is quite a long way to the other side, but remarkably most people are quiet so I do not have to shout.

'Okay. "*Aigh Vie* Tommy Collister" is the title of this poem. "*Aigh Vie*" means "Good luck" in the Manx Gaelic. Ready?' I look into the flames and take one . . . long . . . deep . . . breath.

> Out on a stag night
> Ten pints and a fight
> Says Pam in the Stanley
> 'Boys yer lookin manly'

I screech these last words like the haggard old Lambert and Butler landlady Pam is meant to be. There are a couple of gasps and a few laughs.

> Ten fishermen in drag
> 'Oi moit get a shag'
> Yells Jack on the quay.
> Into the Mitre where the pints are free.

A hand on the hip, a cupped hand over the side of the mouth and the line yelled sideways in a thick Manx accent are the theatrics I invent on the spot for Jack on Ramsey quay. The poem started as the story of a stag night I went on years ago. Writing it I found that the poem wanted to go other places, so it became the amalgam of several stories about boozing in Ramsey, many of which involved Tommy Collister, a lovely man who I used to play rugby with.

> *Aigh Vie* Tommy Collister – in yer pink knickers
>   and yer wig
> By pint number three – easy lads, he's dancing a
>   jig.
> There's Manx at Juan and Orry.
> Quiet lads, but tongues go free:
> '*Breau cassyn. Quoi ish?*'
> '*Shanglaney, ghoinney?*' '*C'red? Mish?*'

This is a conversation between two lads about girls. No one here understands it, but it is easy to suggest the meaning through gesticulation. There are laughs above the flames.

> *T'ad rastagh nish*
> '*Vel shinnyn goll nish?*'
> The best man bawls, running across Market
>   Square
> When Tommy falls.
> 'What'll yer wife say. Reckon yer better lookin.'
> 'Just a cut on the chin, boy, use yer wig for the
>   moppin.'

'*Vel shinnyn goll nish?*' means 'Let's go now?' and I shout it loud, waving people on like a best man who knows he is surrendering his authority to the drink.

> It's the bottom of four
> And they're growling for more,
> So we head for the Plough
> Line up a chaser. Pint five now.

The end of the first verse. Brysor hands me a bottle of whisky. The fire throws coins of copper light on the faces of everyone who sits close about it. There are some jeers to hurry me up as I take a swig. I feel my whole chest warm. I feel relaxed. Is that courage? Or is it simply hot blood let loose by the whisky? The next verse is in a different tone: the narrator explaining why Tommy is getting married.

> Tommy's only eighteen
> So you'd say he's keen
> If ya didna know Catriona's a baby due.
> The old man goes mental, turns the screw.
> 'See you in church, yessa. Over to you.'
> The weddin's on Monday

228

> And that's the way, if you know what I mean,
> Me mate and a good striker, out of the team.

This is the serious bit of the poem. It is a lament for losing a mate, a lament for growing up in a small town and not having many mates in the first place. I read it without the flailing gesticulations of the first verse, in a downbeat voice. And it works. The laughter has stopped. The talking quietens down. Another pause at the end of the verse, then bouncing and reeling into verse three where we pick up the stag night again.

> Into the Brit for number six.
> 'Marilyn Monroe, show us yer tricks!'
> '*Quoid ta shen costal*, boys?'
> Pint seven's on the house, cos I show 'em ma toys.

It is lewd, and I am being lurid, and they are laughing.

> By eight we're caned and partially maimed.
> Number nine's the Central
> Where we're all goin' mental
> Dancin' on tables and breakin' the glasses

Some lads are cheering. We are rollicking along now.

> So we're out on the quay, flung on our arses.
> *Ta emshir olk aym!*
> And we're drinking pint ten.

'*Ta emshir olk aym*' means 'the weather is turning bad' and it is the point, I only realise now, for another gear change in the poem. Just as every big night out on the tear gets ugly at this point, so does the poem.

> Talk goes up a peg
> Seein' as we've drunk a keg.
> '*Ta shoh ny share na shen*'
> '*Ta mish cho mie as eshyn*'

'Shoh yn dooiney share'
'Gowym yn ooilley cooidjagh kiare'
'Aber shen reesht!'

The last line means 'Say that again!' I am trying to raise Cain now. Spittle falls from the corners of my mouth. With arms outstretched and fingers flicking, I am doing the impetuous, 1970s, street-fighting gesticulation that is still popular on the Celtic Fringe and usually found outside nightclubs called Cindarellas or Nitelife and which means 'Come on then, pal. Let's go. Right now!'

> Time for a fight
> And try as we might
> We couldn't stop the Best Man and Tommy
> Hoovin' punches and boots – no comedy.
> Blooded and raw
> We call it a draw.
> See, they both love Catriona
> And that's what I'm sayin' ya.
> In a small fishin' town
> There's ever a frown
> When the one pretty girl gets pregnant, un goes
>   down.

The last three lines get slower and slower and I finish with my arms by my side and my chin tucked into my chest, but I can't stop for long because someone is sure to think it is the end. They do. There is a whistle. I bend my knees and straightening – I am really humming along on this now – I punch the air and yell at the very top of my voice:

Aigh vie Tommy Collister!

Silence again. Then in the assured tone of an old friend:

> Yessa, we had a night of it and yer lookin a mess.
> Treat her right now, and take off that fuckin dress.

I give tongue to the last two words like a drunk trying to kick up a shindy in a nunnery. There is lots of laughter. One of the guitars comes alive for a rousing strum. Cheers and whistles.

'Crackin,' Brysor says. 'There's great you are, mun,' someone else chips in. Gwion slaps me round the back of the shoulders. 'Got the *hwyl* this one has,' he says. This is praise indeed. '*Hwyl*' is a Welsh word for something that is much prized in Wales. It means something like 'speech-song' and describes the musical speech that great Welsh orators have always had, whether they be famous Revivalist preachers, politicians or poets. If the musical notation in your words is like the primeval voices of the forest and the free sound of the wind, then you have the *hwyl*.

I wake up fully clothed on top of my sleeping bag. I taste my mouth and find it little to my liking. Someone has left a stale loaf of bread in there for some reason. As I struggle to regain full consciousness, I realise that the loaf is in fact my tongue. Perhaps I will be able to speak Welsh now. The only liquid in the vicinity of my tent is the dregs of the whisky bottle. A good swig of that and I should be able to speak Turkish.

With a hangover that could start a war, I struggle round the campsite trying to piece my life back together. I am going home today, to see my family, so I start with a shower and a shave to tidy up what is looking like a comic Van Dyke beard. Wandering through the campsite as the rain starts to fall, I am greeted by witnesses to my poetic prowess. It is gratifying, if a little unnerving, as my recollection of the evening's events is not immaculate, to have trendy kids come up and say how much they enjoyed the poem. 'Good stuff, mun' . . . 'Crackin, mun' . . . 'We'll see you round the fire tonight' . . . 'Loved da poo-hm, mun'. The surreal moment of the day comes when a uniformed security guard stops me to ask if I would write a poem about him and his mates, the bouncers at the Maes B pavilion.

Brysor, Rhondrey, Gwion and a few others come over to say

goodbye as I am humping my rucksack on to my back again. 'Tsa pity yew can't stay, mun. Weekend's a riot, see,' Brysor says. They all know I am heading to Brittany for another festival. 'Tek the spirit ar the Welsh to the Bretons. They our brothers.'

The train chugs along the south-west Wales coast, round Carmarthen Bay. The rain is lashing down now. The man sitting opposite me, an Englishman who lives in Pembrokeshire, tells me when we make an unannounced stop in the middle of nowhere that the train journey from London to Fishguard takes ten minutes more today than it did in 1901. It is a long journey and without my daily stimulant of large amounts of alcohol, I go into a physical decline.

To my delight (and surprise), the train is only an hour late so I am home before my son goes to bed. When Vicky opens the door, they both look at me with astonishment, like they have just caught the family dog reading Shakespeare. I have been on the road and on the tear for three weeks and the journey is taking its toll. Lucas runs away shouting, 'Scotland, Scotland,' which is, rather bizarrely, what he now thinks my name is.

11

Vive Lorient

There is an easy way to get from Pembrokeshire to Brittany – by boat. Across the Bristol Channel, round Land's End and over the English Channel and you are there. It is the comparative ease of this journey, in times when sailing was swifter than travelling by road, which fostered the unlikely but remarkable religious and cultural affinities that exist between the Bretons and the Welsh. The problem I face is that there is no boat. This is a pity. I would like to see more of the Celtic Fringe from the sea, though I am no sailor. The beaches and headlands, the soundings, the tidal races and the overfalls must be the same as they have been for centuries. This sort of constancy induces a sense of historical free-fall that few places on the land, even on the Celtic Fringe, have the power to do any more. I suppose I could wait around for a yacht heading that way, but the festival at Lorient is already in full swing and I need to get there urgently. Also, I wanted to travel via London and home in order to convince my son that, though I am there often, my name is not in fact 'Scotland'. So it is a landward route I must take, which barely allows me a lungful of sea air or an eyeful of guano.

From London I take another train through the Channel Tunnel via Paris to my destination, the port of Lorient on Brittany's southern coast. The entire journey from St David's takes two days – twice the time it would take to sail. The one reassuring aspect of continuity, which I gather from looking at a meteorological map in the newspaper, is that the very same rain that was running down my back when I boarded the train in Fishguard is now lashing Brittany.

Now before Francophobes grow overly cheered by the news that western France has the misfortune to cop the same kind of dreadful weather as western Britain does all summer long, I must point out that Brittany is not really France. The name Brittany gives something away for a start. The region was known as Armorica (the land of the sea) when the Romans were here getting duffed up by Asterix and Obelix. When the Roman Empire declined in the early fifth century, there was a great migration of Welsh and 'Britons' from southern England over the sea to Armorica. No one seems to be sure why they migrated – it is classic Celtic history, actually, and about as clear as baby talk – but for two centuries they sailed south. When the Armorican Peninsula emerged from the Dark Ages, it was known (as far away as Byzantium) as Brittania, then Brittany, and 'old' Briton came to be known as Great Britain, to distinguish it.

The Irish and Welsh saints arrived with this migration. Despite the best efforts of the Church of Rome, they developed a distinctive Celtic Christianity in parallel with western Britain, which lasted in the region until at least the ninth century. The legacy of this 'different' Christianity is still obvious today, culturally at least, in the many celebrations and rituals that attend Christian worship in Brittany. The legacy is also there in the place names – often a useful ethnic and linguistic signpost when you arrive somewhere new.

Looking at the map on the train, I find St Malo, Pointe de St Gildas, St Brieuc, St Pol-de-Léon, St Fiacre and many more. There are also plenty of place names with the prefixes Tre (which means 'farm' or 'settlement') and Lan (a religious settlement), just as there are in Cornwall and Wales. One of the districts of Brittany is actually called Cornouaille – Cornwall. In fact, there are signs of Brittany's 'otherness' from France everywhere. It is probably fair to say that Brittany stands in its relationship with France somewhere between where Wales and Cornwall stand in their relationship with England.

To get a real mouthful of what it means to be a Breton, you have to go to the Festival Interceltique de Lorient, the biggest annual Celtic cultural bonanza by far, and a week of madness that is already at full tilt when I step off the train at Lorient late on Thursday afternoon to get slapped in the mush with a bucket of rain.

Folk festivals have always been big in Brittany. In the early twentieth century, as Pierre-Jakez Hélias's elegiac book *The Horse of Pride* relates, they were still spontaneous events rooted in centuries of community tradition. They were not arranged or coordinated, they just happened. Then along came the French centralisation movement and public education which eroded the local traditions and the identities of small, regional communities.

After the Second World War, Celtic Clubs were formed across Brittany with the aim of bringing peasant traditions (dancing, music, costumes and rituals) back into consciousness. At the same time, the notion of being Breton – initially an invention of the autonomy movement – and in the wider sense, of being Celtic, developed. The Grande Fête de Cornouaille, founded in Quimper in 1948, grew to be huge in just a few years.

Brittany then developed its Celtic identity in a different way from the other Celtic Fringe countries, but in the last fifty years it has fallen into a similar cultural cycle. Since 1945 the language has been in dramatic decline and aspects of culture and traditions that had changed so little in centuries have eroded at an alarming rate. Thus the Festival Interceltique is a surviving embodiment of thousands of tiny, local festivals that no longer exist and it recalls many of the traditions that we are in the process of losing.

The festival was first held in Lorient in 1971. It has grown into a byword for pan-Celtic culture. The length of the Celtic Fringe, from Stornoway to Mousehole, it is spoken of with enthusiasm. For many musicians, singers, bagpipers and dancers Lorient, as the festival is usually known, is at the top of the list of places to perform. It completely takes over the sizeable town. It involves

4,500 performers and draws 400,000 people over ten days. It is the greatest gathering of artists, performers and musicians from the remotest corners of the Celtic Fringe. Coincidentally, it is also one of the largest piss-ups on the planet today and it makes Munich's Octoberfest look like a Presbyterian Church outing to a garden centre.

I try five hotels walking from the train station to the heart of the town and they are all '*Pardon, monsieur. Complet.*' I am not too alarmed about this until I am informed at the tourist information centre that there is not one single bed to be had in the entire town. Everything is either full or refusing to take guests during the festival. I do not have to ask why they are refusing. You do not need the imagination of C.S. Lewis to conjure up images of the Diddly Dundonald Pipe Band from Donegal lampposting each other's beds at the Hotel Mercure, or the manager of the Hotel Victor Hugo having to apologise to the other patrons when Finbar the famous fiddler from Fermanagh falls off his balcony on to the patio during breakfast, or the night porter trying to coax the Cornish dance troupe out of the fountain in reception before the whole street is woken.

A bigger blow to me, though, is the news that the nearest campsite is a twenty-minute bus ride away and the buses stop running at 10 p.m. I want to explain to the smug little girl behind the tourist information desk that, on recent form, my evenings have barely begun by 10 p.m., but it would be wasted breath. It looks like I am going to be sleeping on the streets and abluting in the harbour, though I do have one more card to play.

'Em sur soorree, bird ah kent fand yur accumudation registration,' a slip of a girl explains, shuffling piles of paper back and forth across her desk in the festival office.

'Well,' I say, 'with 4,500 people to look after, I am not surprised that you lose a form or two.'

'Eggzaklee,' she says, shrugging and smiling. 'So wet we will dur

is this. Dehr is a rurm free in er school nearby. Angie will tek uh
there neur. You have to sheer uh bafroom wif . . .' – she shuffles
through her pile of papers again and finds the page she is looking
for – '. . . ah, wif a dance troop ef girls from Spain. I ope is okay?'

'I'm sorry?'

'You have to sheer uh bafroom wif a dance troop ef girls from
Spain. I ope is okay?'

'Yes. I thought you said that. That'll be fine.'

'Okay. Enjoiy yur festival and good lurk wif the pottery.'

'Poetry.'

'Aw, yes. Poh-tree. Good lurk, Monsieur Cliig. *Au revoir.*'

My room is a spartan study-bedroom in the local high school.
There is no sign of the Spanish dance troupe when I drop my rucksack off, but still, getting the bed is a result. I merely had to put
my head round the festival office door and ask where a lone poet
from the Isle of Man might lay his head and people fell over themselves to be helpful. They were unconcerned about where I was
performing and when. They had beds. I needed one. Simple as
that. There is nothing stuffy or pretentious about the Lorient festival despite its size and reputation, which marks it as a Celtic
affair from the outset.

As it happens, I have nowhere to perform. In the last two months,
I have rung and e-mailed the festival organisers to find out if there
is a poetry night, a slam or recital or a celebration of the spoken
word of some sort where I could let a few verses off. The response
each time was: '*Non*. No poetry at Lorient.' It seems strange but the
Bretons do not have the tradition in or love for poetry that other
Celtic nations have. What modern Breton poets there are have
invested their energies in song writing rather than poetry; the great
Alan Stivell, who almost single-handedly revived Breton folk music,
stands out. I guess the other problem is language – French, Breton,
Welsh, Gaelic, English and Spanish are all spoken here. So whatever
language you choose to write and read your poetry in, a percentage
of the audience will find it as engrossing as daytime TV. Music and

dancing, neither of which need any translation, make up the majority of the acts and though there is a 'literary tent', that seems to be mainly concerned with selling books and the main language there is French. This is not to say poetry has no place here. Far from it. It just does not get a billing on the official programme. I am going to have to create my own chances, which is fine.

The school restaurant has, Angie tells me when she delivers me to my room, been turned into a massive refectory for the performers at the festival. I dash across the playground to get there as the rain pelts the earth once more. There must be 300 people wolfing down plates of lardons, tripe and boiled potatoes, washed down with full-bodied, dry *cidre fermier*. At 5 per cent, it is not the meanest cider in the world, but drink it for twenty years and, I would say, you stand an above-average chance of going blind.

Many of the diners are in costume, ready for their imminent performances or just back from the stage. It is a very odd collection of costumes, figures and faces. There are thick-armed Scots in military rig and kilts, female Breton dancers in ankle-length velvet skirts and embroidered tops, bearded Irish bodhran players, young lads with faces painted purple, men in white gaiters, and flat leather caps. It looks like the canteen on the set of a David Lean film that he never made about peasant society at the end of the nineteenth century.

Eating my Camembert, I spend a few minutes watching this strange mob, trying to guess the nationality of a dozen people that I pick at random. It may not be much of an empirical experiment but I am having a stab at finding out how similar the physiognomy of the Celtic peoples is. I make my guess, eat another piece of Camembert, and then I go and ask the person where they come from. I get one out of twelve right. And what does that prove? Bugger all, actually, but it gave me something to do and it made me look less like a very sad man sitting on his own sinking *cidre fermier* in a busy room full of people.

At one table, a gruff old Welshman with a white beard (my

survey said Cornish), in a St David's tartan kilt, asks me what on earth I am doing, so I explain.

'Ywll nought tell uh Breton and the Welsh apart,' he states. 'They close-by, see. Mingling fuh centuries now.' He then tells me a story about going on a coach from Cardiff to Paris to watch a rugby match in the early 1970s. On this coach is a teenager from mid-Wales, a farm boy who speaks no English. At the Parc des Princes, they sit next to a crowd of Bretons who are supporting Wales in the match and after the game they all go boozing together. The boy gets on famously with the Bretons with whom he can communicate better than he can with his fellow country-men, who only have English. When they are ready to leave in the morning, they wait and wait and finally this lad turns up. He has been offered a job on a farm in Brittany and that is where he is heading. He never came back.

Actually, I believe it is quite difficult for Welsh and Breton speakers to communicate – though it certainly happens with per-sistence – but this old boy does not look like someone who is used to having his stories ruined by impertinent squirts from the Isle of Man, so I keep schtum. There has undoubtedly been a fluid exchange of ideas, culture, myths and people between the Welsh and the Bretons since pre-Roman times, just as there has been a similar exchange between the Irish and the Highland Scots. Innocently, I had not expected that such an exchange should still be going on, but of course it is.

There is only one small piece of advice that anyone hoping to sur-vive the Festival Interceltique needs and that is – bring earplugs. The defining and indeed deafening sound of the festival is the bag-pipes. From dawn to dusk, and thus to dawn again, for ten days, the skirl of the bagpipes drifts through the streets of Lorient like a bad smell. There is nowhere to hide. It is earplugs . . . or go deaf. And what with the prospect of going blind on the farm cider, Lorient could be a physically debilitating festival for the unwary.

In the road beside the school there are three pipe bands lined up when I come out after my feed of tripe and Camembert. A young man from the Glenalmond pipe band tells me that they are waiting to perform as part of 'Nuit Magique' in the football stadium. A glance at the festival programme reveals more: eight pipe bands, three dance troupes, a male voice choir, *trois ensembles de gaitas* – whatever the hell they are – all on stage, performing before 'giant projected images of heavenly Celtic imagination and dreams'. That is not a precise translation but I am beginning to get the picture. It is a sort of Celtic bagpipe *son et lumière* which I have to say is something that will certainly feature in the torture dungeons beneath my palace if I ever happen to become a tin-pot dictator in a small central African country.

The programme goes on: '*L'imaginaire Celtique s'est toujours nourri de poésie et de magie*,' which, I guess, is why they have designed a show that contains absolutely no poetry and no magic, just a lot of bagpipers in the rain and a series of projected images that the visually challenged might have as screensavers. I endure the show for as long as I do mainly because my seat in the stadium is out of the rain. In this time, the Monkstown Mossley pipe band and the Grupo de Danzas O Fiadiero from Galicia fill the stage with their wind and their folk costumes. When the rain eases up, I wander off.

Lorient uses the term 'Celtic' as loosely as it can be used. It is an inclusive festival, which is a good thing. Not only are there dancers and musicians from the regions of Galicia and Asturias in northern Spain (people who have a reasonably legitimate claim to being here, based on their cultural traditions), but performers come from as far away as Canada and Australia too.

All the main buildings in the centre of Lorient are turned into stages for the festival – churches, stadiums, the Palais des Congrès, cinemas, pubs, the town hall, the chamber of commerce – and in addition there are two huge, specially constructed marquees. All these venues have performances every night and they charge entrance fees. I suppose that is the only way a festival of this size can operate. However, Lorient started as a free street festival and in many ways this is where its lively heart still is.

Quai des Indes and Quai de Rohan face each other across an oblong tree-lined garden that would normally be full of old men flipping their boules about. For the festival, these two streets turn into a spinning open-air venue rammed with bars, food stalls and small stages, where as yet unknown bands from all over the Celtic Fringe belt out beats into the night. It is a great scene.

Tartan is totally de rigueur. Here there is convincing evidence that the kilt has become the most visible emblem of Celticism, despite the fact that there is no historical evidence to suggest that anyone but the Scots wore them in the past. I stop a man called Dafydd who is wearing a tartan I have never seen before.

'Is Jenkins tartan, bach,' he says, his eyes shining brightly with drink.

'Jenkins tartan? What is that about?'

'See, they've goh tartan fah loadsa Welsh family names nooh. Sall bullshit, corse.' He gives me a big wink. 'Yooh carn say ut dates bach a thu hancient tribes aw Wales cus sum bugger made it up last week, see. You know thez nor even ur "k" in a Welsh language.'

I tell him about my Manx hunting tartan and the absence of foxes in the Isle of Man and we both have a good laugh.

'See somit funny, you wanna see Bahree's kilt. Sgoh a ferkin Welsh dragon al oer it. Wet ere, mun. Al gor fend im,' Dafydd says and he dashes off into the crowd.

Dafydd, like me, is wearing his kilt in 'dress-down order' – with a T-shirt, thick socks and boots. This seems to be the fashion young Celts favour. No funny lace-up shoes, no long socks, no short jacket with fancy sleeves, no goat-haired pouch hanging round your bollocks. No fuss. Wearing it this way has taken the kilt away from being a ceremonial garment and made it more like wearing a pair of jeans, Celtic jeans.

Waiting for Dafydd to return, I count eight kilts go by in ten minutes. I can see two Breton bands through the doorway of the bar I am standing in. Both have kilted musicians. The kilt really has become something of a Celtic phenomenon, the most visible and easy proclamation of Celticness. Up to a point, I like the idea of modern Celts having a way of identifying with each other, a dress that distinguishes them. Yet the big question remains: why are these big hairy blokes so keen to get into skirts? A psychologist would have a field day with this, I imagine. There is the notion of collective definition. But could it also be to do with confrontation? Wearing a skirt you are, to a degree, challenging people to have a look at your lad and to snigger at you. It would be easy to end up in a lot of fights wearing a kilt. Or is it simply that the Celts have a deep-rooted taste for cross-dressing that even the classical chroniclers felt was too lewd to mention in the annals? Perhaps the kilt is just the tip of the iceberg, the public persona of an ethnic brotherhood of hairy, warlike men who behind closed doors love to get rigged up in baby dolls and basques and nurses' outfits? I am only half-Celt, so I just don't know.

Dafydd reappears with Barry, who gives me a twirl. His kilt really does have dragons and the Welsh flag on it. It is a rude kilt but there can be no mistaking where Barry hails from. The Welsh do love their flag. It is a symbol of the national libido.

'Now, Ned, yuwll luv this, mun,' Barry says. 'Dyoo knaw wha tha auragins aw tha Welsh flag ahr?'

'No.'

'See, the drah-gone was auriginally a winged phallus ridin awn a chariot.'

'Was it?'

'Aye, it wus. Now, see, you can't say Wales is all bad?'

'I certainly cannot.'

'Tell us, Ned,' Dafydd whispers, tapping the back of my legs. 'Anything awn under, boy?'

I wag my head grievously.

'Sound,' he says. 'Jus a slap a antifoulin oer the bawlacks un you ready a goh awl night, bach.' With that the two of them spring back into the tartan affray.

The rain has stopped completely by midnight and the Quai de Rohan starts to fill up with people. I prop up the bar in the India café (Lorient was built on the back of oriental trade) waiting for a new band to appear on the stage opposite. When they do, I realise that there is one further aspect of the kilt that I have so far overlooked: the tartan mini. There is a long and elegantly legged Breton girl on the stage, in a tartan miniskirt, and she plays the violin – all in all a combination that could do more to stir your sexual impulses than intravenous Viagra. It sort of says: I may be classically trained, but boy do I go like a train too. I pull up a chair and get comfortable.

Their music is good too. I struggle to straitjacket it with a genre, but I guess it lies somewhere between the Edinburgh military tattoo and Reading rock festival. So many of the young bands here are on the same sort of trip and it is a mix-up of traditional Celtic rhythms, gypsy music, funk and rock. It goes by a plethora of names: Celt-rock, kilt-rock, techno ceilidh, acid croft and trip-nobareyourbuttocksfolkadelica, though it is all a brand of folk music. As Louis Armstrong once said: 'All music is folk music, I ain't never heard no horse sing a song.'

Music has always been the most accessible of all the traditional Celtic arts. Ever since the 1970s, it has been the greatest export too. Through bands like the Chieftains, the Celts (though in particular, it has to be said, the Irish) realised that there was an appetite for traditional music outside the Celtic countries. The success of the Chieftains encouraged many young Irish musicians to play within their tradition, rather than going off and becoming glam-rockers or mods, and to update it. Only a decade later, along came what was probably the greatest Celt-rock, or Celt-punk perhaps, band of all time, the Pogues (originally called Pogue Mahone which means 'kiss my arse'), whose anarchic fusion of traditional songs and modern liquor proved to be a success all over the world. I saw them live once – there was and there never will be anything like them. Dozens of excellent bands from Ireland, Scotland and even Wales these days, all with at least one foot in their musical heritage, have followed. I do not think it is too much to say that the success of Celtic music all over the world has been at the heart of the late twentieth-century renaissance of the image of the Celt. Certainly, it has been at the heart of making Ireland – that impoverished, run-down European backwater only a quarter of a century ago – one of the trendiest and best-loved countries on the planet.

Live, Celt-rock (I know, it is an ugly name, but it will have to do) is the perfect accompaniment to strong hooch, just as house music is the perfect accompaniment to designer drugs. So I decide to get with the programme and I swallow a couple of shots of tequila, the second of which the barman shouts me, having me seen me struggle to hold down the first one. Then I leap into the crowd before the stage.

The band – violin (or fiddle – it is the same instrument), bongos, oboe, accordion and guitar – are bouncing out hectic and heady songs in the style of the Pogues. In front of them, we are not so much dancing as leaping like a football crowd in the days before all-seater stadiums, pogoing from foot to foot, prancing higher and higher like the sea being whipped up by a strong wind against a current. It is a delightful kind of anarchic release. At one point, I am linked by the arm to another man. We are jumping and arching when we completely lose our balance and we fall through some people and on to a table, wiping it clean of glasses and bottles, for which social transgression we are grasped firmly by friendly hands and put back on our feet. With slaps on the back, we are set to start all over again.

I find out that the band is called Fiesta Dogs. The cavorting crowd gets thicker and thicker beneath their feet. The music is the sort of stuff that makes you want to pull up the front of your kilt in front of a nun and shout, 'Get yer ya yas out!' Well, that (and I suppose the tequila too) is what it makes me want to do and in the absence of a nun in this mosh-pit, I just start flashing anyone. In no time, there is another man in his kilt, hoiking it up and yelling something equally unintelligible back at me.

The Fiesta Dogs play two encores. Tables and chairs have to be hurriedly cleared away in front of the café because people, in their eagerness to dance, are climbing all over them. When the band does finish, there is not a dry patch on my T-shirt. Someone pours beer on my head and someone else sticks a bottle of beer in my hand. Feeling like I have just been in a boxing match, I wander off down the still throbbing street. More bands are at it. More people are dancing and drinking and shouting. 'Get yer ya yas out!' I shout back. But I am spent. I eat two pork baguettes and, tracing a path that is something like the flamboyant and whirling circles of a Celtic capital letter, I stumble my way back towards the school, eagerly anticipating finding the Spanish dancing girls taking a communal shower.

It is the only disappointment of a tremendous evening to find that the Spanish dancing girls are, in fact, a Scottish pipe band. Wondering what might have been, I pogo off to sleep.

I wake to the sound of bagpipes ringing in my back teeth. There is getting out on the wrong side of bed in the morning and then there is being sprung from your slumber by the airy skirl of some tosser wetting his warpipes. No matter how you look at it, it is not a good way to start the day. I would rather be cleaning the bogs in Guantanamo Bay. My enthusiasm for the signature instrument of the Celts is waning. I shovel in ibuprofen and try to go back to sleep.

I have managed to convince myself that mornings at these festivals are for folklorists and language enthusiasts and generally people a little too keen on all matters Celtic. To take part in any a.m. activities suggests an ingenuousness that I feel I should now be above. Better to stay in bed and compose verses about the sad but ghastly demise of a band of once celebrated bagpipers, murdered gratuitously in the shower at a folk festival.

When I do get up at lunchtime, my day hardly improves. As I am walking through the 'Celtic village' looking for some greasy comestibles to stabilise the revolt that is going on in my stomach, a very small man accosts me. He grips his chest like he is looking for the role of JFK in an amateur dramatics production, and then he barks in a stentorian voice, 'Asturias.'

I think I see what is going on, so I place my right hand tenderly on my left breast and whisper, 'Isle of Man.'

This fellow then throws his arms around me. Now there are not many people on this planet who are over the age of eight and who only come up to my chest in a bear hug, but one can be sure that most of those who do have Celtic genes. The Asturian man's forehead cracks against my breastplate.

'*Vous parlez français?*' I ask.

'*Eh, non,*' he replies, giving me a 'what to do?' shrug.

I am wondering if we are just having a spontaneous and public expression of Celtic fraternity here and that this encounter is otherwise pointless, when he pulls from his pocket a camera. It is a digital camera and on the small screen up come images of the festival. This is rather good – I am getting an eye, albeit a waist-high eye, on the events of the early part of the week. We must have looked at forty pictures and I am still not sure why we are doing this. Then a photo of the Fiesta Dogs pops up.

'Argh, argh, argh,' he exclaims.

The next two images are of people who are either dancing or running away from a terrorist attack. It is difficult to tell which. The next photo is a strange composition. A third of it is blitzed by flash, and white. I look again. It is human flesh: a most unattractive thigh and a set of gleaming buttocks, and in the corner of the screen there is a square of tartan, a tartan that belongs to those buttocks, a tartan that is for any man who really knows his tartan, unmistakable. It is Manx hunting tartan. Shit! That's my arse.

My Asturian friend flicks a switch and slips the camera back into his pocket before I can locate the delete button. He gives me a big grin. Then he taps his watch and shuffles his feet to suggest that his dancing skills are imminently required somewhere. He head-butts my breastplate again and he is gone. He has probably e-mailed these pictures home to Asturias and I am left with the sinking feeling that global subscribers to a niche tartan fetishist website are already downloading my bum on to their hard drives. This is not going to be easy to live with.

I am sitting outside a café on Quai des Indes, ruminating the consequences of this, over a coffee and a croissant, when things get worse. The bongo player from the Fiesta Dogs walks by. It could just be a passing reminder of my meddling with infamy, but he stops, looks at me, smiles and bounds over.

'*Salut, Ned*,' he says, clasping my hand and pulling up a chair. '*Ça va?*' Actually, *ça va pas du tout*, I am thinking. '*T'as la forme?*'

Ned? Oh, God. We have met? There is an outside chance that this encounter took place in a previous life, on another planet, perhaps even in a different dimension. However, a more rational analysis suggests it happened last night, which means my recollection of events is not exactly peppered with brief blank spots, but rather that it has been vacuum extracted. I have had a tequila memory abortion and I feel quite sick.

Being Ned Clague has never been simple. Having an alter ego is like walking along an uneven path in the dark. You start very warily, frightened you are going to trip, but you slowly get the feel for it and your eyes adjust. In no time, you are breezing along at a good pace, your confidence is back and before you know it, there you are thinking that you can manage this walking fast, perhaps even running, in the dark with half a bottle of hooch inside you. Hubris has struck. Last night, as is clear with every word this musician says, I was guilty of the most heinous offence that an international poet of mystery can commit – I was drunk in charge of a disguise.

Clearly I have got to get to the bottom of this and fast: '*Tu parles anglais?*' I ask.

'*Non, mais toi, tu parles bien français, Ned,*' he replies. If I was speaking good French then I must have been very smashed.

Slowly I begin to piece it together: he is called Mattieu. Thankfully, he thinks it is funny that I cannot remember his name. We were all drunk? No, I was the only one really drunk. After the gig we drank whisky in the bar. A lot of whisky. Woo hoo! I stood on the table in the bar and recited a poem. I fell off the table in the bar. The poem was great. Tifenn loved it. Tifenn is? The girl in the band. Uh oh. Tifenn writes poetry too. We spent a lot of time talking about poetry. Agh.

Rob Penn's *Thoughts on Poetry* would be a slim volume. It may be even slimmer than the book of Italian war heroes. So what can I have possibly contributed to a conversation about poetry? Well, I am about to find out because as I am masticating the last mouthful of my croissant and pondering this, Tifenn appears. Thank Lugh, she is not wearing the tartan miniskirt. Though I am not suggesting that I look anything like Adonis on this particular morning, Tifenn is less like Aphrodite than I recall. The tequila was talking. She kisses Mattieu no fewer than four times, which seems to be the standard around here, and she moves to do the same with me. Rather than stun her with my rotting venison breath, I gulp and purse my lips. We both go to the left and bonk noses. By the time we are through four kisses, I am gurning like a free-diver who has pushed the outside of the envelope.

'*Salut, Ned.* Ow air you? A bit pearly?'

'You speak English?' I blurt and they both laugh.

'Ef curse. You daunt reh-member? We ave a leurng discussion abet poo-hetree lest night.'

'Yes, well, I'm afraid I don't recall everything I said. What I mean is, I don't recall anything I said.' We are all laughing now. 'Can you tell me?'

'Well,' Tifenn says, trying to catch a waiter's attention with a flick of an elegant hand. 'You av ze belief in Celtique poo-hetic tradition, in a linguistique un technical connection between ze Celtique countries which make zem distinct, unique. Yeur believe zis vehr strongly . . .'

'I do?'

'*Oui* . . . yes . . . but you sink Celtic poo-hetree hez to mudernise, but wiff zese traditions un techniques. You daunt lack strict metre for itself. You duh lack *vers libre*, free verse. Yuh sink zuh Welsh poht muss rat en English, mais en vernaculaire, en the Gallic poht too, to be red meur.'

That all sounds reasonable. No howlers. It is not as bad as I thought. Perhaps I have learnt something this summer.

'Yuer favouret poo-hets air Heaney, MacDiarmid, I sink two Thomas, Kavanagh, Maclean, yeur T.E. Brown. We ev different opinion abet some of zem . . .'

Okay, so apart from Dylan Thomas, R.S. Thomas and Brown, I have not read much of any of these poets, but as a list it is pretty good.

'. . . end yeur fehvoreet poo-hetical dehveec is yehr iambic tetrameter.'

I didn't even know I had a favourite poetical device. Where did that come from? English A-level notes? I can't be absolutely sure what an iambic tetrameter is.

'It is?'

'*Oui* . . . en ah like yeur poo-hem you read . . . until you fall off the tabla.'

All in all, there is nothing to be even remotely embarrassed about. I do not have to leave Lorient immediately. I do not have to put in an emergency phone call to Vicky. I do not anticipate being berated and spat at on Quai de Rohan this evening. In fact, I think my behaviour was quite reasonable and so, it appears, do Mattieu and Tifenn. They are playing again this evening, in another bar on Quai de Rohan, and they ask if I will come along and recite a poem during their gig. Clearly, this is the way Celtic poets are expected to behave and I feel myself warming to the task. I feel like a man who has just had a death sentence reprieved. I think I should celebrate with a little 'hair of the dog'.

'*Garçon!*'

Lorient is a very fluid festival in that there are always a dozen things going on at any time of day and most of the night. With my laminated performer's pass, I seem to be allowed in anywhere without having to put my hand in my pocket. In the last couple of days, I have been to a continuous stream of events: bagpipe competitions, dancing classes, art exhibitions, films, a traditional *fest noz* (a Breton ceilidh), book markets, uilleann-pipe concerts, harp recitals (albeit briefly) and I must have heard fifty different bands. In the evenings there seems to be a band playing outside every bar, and there are lots and lots of bars. This is a port, after all. When the heavens open and the street party gets a good dowsing, I slip into Le Pub, a semi-permanent marquee half the size of a football pitch at the end of Quai de Rohan, where a seamless string of bands are rolled out to rock the honking crowd.

The festival is dominated by Breton performers and first and foremost it is a remarkable testament to the survival of Breton culture, particularly music and dancing. These traditions hit a nadir in the middle of the twentieth century when they approached being folkloric oddities rather than the expressions of a living culture. Brittany had quite an inferiority complex at this time, in which respect you can liken it to all the other Celtic countries. That trend has been reversed and what happens annually at Lorient is both the cause and effect of that. In terms of artistic creation – recording and publishing, most notably – Brittany is now one of the most progressive regions in France. But Lorient holds itself out as something bigger than even this. The festival calls itself Emrod ar Gelted – the Great Celtic World Gathering. As well as the bagpipers, harpists and singers from North America and Australia who compete here against the best from

Scotland, Ireland, Wales and Brittany, the organisers of Lorient also take the managers of Celtic festivals from all over the world on internships and as guests, placing Lorient at the centre of a global web of Celtic celebrations. The festival produces books, CDs and TV films. There is even a club set up for Celtic business networking.

Crucially, it seems to be a protean festival – how else could it draw such large crowds every year? – changing shape and emphasis as quickly as the notion of what it means to be a modern Celt alters. It would be easy to knock the festival for being fickle and perhaps for losing sight of its original mission, but how the people of the Celtic countries see themselves has changed dramatically in the last quarter of a century, and Lorient has always managed to be a barometer of this, which is no mean achievement.

What cannot be disputed is that an awful lot of people come here and have a sodding good time. Most of the young Bretons I have met (many of whom have left their homes in rural Brittany to find work elsewhere in France and are back for the weekend) are barely conscious of the Celtic fraternising that goes on. They are here to drink and make merry and dance like live fish being barbecued, long into the nights.

One night I fell in with a gang of young Bretons who all live in Paris. None of them spoke Breton, or cared to (other than to say 'Yer mat' or 'Cheers'). For Marina, Patrice and Sabrina, this was like Glastonbury or any other tribal gathering – a chance to get your rocks off with like-minded people. That they or I were Celtic mattered not. In fact, they thought it odd that I had come all the way from the Isle of Man to be here. Marina asked if, as it was Sabrina's birthday, she could have a look up my kilt. It was as if they had never seen a man in a kilt before. (Sabrina actually wrote in my notebook later 'Tu as un beau zizi' which is a personal milestone for me. If I take only one thing away with me from my first visit to Lorient, it will be that a young woman described my penis as 'beautiful'.)

The one great omission in all of this is poetry. I have heard none, and apart from Tifenn and a random Irishman, I have not met another poet. There were more poets within thirty feet of my tent in Maes B at the Eisteddfod than I have met here. In the absence of a formal venue and in addition to hopping on stage with the Fiesta Dogs, I have taken up what I choose to call 'guerrilla poetry'. When the mood catches me, when the wind is blowing the right way or I am feeling a little tipsy, I hop up on to a bench or a table in a public place, give a loud whistle and let a poem off to whoever will stop long enough to listen. Depending on how drunk I am, it might at times be more appropriate to call it 'gorilla poetry' as that is what I must look like, beating my chest and howling at the moon. A gorilla may also be what I smell like as I seem to draw dogs faster than humans.

It is not easy to draw a crowd and I now know why street performers have such protracted preliminaries. There are all the bands to compete against (on one occasion I am howling out, 'I've Got Whiter Buttocks Than You,' when a full twenty-man pipe band sets off right behind me, rousing legions of long-dead Highlanders to fight once more and sending me out to sea in a gale). Then there is the language problem. With the help of Tifenn, I have learnt a short preamble in French, which says who I am and what the poem is about. But the poems are, of course, in English with a bit of Manx so the majority of people cannot understand them. The performance then becomes the key to stopping people, rather than the poems. To this end, I have done some work in the mirror in the bathroom back at the school. My gesticulations have grown excessive – whirling my blackthorn stick about my head, foot stamping, pointing, throwing punches – and they suggest a religious zealot outpouring a 'the end is nigh' type speech. It is important, I am also learning, not to go on too long, and also to adopt the right voice: not too soft, but not too tortured and agonised either.

I might get a better audience in here, I think, as I walk into and feel the warmth of the Quay Street Pub, a bar on a pedestrian street above Lorient's marina that could be situated in a village in Connemara. It is clearly based on an Irish tavern. When I turn up there is a proper music session going on: two mandolin players, three fiddlers, a flautist, two bodhran players, two uilleann pipers and a guitarist are crammed around a table hammering out rhythms to the foot-tapping drinkers. It is a familiar scene.

I order a pint of Guinness in my reluctant French and the barman says, 'Thas noh need ah try the funny stuff in ere, pal. Whoaza tartan, then?' He is a Glaswegian. I have a couple of pints – I still need them for courage – before my moment comes. When the musicians drift out of a tune that has been jigging along for ten minutes and reach for their glasses, I hop up on a bench. There is the customary problem of getting the drinkers who have been talking eagerly in order to be heard over the music to listen up. I am getting better at this. I deliver my brief introduction in French and English and say a few words in Manx, then I hold a long pause before bellowing, '*Aigh Vie* Tommy Collister!' It is a rousing call and the pub falls quiet. Then I am off.

The barman shouts me a pint afterwards and there is a delightful Welshman at the bar who puts a silver cap from a hip flask in my hand.

'Thas good whisky, it is,' he says, 'for tha poem. Yer mat.' He takes a slug himself. Donald is tall and lean – not your typical Welshman in name or stature – and he has a weirder accent than mine. He grew up in Canada where his dad emigrated. His dad appears: father and son are on tour together. They are musicians. They seem knowledgeable about Celticism and they are full of enthusiasm for what they have seen at Lorient.

'Are you performing here?' I ask Donald.

'No, no. Just lookin, just listenin. We've heard some great music, we have. Even from Canada, we've heard some great musicians from Canada. You know, descendants of Scottish emigrants in Nova Scotia. Wicked, you know.' I have read a little about the influence of the Celtic diaspora on modern Celtic identity. It has been profound, particularly in the last twenty years. 'It's mad,' Donald goes on at breakneck speed. 'Ya hav the descendants of emigrants who made it to Canada a hundred un fifty year ago, they're back here un they know songs un poems un dances that have actually been forgotten on Skye and Lewis and everywhere else. It's like the culture the first emigrants took away with them has been pickled and preserved, like some family relic, it's bin untouched, and they bring it back and freak out the relations because back here no one remembers that song. Nother dram, man?'

An old, local man who beamed a kind, toothy grin at me as I recited the poem grasps my arm and tells me that he did a farm stay in the Isle of Man when he was a boy in the 1950s. I know the farm and I set him off on a happy trip down memory lane when we talk about the hills and villages and pubs that he knew for a summer. I could stay in the Quay Street Pub all evening. It is a fine boozer and the music is good, but Ned Clague has a date with destiny tonight, so I move on.

It is Sunday night, the last night of Lorient 2003, 'Survivor's Night' or 'Saliva Night' as some choose to call it. Performing my poetry in front of a large crowd of Celtic enthusiasts and revellers at Lorient has been my goal since I first set foot on top of Cader Idris nearly four months ago. We all need goals and the Festival Interceltique was mine. When I arrived here on Thursday, I busied about chatting to venue managers and festival organisers, looking for an opening, looking for a gap in the programme that Ned could boldly step into with a swish of his skirt and a stab of his stick. But I was dismayed to find that everywhere I went, people said '*Non*'. They said it in the kindest possible way, and apologised profusely, but it was always '*Non*'.

Only on Saturday morning did I eventually see some light at the end of the tunnel when I went to see the *responsable* or manager of Le Pub. Above the disconcerting sound of my knocking knees, I asked Maurice for a ten-minute slot between bands – time enough for me to read two poems. He was a Breton but he had lived in Dublin for a long time and he liked poetry. He thought the idea was good, but there was some bureaucracy to hurdle first. He sent me off to try and find the Manx delegate who is supposed to look after the acts and performers at Lorient. There is only one lone band from the Isle of Man at the festival this year, so this delegate was not easy to find. I hunted and hunted all day without luck and I even met her Breton fiancé – by an incredible chance he poured me a drink in a bar and asked where my tartan was from, but even he did not know where she was.

On Sunday morning, I went back to Maurice. He was a bit bleary-eyed and I pestered him until he finally said he would organise it. I could have a crack on the main stage of Le Pub. 'Hokey, hokey,' he said. 'We do it. Yuh cum ear at eight o'clock. Ah get yuh ten minute.'

It is quarter to eight now and I am walking through the crowds back down Quai des Indes with purpose, or it might be fear. Yes, it is fear. I am frenetically nervous, like I have just overdosed on diet pills. I have been like this most of the day. My last day at Lorient has been ruined. I have wandered the streets in an unrelenting dither. I am only being honest when I say that the thought of reading my poems out aloud to 1,000 people fills me with complete horror. I would rather be doing PR for A.A. Gill in Wales. But I am going to do it.

Le Pub is, as you would expect on Saliva Night, heaving. There seems to be more beer going on the floor than there is down the gullets of the festival patrons, who are raising their game for one last heave-ho. The bar-scrum is six deep. A band of Breton Goths are hammering out their stuff from the stage. I have a look around the mixing desks, but no Maurice. Round the back of the marquee, one of the security guards checks my pass.

'*Je cherche Maurice*,' I say.

'*Maurice? Il est pas là*,' the guard replies, suggesting conspicuously with those five simple words that he does not care where

Maurice is, nor would he even if some news of the man's where-abouts won him a night in the scratcher with a youthful Brigitte Bardot.

'*Uh? Mais il est le responsable.*' Urgency springs into my voice, but in reply I merely get a look that intimates, 'Hey, it's Survivor's Night, son . . . order has broken down . . . we're all in free-fall.' This is followed by a Gallic shrug combined with a throaty grunt that says something about how little progress the human race has made since the Neolithic Age. I am still outside the eight-foot security fence at this point. Knowing full well that I can't goose him, the guard turns round and walks away as my platitudes get more and more urgent. When I start shouting in Manx – I am not sure where this comes from – he does come back, whereupon we have precisely the same conversation. It takes five minutes of pleading before he agrees to go off and get Maurice's assistant.

No Maurice is a setback, but it should still all be fine. A girl in a baseball cap comes out. She looks like she has done six Survivor's Nights back to back and run a marathon each day, in between. I guess it has been a long week, working in Le Pub. She explains to me in French that Maurice has disappeared and nobody knows where he has gone. He has done a bunk. He was spotted at lunchtime and he was drunk then, so he must be really howling by now.

'*Alors. Peut-être vous pouvez m'aider.*' I am trying to muster my best French.

'It's all right,' she butts in. 'I speak English. I'm from Wales.' It is a small mercy at a time like this. I explain the whole run of con-versations and events that have brought me here. Her eyes begin to glaze. At the end of my pleading speech, she says, 'Look. I'm really sorry, but there is no way we can get you on stage now. The sound checks for all the bands were done hours ago and all of that information is programmed into the computer. And one of the other venues packed up this afternoon, so we have twice as many bands to get through here anyway. If I tell the sound technicians to do what you want now, there will be a bloody revolution. They will walk out, but they will hang me first.'

I am really uptight now. I start swearing and battering the fence with my stick. This is not for show. I am angry. Fuck it! A minute or two of impersonating someone with Tourette's syndrome and this girl drags herself back inside muffling, 'I'll go ask.'

Clearly the idea of seeing me again is more than she can handle and the guy who comes out next is a sound engineer. He is very nice. In Franglais, he explains how it just can't happen. He leaves me hanging from the steel fence. I really am disappointed. Not just because I have spent the whole day dropping a trail of small fired-clay blocks from beneath my kilt, marking my meanderings round town, but also because I was good for this. I was up for it. I have managed to convince myself that I could pull it off on stage. I wanted those people to hear my poems and judge them.

What do you get if you cross the Tweenies with a case of Stolichnaya? The scene in the Olympic bar on Place Aristide-Briand at 2 a.m. It is a four-cheese meltdown. I am not sure if I have ever seen so many people, so drunk. Most of them are part of a pipe band from Kerry, but I only learn this from the Breton barman who is wearing a Kerry football shirt. The members of the pipe band have long since forgotten where they are from. They are all absolutely nutted. In the first five minutes I am in there, I am taken off my feet by a revolving scrum of men, a girl gets pushed through a window and the lead singer of the band is mobbed, thrown to the ground by three women while a noteless oaf takes over the singing of 'Wonderwall'. And as all this happens, nobody even misses a beat.

The barman is a real professional. He is dispensing cocktails as if he has just started his shift. Knowing that I can't beat them, I play my favourite Celtic festival cocktail game, which entails identifying the person most obviously crazed with drink and ordering a large one of whatever he is having.

The Olympic bar is no place to try and think cogently about anything, least of all the opportunity I have missed here at Lorient, but I can't stop turning things over in my head. I have fluffed it. There is no other festival between now and Samhain where I will have the chance to get up in front of a huge crowd. But two thoughts emerge out of my impenetrable sulk. First, why do I have to end this bardic lark at Samhain anyway? Well, there is my family and my health to think about, but I could happily continue writing poems and going to the odd festival from time to time. But further than that, and I only realise this now I am well into this journey and steeped in all things Celtic, wanting to achieve something as nakedly ambitious as being on stage in front of 1,000 people at the Great Celtic World Gathering was something of a metropolitan, dare I say it English, goal – an achievement without substance, something to boast about but which really means nothing. I am, and will continue to be, happier in a dingy pub facing a dozen dwarfs and a wet dog.

Just when I am rising out of my fury, a wiry little Kerry-man sticks his tongue in my ear and then blurts, 'Shoite! Pairdon me dar fella. Oi tairt you wuz moi suster.'

I have already lost my temper once this evening and that got me nowhere. 'Had a good week?' I ask.

'Toime a moi loife,' he exclaims, with an expression that suggests he is about to park a week's worth of croque-monsieur in his lap. I shift out of range.

'When are you going home?' I am trying to keep the questions simple.

He stares at his watch-less wrist for some time. 'Air floight's in two hairs.'

'Good luck,' I say, swallowing my menacing cocktail.

'Air, good luck to yaeow too.'

My train is only four hours away, so I see no point in going to bed. By 3 a.m. almost everything is closed and the human detritus of one mother of a belting festival gets flushed down Quai des

Indes and Quai de Rohan and out of Place Aristide-Briand, into Le Pub. A few of the people I have met are here. Mattieu gives me a hug and a kiss and a tot of whisky.

When I stumble out into daylight, I realise what a Herculean task getting to the train station is going to be. I stop to spectate at two fights, I get lost, I stop again to ask an old lady directions and she defies her age by launching into a run in the opposite direction, I fall and cut my knee badly and I throw up twice. The second time, I am bent over double, leaning on my stick, filling the gutter outside the railway station. When I think I am through, I straighten up and a voice beside me says, 'Well, well, well. If it's nought de poo-ht himsilf naw. Un how air ya?' Clearly I do not have to answer that. He is a charming Irishman, and a poet, who I met a couple of days ago. He slips his arm round my elbow and looking just a little like Humphrey Bogart and Peter Lorre in the final scene of *Casablanca*, we walk on to the platform to catch our train.

12

Flying at the Fleadh

'Wanna personality optimiser?' Gerry asks.

'A what?' I retort.

'Personality optimiser.'

'Yes, I thought you said that. If I have one will I wake up in a strange room with a funny taste in my mouth and a sore arse?' He doesn't laugh. Not so much as a dimple appears on his tight cheeks. It is just my luck that among the Irish, a nation of people famous for their conviviality and quick-wittedness, I get an Irish-American with all the allure and sparkle of an old cow pat for pub company.

'Naw, buddy. Personality optimiser suh name fuh yuh antidepressants. But see weez in Ireland so iz a drink, yeah? Wan one?'

'A-ha. Guinness. Thank you.'

The pints get passed overhead from the bar back to where we are sitting in the corner, so great is the press of bodies, the inflated bodies of Irishmen who have spent half their lives in pubs, that pints cannot be safely carried. Gerry shins along the bench and drops back into the seat next to me.

'Phwooah,' he says, 'either this publican gotta make a bigger bar ar the customers gotta work out some, hey? Wha ya writin there, buddy?'

For various reasons – though mainly because I don't want people to know that I am writing a book and I feel self-conscious about that deceit – I try not to let people catch me making notes. It merely encourages questions, as if the Celts need encouraging, which I then have to deflect with half lies. So I am often to be found scrawling out my notes in bogs, outside pubs, in moonlit doorways, in phone boxes and crouching down on quiet pavements. Occasionally, when I fear that I may forget something important, I slip my notebook on to my lap in a pub. Eagle-eyed Gerry has spotted it.

'Oh, nothing,' I say. 'Just some notes for a poem. I'm a poet.'

'Poet, huh? Okay. I thought you were some English spy, y'naw' – he pokes an elbow into my ribs – 'keepin un eye on the Ahrish pay-triots. Huh? If these guys catch yer, er if ah blow the whistle, buddy, they'll kneecap yer un heave yer awf the Cliffs a Moher. Paddy never furgats hez bun betrayed bah the English. Am I right?'

Wrong . . . I think. Uncannily, Gerry has hit on the very subject that I was just making some notes about. The pub we are in is thick with a perceptible sense of Irishness and in a former age, as little as ten years ago, an Englishman might have felt extremely uneasy in this environment. But not any more.

Nationalism and hatred of the English were the two major collective passions of the Irish for most of the twentieth century. A decade of unprecedented prosperity – the 1990s – as well as a new and coherent sense of Irish identity have dissolved that fervent nationalism. In the process – and this is the remarkable bit – the English, the cause of several hundred years of unremitting misery in Ireland, have been forgiven.

These thoughts are only dawning on me right now, and I have already had a few pints to obstruct my stream of consciousness. I do need to think this through because it is not a matter that can be taken lightly. As I have previously said, hating the English – which entails a perverted sense of strength derived from dwelling on disaster – has been one of the defining features of the modern Celtic identity. Take it away, and . . . well, I am just not sure what that leaves behind.

I am trying to think of an articulate response to Gerry's question when a young man pushes past our table on his way to the gents. His T-shirt says: 'Have fun or fuck off – The Fenians'.

'There's your modern Irish political statement, Gerry,' I say, pointing to the T-shirt. 'No Englishman gets heaved off the Cliffs of Moher any more. They just make you buy a lot of postcards. You're one crucial decade out of date.'

The pub, the Arch Bar, is the home venue for the Listowel Gaelic singing club and today it is packed with singers and enthusiasts from every corner of Ireland who are gathered in the town of Listowel, deep in County Kerry, for Ireland's most important annual music and culture event, the Fleadh Cheoil na hÉireann.

Traditional unaccompanied singing, or 'Sean nós' as it is known, is the most loved and the most reviled, the least often heard and the worst understood part of traditional Irish music. Sean nós is a hazy, blanket label used to describe singing traditions in both Irish Gaelic and English that are obviously outside the standard European musical aesthetic. I am no expert, but characteristics of Sean nós include a bare, unaccompanied voice, the absence of vibrato, the use of vocal ornamentation, occasional nasalisation and the use of glottal stops or dramatic pauses. It is a distinct and obviously un-operatic way of singing that I happen to like, but in the wrong hands, or rather in the wrong larynx, Sean nós will set dogs howling at the moon whilst little children run around screaming with their hands clamped over their ears, begging forgiveness for past misdemeanours.

The Sean nós tradition is most readily associated with the west of Ireland, and in particular Connemara, which is where I first heard it and where, as a gentleman I met in a pub on Inishboffin once told me, 'a let of people air deaf un so content to be listenin a tha singin erl noight long.' Just as the ancient Celtic bards composed songs and poems about contemporary episodes, so in the eighteenth century Gaelic songs were written about almost every national event. Ballad sheets were printed recording news, rebellions and hangings and in this way political news was disseminated across Ireland.

As little as thirty years ago, a gathering of singers like this from all over Ireland would have been a place to exchange news and opinions, a political meeting as much as a cultural one. And as Gerry intuited, an Englishman showing his face back then probably would have ended up kneeless, face down and flailing around in the white water beneath the Cliffs of Moher.

The session in the Arch Bar today is informal. There are many singers in the pub and they take it in turn. There is a sort of compère who busies himself about the pub, shushing and tutting and cajoling us into respectful silence, identifying and introducing the singers and generally giving the session some sort of order and occasion. Most of the singers are men, though there are a couple of women with beautiful voices who have their turn. They come from Cork, Wexford, all over, even from Derry in Northern Ireland. The men are my age and up, up to Paddy Mulholland, an eighty-nine-year old from County Kildare who seems to be well known.

The singers never stand up to fill their lungs or raise their heads heavenwards. They actually do the opposite. They stay seated, dip their gaze and tuck their chins into their chests. They sing not in an explosive operatic way, but in a curious sullen fashion, using the nasal tone that is distinctive to Gaelic singing. I am not sure if this is a reflection of the subject matter, for so many of the songs are woefully sad. They are mournful songs of emigration, of loss and misery, of lovers wrenched apart and families dying of starvation, of the hardship and poverty that Ireland knew too well. There are also witty songs about the dreaded drink, angry wives and the Catholic Church, but it is the former which have weight and which resonate within the walls of the pub and in my head long after they are completed. Some songs are in English but most are in Gaelic. Gerry and I keep up with the titles of the songs and their subject matter with the help of Dermot, who is sitting across the table from us.

I may be a hopeless romantic, but I find the songs very moving. I wonder if there is any other form of singing that inspires such immediate and remarkable access to the subconscious. The chapel at King's College, Cambridge may have little to do with the Arch Bar, but I feel you have to go that far to find unaccompanied singing that is so able to transcend thought.

Gerry and I are both carried away. We sit in our reverie for song after song. I am completely unaware that the middle-aged man (that is a guess – I find it difficult to tell a forty-year-old from a septuagenarian in rural Ireland) sitting next to me on a stool has fallen asleep and slumped over the table on his folded arms. It is only 7 p.m., but then again the Fleadh Cheoil is a time when all established drinking customs are abandoned in the communal glee of tens of thousands of cavorting Irish people.

A local man with a perfectly rounded stomach caught in a brown cardigan with a face like a bruised peach is introduced. He has another song about the 'American wake' – saying goodbye to children and darlings as they boarded the ships for America. His shoulders heave as he starts to sing. The compère whistles about, ducking between tables, holding out his hand for quiet. The last quips are made and the laughter falls like rain on a warm road, into silence. I am, again, quickly transported into a melancholy that I can hardly call my own. Two verses, three verses . . . I am not sure how much of the song is sung but the plaintive notes are still filling the hushed bar when the slumbering man beside me erupts. His head springs from the table as if he has just taken a punch on the chin and he glares at me with red-rimmed eyes and shouts, 'WHERE'S MY DOG?'

I am still searching for something suitable to say when his head falls as quickly as it rose. His twitching hand shoves a pint glass off the table. It smashes on the floor, but he is snoring again, like a colonel beside the hearth.

'That was close,' Gerry says. 'Reckon he smelt hun Englishman.'

'Hus yer friend?' someone shouts and another man says, 'No matter the glass. Twas empty anyweh,' before the compère casts a glare at our corner.

Flying at the Fleadh

It has been in my mind to chat the compère up and suggest I read a poem but I am just not sure if this is my place. There is a sanctity attached to *Sean nós* that suggests it should not be adulterated, even with poetry. And poetry is, I have to remind myself, the reason I am here. I have been in Listowel for half a day and I haven't left the Arch Bar yet. It is time I took a walk.

Gerry comes with me. It is alarming to find that it is still light outside. The bar was so dark and full of smoke that it felt like the early hours of the morning.

'Gotta switch on ta festival clock,' Gerry says.

'What's that?'

'Tha's when ya stick ya watch in yer pocket so ya never feel its time a leave.' Gerry still has the faint trace of a bog Irish accent. He emigrated to Boston when he was eight, twenty-five years ago.

'Why are you over now?' I ask.

'Come to see family. For the Fleadh . . . culture, roots, ya know. It's the first time ah bin over fur eight years.' We have arrived at the junction of the two main streets in Listowel where our ways are parting. There are hundreds of people trying to thread their way through the maelstrom of bodies. The festival is really coming alive.

'And what is different this time?' I probe. Gerry scans the shop windows and pub hoardings in front of us.

'The history,' he says thoughtfully. 'The hellish history of Arland, thas wha held the country together. It was so darn easy to identify wif. It's going, bein fawgatten. Am gonna miss that.'

To get away from the centre of town means going against the crowds which are pouring in. It takes the skill and determination of a Maori prop forward making for the try line. Each time I find the path of least resistance, I am checked by the contraflow of people exiting a bar or by a band who have found space on the pavement or by a woman in a Gaelic football shirt who briefly needs a dancing partner just to stay on her feet.

I had no idea there would be this many people here, just as I had no idea I was going to be one of them. After the bonanza of events around the time of Lughnasa, I was planning to have a couple of weeks off. I was going to stay at home in London and catch up with myself, catch up with Rob Penn. I was going to open some post, take breakfast in bed to my wife, paint the spare room, fix my bicycle, take Lucas to the park (we need to spend some time together – he has got over the fact that my name is not Scotland, but he has chosen to call me Ken Dodd instead and I really have no idea why), chase some invoices, go on a diet and talk to my GP about the precise symptoms of liver cirrhosis. Then, with every-thing back on an even keel, I was going to warm Ned Clague up again – write a new poem, varnish my blackthorn stick and press my kilt – in time for the autumn equinox and the final festival thrash (the Scottish Mod and the Lowender Peran in Cornwall) that leads up to Samhain.

But it didn't work out. I got frustrated. I got on everyone's nerves, including my own. I thought of the poor, bent men who did long-range reconnaissance operations in remote jungles for months on end during the Vietnam War. When they were sent back home on leave to the white picket fences of suburban Toledo and warm apple pie they realised, with horror, that they would rather have been in the jungle. Okay, so drinking myself senseless with the Celts is hardly comparable to fire-fights with gooks, but when my wife went out for lunch one day leaving a pan of 'skinny soup' and an introduction leaflet from Alcoholics Anonymous on the kitchen table, I knew I had to get back in the field. PJ, who I got trousered with in the Merry Monk in Mayo, mentioned the Fleadh to me. 'Tis nat ar pan-Ciltic affair bet tis the best place fur mew-sic in de hool world,' he said, which was a good enough rec-ommendation for me.

I am fighting my way out of town to get to the Fleadh office where, I have been told, there is a lady who knows all about the history of the Fleadh.

'Are you Coleen?' I ask a rather prim middle-aged lady when I finally get there.

'I am nat,' the lady says in a very clipped tone that suggests I just asked if she was the Listowel hooker.

'Um . . . is she here?'

'Nat exactly.'

'Not exactly?'

'Whoi?'

'I would like to talk to her.'

'Ar, then, she is nat.'

'Eh? And if I wanted to present her with this week's lottery prize, would she be here?'

'She wud nat, nor.'

'So she is not here at all?'

'Nat at erl.'

'But you said "not exactly" before and now you're saying "not at all".'

'Oi foind yer questions confusing, young man.'

'She was here before?' I am searching for clues now.

'Perheps. She will be here lah-ter, at eight a'clock.'

'Eight o'clock this evening?'

'Naw.'

'Eight o'clock tomorrow morning?'

'Naw. Eight a'clock Sunday morning.'

'And are you sure about that?'

'Nooh.'

'Thank you for being so helpful.'

'Aw, tisa pleasure. Enjoy the Fleadh.'

While I am trying to work out what I have learnt from this conversation, I stumble across an exhibition of press cuttings and photos from Fleadhs of yesteryear, which actually tells me all that I want to know. The festival started in the 1950s. The press cuttings suggest it was still a small show by the early 1970s – a few old fiddlers, a storyteller and singing sheepdog – attended by what must then have seemed like the ardent devotees of a dying musical culture. Much has changed in Ireland since then, and the Fleadh Cheoil is now a very different beast – it is a massive week-long celebration of Irish traditional music with a programme that runs to sixty pages. I head off back to the town centre to have a taste of it.

The Fleadh, like the Eisteddfod in Wales, travels round Ireland but it has been to Listowel a record fourteen times. If you did not know better, you might assume this was because the small, well-defined town on the banks of the River Feale in the green Kerry hinterland offers no fewer than sixty pubs in which to sample the delights of Irish hospitality. If you did know better, then you would be aware that the town has gained something of a reputation as a literary and cultural capital in recent times. Culture is very fluid in Ireland. It does not find a home, put down deep roots and settle in for eternity. Rather, it likes to drift around the countryside, just as the Irish musicians and poets and writers do. Yet it did not arrive in Listowel by chance. John B. Keane, a famous Irish playwright, was also a publican in the town. His popular quote: 'Give it your best, your almighty best' might be the motto for the Fleadh Cheoil and I decide to give the occasion just that, starting at the bar John B. used to tend.

The Fleadh Cheoil is a music festival packed full of competitive events. There are competitions for different age groups (from twelve to fifteen years up to eighteen plus) in every imaginable Irish instrument: harp, fiddle, flute, melodeon, concertina, mandolin, banjo, mouth organ, slow airs whistle, button accordion and bodhran. There are also competitions for pipe bands, ceili bands and step dancing groups, as well as something called 'lilting', whatever the hell that is. The competitors are at it in venues all over the town, all day. At night they spill into the pubs and on to the streets to bring their music to the masses.

I have never seen so many musicians before in my life. The town is, as the Irish say, 'black' with them. There is a music session inside every pub as well as a session outside every pub and a smattering of sessions on the pavements between the pubs. There is a rare urgency about the festival that I have not witnessed at any of the other events I have been to this summer. It is like Hogmanay in Edinburgh, or Mardi Gras in Sydney. The profusion of energy being spilt on to the streets of Listowel might make sense if there was a nationwide ban both on festivals and the consumption of alcohol that started at midnight tonight, but of course there is not.

I find myself back in the main square in front of the 'Guinness gig-rig' wondering where this vibrancy comes from when I get a big slap on the back. It is Donald, the Welshman from Canada who I met in the Quay Street pub on the last night of the Lorient festival. He looks madder than ever, beard and hair all in one tangled mess, encircling his smiling face.

'How the hell are you? Have a pint?' He has to shout over the music. He is carrying two and he thrusts one at me. 'Great to see ya.' He is, as my dad would say, 'moving nicely'. We exchange stories about our respective strategic retreats from Lorient, then he takes me over to meet his crew. It is a great chance meeting – there are tens of thousands of people here – but that is the kilt. I am the only person in Listowel wearing one. Donald is over with a band of musicians from Wales. His father is here too.

'Pop, Pop, look. It's the Manx poet from Lorient.'

'Huh? The Manx pillock from L'Oréal? What are you talking about, son?'

'No, Pop. It's Ned, the Manx poet from Lorient.'

'Hey, hey, hey,' Ronald says. 'How about that? How are ya? Now, it was an Irish pub, the Quay Street pub, wasn't it? You had a good poem, boy. Hell, I remember. With a crackin last line. I like a poem that goes boom at the end. What was that last line now?'

'Treat her right now and take off that fuckin dress!' I exclaim.

He roars with laughter, and sounds like an old bear.

'What d'you think of all this?' I ask, looking over my shoulder across the horde that fills the square.

'Marvellous. I think it's marvellous. The Irish really know how to do it, don't they? It all slightly takes my breath away. I'm an old fella, see, but it's so bold. The Irish culture is so bold. Ah reckon these Irish know who they are now . . .' Ronald, like Donald, is a huge man – well over six feet. He waves a gorilla-length arm over my head. 'And this is it.'

I need to eat something, so I make a plan, inasmuch as you can plan anything at the Fleadh, to meet Donald back here later and I head for the gigantic burger bus. Ireland has changed out of all recognition in the last ten years. Emboldened by a decade of near miraculous growth (probably the greatest era of economic prosperity in the entire history of the country), the 'Celtic tiger' has gained a true and coherent sense of its own identity. European Union cash has poured in over that time and the Irish have spent it swiftly, and then asked for more. What was a faltering and impoverished island on the edge of everything for most of the twentieth century managed to Europeanise itself while the rest of Britain was not watching. There were occasional features in the British press about stag nights in Dublin's Templebar district, the burgeoning film industry and property prices in West Cork, but no one was really watching the big picture. Ireland used its relationship with Europe to prise itself away from Britain. At around the same time and without much fuss, it suddenly became cool to be Irish (coincidentally, just as it became dire to be English). And these people, the thousands that have come here to celebrate the phoenix that is Irish culture, know it. Their time has come. Being Irish rocks.

We all know this. Even the English have acknowledged it. The English have responded to being forgiven by the Irish by falling in love with absolutely everything and anything Irish. It is a mad, mad, mad world we live in. The English support for the Irish football team in the World Cup this summer is testament to it (compare this to the way the Scottish team are vilified south of the border), even though that 'secondary support' is not reciprocated. Adorning the backs of young Irish lads you will find Australian and South African rugby shirts and a profusion of Italian and Brazilian soccer shirts, but throughout Ireland, and indeed, the entire length of the Celtic Fringe, you will never, ever see anyone wearing an English football shirt.

But I am interested in something else that has been on my mind since I left the Arch Bar. I want to know how the resurgence of the Irish identity has affected how Celtic the Irish feel. With my jumbo sausage and chips, I head back up William Street towards the Arch Bar again. I have been told that the music session going on there is as good as it gets. The courtyard behind the pub is packed with young revellers. I get my pint from the bar and head for the golden glow and the sound of fiddles that comes from the shed. It is a tremendous rural music scene inside, so perfect it could be a set from a Brian Friel play: whitewashed brick walls, concrete floor, corrugated tin roof, wooden benches and, in the middle of the fifty-foot-square room, one table with a hundred empty pint glasses. Crowded around the table, under one bare light bulb and a blanket of smoke, are a dozen musicians, playing whistles, fiddles, accordions and banjos, riding along on the back of a furious reel that no one can stop. As I try and ease my way through the audience, a strange man grabs my arm and spits into my ear, 'Best feckin banjo oi evar here-d.'

I find a corner of bench and I perch next to a girl with long, curly hair and arms as white as haddock fillets who chinks her pint against mine. When the reel does finally finish, she looks at me and says, 'Dat reel wuz saw good, oid sear it is run offa darn der street ta foind anuther bend ta play it. Well, look at you hear, all in yer teirtan and efter havin yer dinner. Where us it yer from?'

'The Isle of Man.'

'The Haila Man is it? Now thel noh be wearin kilts in the Haila Man. Tis the Scots as wear the kilt.'

'The Manx too, actually, and the Cornish and the Welsh. There is even an Irish kilt. I think it is worn by pipe bands in one of the Irish regiments.'

'Un oirish kilt? Ballox. There is nat.'

'Well, I don't want to argue about it, but I have seen it.'

'Ballox to tha, ballox to you wearin a kilt un erl.'

To describe this girl as feisty is an understatement to rank alongside saying Red Rum was a decent nag. She is also lashed and spitting and I have just walked into the line of fire. On we go . . . bollocks to this and bollocks to that and bollocks to this again. I tell her a bit about my journey. I try to suggest that the kilt has become something of a sartorial symbol for the Celts, a sort of badge of otherness. She disagrees emphatically which brings us neatly, if completely unintentionally, to a feeling that I have been discreetly rummaging around for all evening.

'Ballox ta the Celts!' she shouts in my face.

There, in four words, is the sentiment that I have suspected exists since I first arrived in Ireland on this journey. It was not obvious at the glorious gathering I was part of on top of Mount Brandon, nor in the cordiality I encountered in the Merry Monk in Mayo. But with hindsight, I feel that it is something that has surreptitiously trailed me back and forth across the Emerald Isle. It has managed to keep a pace ahead of me in the dissembling, or linger behind me like a shadow in the slightly embarrassed expressions of Celtic solidarity. This is the first time I have come fully face to face with it.

'Ballox ta the Celts,' she shouts again, shaking her locks off her shoulders and sticking her face up against mine.

To a great extent, I am a victim of my own hopes and desires. I have allowed myself to be indulged by the sweet brotherhood of Celticness in the last four months. I have been carried away by the similarities between the people of these Atlantic realms and consumed by the notion that the unity of these different nationalities delivers them strength. To hear, then, these words from the flush lips of a pissed-up Irish pig-scarer is a total affront.

'Air you naht hearin me? Oi said ballox ta the Celts.'

I want to whip a fist up into her chin and send her flying off the bench, but I know she will be on my back scratching at my eyes like an epileptic cat.

'When you say "ballox ta the Celts" do you mean bollocks to the whole notion of there being a distinctive group of people who inhabit the western Atlantic seaboard of Britain, who share language and culture and traditions too numerable to mention?'

'Yes, oi fuckin do. Tis arl a-made up and yeur too tick ta now it. Dez em Scots, dez da Welsh, un oim Oirish. Das ut.'

'Well, it was all made up by the Irish, you might like to know, and when it suited your purposes, when you needed the wider notion and community of Celts to strengthen and define your nationalist cause, then your people believed in it. You clung to the idea of Celticism. And now you're rich and independent and the rest of the Celts can go screw themselves. Is that it? Is that what you are saying?'

'Gaw an wit yer. Feck awf hawm.'

'I will, but before I go I encourage you to consider washing your mouth out with a dog turd. It will improve your breath, you stupid little bog-trotter.'

As I step out of the shed, the musicians are beginning a new tune which drowns the trail of invective that is streaming after me. I am so angry. I really need to stop at the bar for five minutes, have a drink and calm down, but I cannot chance meeting her again. Nor do I want to talk to another Irish person right now, which means I have to keep moving. I shoulder my way through the bar on to the street and I head away from the crowds. I need space.

It only takes me ten minutes to calm down. I soon see the funny side of it. Bloody Irish woman. I suppose I should be grateful she was not a bloke. If she had been, I would already be queuing up on plastic seats with all the other festival casualties at the Listowel cottage hospital, waiting for a grizzly nurse to patch up my face with butterfly stitches.

As I walk back into town, I can feel the meltdown happening. It is midnight and the street is awash with bottles and stumbling people. I see a few fights and I stop to help a couple who appear to be looking for a contact lens.

'Can I help?' I offer.

A middle-aged man looks up. He has three or four goes at fixing his eyes on me, giving his head a good shake between each attempt, then he addresses my knees. 'We hev mohmentarily lest air relationship witt der perpendicular.'

I am back near the square, crouched in a doorway, writing something in my notebook when a voice beside me says, 'Ar ya wroightin da poo-hms dar dat will change de wurld?'

'No,' I say without looking up, 'just writing notes about what an artificial people the Irish are.'

The man standing before me makes a small 'o' with his mouth. 'Is it daht yav bin oarfended now? Well, tis an earful noight, wot wit dis foine street peartee en all not to be hanjoying yerself.' He stands to attention and draws his shoulders back. He has two pints in his fingertips and he holds these out in front of him. 'Un beherf a de people a de moast distressed republic a hairland, will ya accept a point a happeasement?' He thrusts one of the Guinnesses at me and it sloshes over on to the pavement.

'I will.' I take the pint.

'Ta peace un ta points,' he exclaims, spilling some of his own pint on his head as he hoists it like the FA Cup.

'To peace and to pints and to girls who don't wear pants,' I toast as we clunk glasses.

'Yar a gas, lad. Oim Stevie.'

It is one o'clock but the streets are still rammed and it takes us ten minutes of crowd-frotting to go a hundred yards, to find Stevie's friends.

Fergus, Daniel, Karen and Stevie are all in their early twenties. They are from Cork and they drove up to Listowel on a whim today. It is not far – Kerry and Cork border each other – but they spent several hours in the car and I feel that anyone making even the shortest road journey in Ireland deserves a medal for bravery.

'Tis Ned,' Stevie says, introducing me. 'A gas man from da Oisla Man un a poo-hit too. He has bin foightin with air people tonoight, saw mek im welcome un give im sum a dat potcheen now.'

Potcheen is illegal, home-distilled whisky. It can be fiery stuff. Fergus pulls the bottle of white spirit out of the poacher's pocket in his parka.

'Naw, d'ya tink he can handle ut?' Stevie asks melodramatically.

'Naw, but he looks loike a fella who will doi troyin,' Karen adds. I have drunk enough this evening. I don't suppose this can do any more damage. I have a big swig. It is aggressive liquor. My throat burns and my stomach endures minor paroxysms. Drinking vinegar can be no worse.

'Naw den,' Stevie exclaims, 'weel hev a poo-hm, eh, Ned?'

We are standing on a raised triangle of pavement in the middle of the road at the point where the two main streets, William Street and Church Street, meet. It is a small island in the middle of the river of people who are flowing about us.

Stevie springs up on top of the traffic bollard and yells over the heads of the milling crowd, 'Cem awn naw . . . cem awn wit yah.' A couple of people stop, looking up at Stevie. Someone whistles. Stevie thrusts an arm down at me and shouts, 'Oi give yer Ned Clague.'

'*Jee banner mee, ghoinney*,' I cry out slowly, leaning back and looking up into the night sky. Then a pause, and I rock forward, levelling my blackthorn stick at Fergus. My kilt is swishing. I am off. A few more people stop on the road beside us. By wheeling towards them and gesticulating, I try to include them before they drift off. It is some time since I have recited this poem and, full of drink, I get completely lost on three occasions. I crash into the end of a line to realise that I have forgotten the next one. It is hardly the mark of a professional but I use the gaps to scan the dozen people who are now listening, trying desperately to make these hiatuses look like dramatic pauses. Then, like the first strike of lightning in a summer storm, the next line flashes into my head. In this staccato manner, I dash and stagger my way through the poem. When I finish, Stevie and the others howl and applaud. Someone blows a flourish on a tin whistle. 'More!' Fergus demands, but two whistles are going now and people have begun to clap. Then a man with a fiddle stops beside me. He tucks it under his chin and raises his bow. Within minutes, there are eight musicians playing and a young man has managed to clear a small patch of tarmac, to perform a knee-dislocating step dance.

'Tis er woild scene,' Karen says, coming to stand next to me. 'Der stone mad fur da music tanoight. Tis a really professional delivery ya hav, Ned. I was tinkin da poo-hm wuz finished at toimes der, but naw, there wuz mere ta kum. Deh great, da pauses. Dramatic, loike.'

'Actually, I kept forgetting the lines of the poem.'

'Aw, well,' she says, laughing. 'It turned out aroight than.'

It is 3 a.m. when the pubs start closing. We are still on our little island, drawing the entertainment to us. The number of musicians wax and wane whilst we clap and 'tup' out the rhythm on the bollard and with our feet. Stevie, Fergus, Daniel and Karen are great fun and with a mixture of charm and enthusiasm they keep the night swinging along.

We manage to trick and talk our way past tired bouncers into the pubs a couple of times, to score pint bottles of Bulmers cider. The clock in the main square is striking five when we roll back down the hill to the river, scuffing our heels on the detritus that blankets the streets. I completely forgot about going back to meet Donald again, but I know that he will be having a roaring time somewhere. There are a couple of bonfires burning in the campsite, surrounded by the last delirious revellers, who are propping up the dawn.

'Fancy a joint, there?' Fergus says.

'No way. I'm Ned and I'm going to bed.'

'Awee wit ya, then. Y'are a gas, man. Now, didya give it yer best, lad?' he asks, clutching my shoulders. I am on my last gasp.

'I did,' I blurt. 'I gave it my almighty best.'

'Guinness is good for you.' Yeah, right. When I first wake up I wonder why I am sleeping in a chicken broiler. I cannot feel my toes – a condition that the Irish call 'Jake leg', got from drinking too much contaminated alcohol. My eyes ache to witness the nightmare day. I have the skin complexion of someone who lives beside the Aral Sea and the adipose ankles of a great-great aunt. My first coughing convulsion is alarming. My head thumps metronomically with the sound of bricks being dropped from a great height into a plastic dustbin. I feel as if my teeth, hair and nails are all about to leave my body, probably with the next exiting of wind.

I am a mess. Is this alcohol poisoning? Certainly, you would be unlucky to feel like this after a few pints of carrot juice. I think my body is growing intolerant of the abuse and I am growing intolerant of my body. I would like a Keith Richards makeover. Now that is a body. My diet of Guinness, Drum tobacco and pretty much anything wrapped in pastry is taking a heavy toll. I have my last three ibuprofen and a litre of apple juice before going back to sleep.

It is 3 p.m. when I get up. I have to dunk my head in the river to get a clear start to the day. I still feel dreadful, but recalling last night, I am weighed upon by something other than a hangover. Too precipitous an intimacy – particularly when encouraged by drink – so often leaves in its wake a dirty awkwardness. Well, it does for me anyway. I wonder if this is the vestige of the emotionally bound-up Englishman in me. Added to this, I cannot remember how much I told Stevie and the others about my journey. I walk up towards the town hoping not to run across them.

But this is Ireland, where your hang-ups are seldom reflected back at you. I am barely on my way before I bump straight into

them all and they are delighted to see me. They are on their way
back to Cork but they have time for a joint. 'It'll tek the edge affa
yer hengover,' Fergus assures me.

'Naw yell nat be foightin wit naw Oirish girls now if we leave
yer alone, Ned?' Stevie asks, squeezing my arm.

'No, no . . . no. Oh dear, did I bore you with stories about my
trivial arguments last night?'

'Ya did. But then, maybe ya hav a point in yer foightin. Wull ya
pass tha joint naw?'

We are sitting on the grassy bank beside the river. Stevie watches
the water for a minute and carries on: 'Airland's on a roll en all –
prosperity, da film industry, de football team, Seamus Heaney getting da Norbel Prize, whaz happenin here en all' – he waves a hand
back towards the centre of the town – 'traditional Oirish music
hes never been saw parpular, nat internationally, nat even here.'

My head is still ringing with the sound of a fiddle and the tump
of a bodhran. I am not quite ready to be reminded about music.

'De music' – Stevie's tone is increasing in emphasis – 'is a rural
tradition un if all de boys what wraught dem tunes dey're playin,
what wraught dem about de hearth, if dey knew deir music was
heird boi millions erl awver da world, well dey'd fall in de fuckin
foire.'

'D'ya hev a point here, Stevie lad?' Daniel interjects.

'Shut it. Soh, tis loike dis. Airland is an a crest huv a wave. We're
roight dere, in de heart a modern Europe. De h-economic boom
hez brought a load a new problems . . .'

'Such as?' I ask.

'Such as, well, racism.' I am not the first observer to note that
Ireland – and this goes for the whole of the Celtic Fringe – is about
as ethnically diverse as Enoch Powell's memorial service. The
decade of prosperity has made Ireland attractive to immigrants
from the undeveloped world and I know from the newspapers the
Irish people are struggling to accept the new arrivals. Racism is
rearing its hideous head.

'Un there's more prablems,' Stevie goes on, 'un we need erl air attention on da future to face em. But yer roit, Ned. De Oirish hev turned der becks un bein Celtic. See, un oidentity stuck in . . . em oi jabberin an now?'

'No, you're doing fine,' I say, 'just pass the joint.'

'Oh, yes . . . where wuz oi?'

'Stuck on oidentity,' Fergus says.

'Good man! An oidentity stuck in a very distant perssed is jes nat impairtant nar appropriate tah modern Airland. Near will it be tah Scotland un Wales un da rest when deh hev de pawlitical empowerment un da prosperity too. D'ya get it?'

'Something about Seamus Heaney throwing himself in the fire,' I say, flopping back in the grass.

'Un whoi do oi bather? Whoi do I . . .'

'Kidding, Stevie, I'm kidding. I get it. But I will have to think about it and now may not be the time. I will send you a postcard with my answer.'

They all jump in their old banger and head off hooting. I walk up to town, tripping on bottles and stumbling over my thoughts. According to Stevie, Celticism in the ethnic sense is like a prop or an aide, a political and cultural crutch that helps crippled national identities find their feet and learn to walk alone. When they can walk, it is cast aside. It is an interesting idea, but I am not sure about it. The Isle of Man has its own government (it is a crown dependency and not completely autonomous) and it is rich, yet it shows few signs of abandoning its Celticness. In fact, to a small degree the opposite is happening. But if Stevie is right, and if Ireland is ahead in a cycle that all the Celtic countries will ultimately follow, then in fifty years' time there may be no modern Celts and the ancient Celts will be relegated to the role of honoured ancestors.

I know very well from the time I spent in Ireland in July that not all the Irish are so quick to assert themselves as Irish only and not Celtic, and in terms of the global perception of what is Celtic, it does not really matter anyway. Whatever the Irish think, they will continue to define the word, most especially through their music, and I head off now to get a final taste of it before I leave the Fleadh.

Just because it is Sunday, it does not mean there is any respite. In the Listowel Arms Hotel, every corner and chair is jammed with musicians giving it some. On the fire escape at the back of the hotel, overlooking the river and the racecourse, there are twenty or so musicians playing in the sunshine. They are aged from sixteen to sixty-five, male and female, and playing all the usual suspects. There is even one teenager playing the bones, the Irish answer to castanets. I realise that I am leaning against the railings next to Paddy Moriarty, who runs the post office in Cloghane, and who I walked up Mount Brandon with. He does not recognise me at first, but when I step back and he sees the kilt, he is delighted. He has the most mellifluous brogue I have heard and he chats happily as we walk over to meet his wife.

'Hear uss a famous poo-ht frum dur Aisla Man. Did oi net tell you about the yung man up Mount Brandon.' He is very complimentary about my poem, though I am sure he cannot remember it. He seems to be in a state of permanent grace, moving and speaking very slowly. We talk about the importance of the Fleadh. He asks me if I will be back in Cloghane for the Feile Lughnasa next year. I try to evade the question, but Paddy presses and cajoles me for a promise that I will return with a new poem. It is unlikely, since the short life and fast times of Ned Clague will be over in two months.

'End will you be stayin un Listowel fur tonight, the lerst noight of the Fleadh?' Paddy asks.

'No, I . . . I think I need to head off somewhere quieter.'

'Oid tink again. Der will be woild scenes a carousal.'

'Wild scenes of carousal?'

'Noh less.' He winks at me.

'Well, in that case . . . Can I buy you a drink?'

13

Encore Bretagne

For all the joys of being on the Celtic Fringe, travelling to and from it is enough to test the equanimity of a Buddhist priest. Motorway pile-ups, delayed trains and bolshy conductors, cancelled flights and budget airline hostesses with the courtesy of a Gestapo commandant suffering from piles. I have had it all, and I have re-mortgaged the house to pay for it. The transport network in the British Isles (especially in and around London, for which I blame the Romans) is on its knees, but we all know this. It takes a ferry journey across the English Channel to St Malo to revive my enthusiasm for travel, and it will surprise no one to learn that it is on a boat operated by a French company.

The early Christian saints most probably made this sea crossing in coracles – small wicker-framed craft covered in the skin of a goat. I feel substantially safer on this colossal ferry, which has enough room to land Tomahawks on the deck. My good favour with Brittany Ferries began when I rang at the eleventh hour to change the date and time of my sailing. I was wondering which credit card to burden with the financial penalty when I was told that this meant there was a refund. When I boarded my humour only improved. There is a flashy restaurant and I was keen to squander my refund and acquire some heavy cholesterol. The maître d' took my table reservation, explained that it would be announced over the Tannoy and told me the best place to catch the sunset armed with a cocktail. This is really travelling.

It is a far cry from the ferries I used to take between the Isle of Man and Liverpool as a kid. They were operated by a company called the Isle of Man Steam Packet, nicknamed the 'Isle of Man steaming packet'. The boats themselves were fine but the refreshment highlights extended to a cup of Bovril with salt and cheese sandwiches that people used to pocket and sand floors with when they got home. I am sure the saints' coracles were better victualled. Anyway, I do as the maître d' says and sit on the deck listening to the civilised sound of ice chinking on glass as we ease past the Isle of Wight.

After dinner I return to the bar, where there is a cabaret (the only cabaret on the Steam Packet was a couple of scousers having a scrap). The cover band, called Picasso, play Fleetwood Mac and Thin Lizzy hits mixed up with some r & b. When they take a break, the lead singer, a rough rock chick from Portsmouth, whispers into the mic, 'You're the tops. Don't go away.' It is great stuff. The band is followed by the illusionist, who I feel has timed his run this evening, and perhaps in life, all wrong. People have been in the bar for a good few hours by the time he comes on. The group of lads in front of me have been cruising pints of Stella solidly. When the illusionist thrusts the first sword into a case and through the plump midriff of his ever grinning assistant, to a crashing of drums, the heckles start – 'It's all done by mirrors,' 'Don't stab the stripper,' 'Come back, Paul Daniels, all is forgiven' – and it goes on in this vein long into the night.

I chat with the barman. Arnaud is a nineteen-year-old from the north coast of Brittany. He cannot place the Isle of Man on a map and when I ask him if he feels proud to be Breton over and above being French, he gives me a look that suggests he thinks I am one crucial ingredient short of a good cocktail.

'Do you speak Breton?' I persist in my questions.

'*Non, non,*' he says. 'Mah granmuvver was from the sou-west of Bretagne. She did speak Breton but she is dead. Iz few people oo speak it now.' This is only half true.

'Don't you wish you could speak it?' I ask.

He shrugs his shoulders and shows the palms of his hands. I

have read that there may be as many as half a million people who can speak Breton. However, perhaps only half this number actually do speak it and many of these are endogamous, which does not mean they sleep with their household pets. It means they only speak Breton with their milieu, or their family, friends and neighbours.

The taboo attached to speaking Breton still lingers. The story of how the language became a taboo is all too familiar and similar to what happened with the three Gaelic languages. The 'one and undivided' French Republic knew best: the French language and national unity would liberate individuals from community oppression and give them access to modernity. From the beginning of the nineteenth century until after the Second World War, Breton was suppressed. Signs in public places actually said: 'No spitting or speaking Breton'. School children who spoke it were punished and images of the backward Breton peasant speaking his defunct tongue were spread across France through literature, songs and comics. The comic book character Becassine – still well known today – is the best illustration of the devoted and honest but stupid and ridiculous shadow that the image of Brittany casts. English jokes about the Irish come to mind. It is hardly surprising many Breton speakers grew ashamed of speaking their language. The irony today is that Breton, having survived nearly two centuries of state suppression, continues to fade, as my shrugging barman suggests, because of indifference.

I probe Arnaud with more enquiries about the depth of his Celtic identity, only to be repulsed by the same shrug, again and again. Eventually Arnaud feels that cleaning glasses would be more stimulating than talking to me and he goes off to do just that.

I had something of a blitz of all things Breton at the festival in Lorient, but I was trying to consume information there at the same rate as I was consuming alcohol, which does not really work. So I have returned for a week of sightseeing and walking. There are no festivals going on and my plan is to roam around the region looking for Celtic clues. The first one I stumble across only an hour by road from St Malo is the legend of King Arthur.

Arthur even made it to Brittany, it seems. It is more likely that the legends and stories came over in the early medieval period (possibly with knights returning from taking part in the Norman Conquest) and took root, but the legend of Arthur is here all right. Actually, it is Merlin, Viviane and Lancelot who figure most prominently in the web of Breton Arthurian legend, though Ile d'Aval off the south coast of Brittany is a contender for Avalon (where Arthur sleeps until the time when the two Bretagnes – Britain and Brittany – need his services again).

The main legends centre on the Forêt de Paimpont or 'Merlin's Forest of Brocéliande' and it is here, in a bookshop in the sleepy town of Paimpont, that I start my second, slightly more organised and sober search for Brittany's Celtic soul.

'*Soupe?*' the old lady who runs the bookshop asks, plucking her specs from her nose. '*Comment soupe?*'

'*Non, pas soupe . . . um . . .* soul *. . . soule, ça veut dire comme . . .*'

'*Pas soupe! Bien sûr pas soupe. C'est une librairie, pas un restaurant, monsieur.*'

So how do you ask for books about the soul of Brittany in French? Asking for books about the soup of Brittany in Franglais was a bad start and it appears that I have completely unhinged this old lady. She is on her feet now, strutting like a chicken between the stacks of books and the bowing tables in her shop, muttering, '*Soupe? Soupe? Soupe?*'

'*Pas soupe, madame! Je veux dire quelque chose comme . . . l'essence.*'

'*L'essence?*'

'*Ah, oui, l'essence.*' I think I may have cracked it.

'*Monsieur, pour l'essence il faut aller au garage.*'

'Ah.'

She resumes her highly agitated and peculiar perambulations, mumbling now: '*Soupe? L'essence? Soupe? L'essence? Soupe . . .*'

'*Comme . . . le cœur de Bretagne . . .*'

'*Le cœur de Bretagne?*'

'*Oui.*'

'Ah.' She smiles. I sense that the threat of this lady having a stroke is receding. She takes a few more strides and stops. Her clenched hands are held rabbit-style beneath her chin and one of them springs out like the tongue of a lizard, to point to a poster above her on the wall. I follow the angle of her arm and there, between a portrait of James Joyce and a print of the Forest of Brocéliande, are my old friends Asterix and Obelix, with their tumescent noses and their joyful grins. Across the bottom of the poster is written: '*Occupé seulement, jamais vaincu!*' That could be the defiant motto of the whole of the Celtic Fringe. What a treat. I laugh out loud and she has a cackle too.

As a kid, I read Asterix books avidly. I still have a stack of them. Asterix and Obelix and all their wonderfully named friends were Celts. They lived, according to the map inside the cover of all the books, in a village on the north coast of Brittany, where they resisted the might of the Roman Empire. They were able to resist because the druid, Getafix, had a recipe for a magic potion that made them invincible. Thus, they were never conquered and they feared no one. The only thing they did fear was that the sky would one day fall on their heads. This phobia set them spinning like dervishes in paroxysms of terror. It was not a phobia that the authors of Asterix made up. It comes, as I mentioned at the beginning of the book, from the account by the historian Ptolemy Soter, who recorded the exchange between Alexander the Great and a Celtic envoy. Alexander asked what man the Celts feared, presumably expecting the reply: 'You, Big Al. You're the man. My people generally need to change their underpants if they so much as think about you.' But the envoy was made of sterner stuff. Setting the mark for over 2,000 years of Celtic defiance, he replied with the famous sentence about fearing no one and nothing, save for the sky coming tumbling down.

I can still hear the old lady chortling as I walk among the moss-covered oaks and the ancient beech trees in the Forest of Brocéliande. It occurs to me that there may be something in what she was getting at. For many Bretons, the notion of being Breton is relatively new, and I wonder if it actually coincides with the publication of the first Asterix books. The authors – the weirdly named Messrs Goscinny and Uderzo – probably have more to do with modern Breton identity than they might ever have imagined.

It is a beautiful forest. By guesswork and perseverance, I manage to find the Fontaine de Barenton where Merlin and Viviane are supposed to have exchanged love for knowledge. There is a double spring encircled by a small stone wall. One of the legends of the Fontaine is that local nobles have the power to make rain or even cause tempests by pouring water on a certain stone near the spring. Up until the mid-nineteenth century, processions from villages would come here in times of drought. As with Madron Well which I visited in Cornwall, all this derives from Celtic pagan well-worship. There is evidence that people still come here, probably for reverential purposes. There are burnt-out candles and fire-pits, and only a few yards away someone has made a sloping canopy of branches and bracken between two trees, which would make a great overnight bivouac. It is thought that the name Brocéliande derives from Bar'c Hélan, which means 'Empire of the Druids'. Certainly, on this afternoon with dappled sunlight playing kaleidoscopic tricks on the forest floor and single, disconnected breaths of wind whispering through the canopy, it takes little imagination to picture them here. I feel like I am placing my feet in the footmarks of the ancient Celts.

As at Dozmary Pool and Emain Macha, I sense a spirit alive in this place. Remembering again that the ancient Celts imbued stones with the power of the place they came from, I dig out a grey stone the size of a watch face from the bottom of the pool and put it in my pocket.

In the abundance of mystical vibes, in the pulses that tell you to abandon reason and greet the fairy that must surely be sitting on the footpath round the next corner, in the perception of all the things that the land must know, Brittany is strikingly like the other Celtic Fringe countries. I guess this is partly because the pagan and then Celtic Christian faiths have revered the earth – the springs, the woods and the rivers – in the same way. It is also because the human imprint on the earth has been similar.

I have heard people describe both the Western Isles and the west of Ireland as 'landscapes of memory'. This is a reference to the abundance of menhirs and dolmens and standing stones, the springs, the Iron Age hill forts, the fields of 'lazybeds', the ecclesiastical ruins and the squat antique cottages that provide tangible evidence of every stage of the human involvement with the land over the millennia.

The beach at Bréhec is a beauty – a mile of unbroken sand, 200 yards wide with the tide out. Waves are crashing just offshore, flicking iridescent flecks into the sky, and wiping the beach with white foam. The afternoon sun pours out of a clear blue sky, filling the riddles in the sand and bleaching the rocks. There is a swift and chilling wind, which has gathered a myriad of muscle-bound young people to play on it. There are windsurfers tearing up the sea beyond the surf. One moment their shoulder blades are clipping the water and the next they are ten feet up, like rockets shooting for the moon. Closer in, boarders are bursting through the surf, hauled up and down by big kites. It looks like a perilous enterprise and I watch them carefully, waiting for someone to fall and be dragged out to sea like a torpedo. On the strand, cruising passed me intermittently, is a barrel-chested bald man on a plank with wheels, a sort of skateboard on steroids. He too is attached to the wind, by a kite which whooshes across the sky looking like a huge piece of purple rigatoni. There are also kids learning to surf and a chorus of people flying conventional kites. Their movements mimic each other as they wrestle with the gusts, giving the appearance of an informal synchronised beach dancing team.

I have spent a glorious morning walking along the pink granite cliffs from Plouha. I was on my way to the famous port of Paimpol, formerly the heart of Brittany's cod fishing industry and a town awash with the tears of sea-widows, as the romantic image goes. But the beach at Bréhec is too much to pass up. It seems weeks since I have swum in the Atlantic, so I have a dip and I decide to blow the afternoon here.

The relentless roar of the surf means that I can hear no voices, no French accents. The sound of the sea, the dynamic of the sunlight on the water, the cars on the beach, the V-framed men in wetsuits, the frenetic kids, the fluorescent Frisbees ghosting on the air, the families gathered close in pockets, away from the wind in the lee of jagged rocks – it is a familiar and joyous scene and it prompts me to wander in my mind back to Barra, then to Cornwall and on to the end of the Dingle Peninsula: to all the beautiful places where I have swum in the Atlantic this summer and laughed in the face of impotence.

When the sun weakens, I walk along to the village. Next to the harbour where the boats are hauled up on sand, there is a small bar, the Café de la Plage. Again, it is familiar, if only from memories of Cornwall. There is a CD playing the sweet soul music of Otis Redding. The walls are covered with a black and white photography exhibition of the region, the Côte de Granite Rose. The furniture is a random collection. The barman, with a gold loop in his ear and a tattoo stretching down his arm, looks like an extra in *Mad Max*. The bar is cool, with a small 'c'. In a way, it is far too cool for a fishing village in a remote corner of Brittany. Not so long ago, it would have been a rough fisherman's bar. But the fishermen have gone and surf culture now throws up incongruities the length of the Celtic Fringe. Surf hangouts are beginning to look like part of the furniture, just as the surfers are them-selves.

'*Je prends un demi, s'il vous plaît,*' I say to the barman. He plucks a glass from behind him and hooks it under the tap.

'Where are you from?' he asks in perfect English.

'Is my French that bad?'

'*Non*, but I can tell.'

'The Isle of Man.'

'Mmmmmmm . . . you ev surf there?'

'Not really. It is in the middle of the Irish Sea, so shadowed by Ireland from Atlantic swells. Plenty of wind, though.'

'*Voilà!*'

After a day in the sunshine and a swim, the beer tastes sensa-tional. Not having to pay for it immediately – 'Pay me when yeu ahr finish,' the barman says – adds a little to the pleasure too. Outside the café is a trap for the evening sun. Customers come and go, stopping for a quick chat and a beer while they strip off their wetsuits on the road. When there is no one to serve, the barman – he is called Alex – comes and sits next to me in the pocket of golden light. He looks at my rucksack and I tell him where I have come from. Quickly, this spins out into an account of my Celtic journey. Alex has surfed in Ireland and Wales and he lived in Cornwall for a year, though he comes from a village near here. He is well informed about the Celts. I make a joke about how seem-ingly incompatible surf culture and rural Breton culture are and he looks at me with surprise.

'Ah daunt sink so. I sink zey are very alike. I sink zis is wha we can be ere, and in Cornewall and in more places you av been at. Suh bourgeoisie, zey cum here from the cittays to buy farms un cottages. Zey av ur different culture. Zis se people ere daunt like. But surfeurs is okay.' He nips back inside, lifting his sunglasses on to his forehead, to serve some drinks. When he returns, he carries on.

'Know what ah sink? I sink suh surfeur and suh Celtic peasant who work is land av many fing in common. Se weather. Suh fir-meur un suh fisherman, he is sensitive to weather. Un so is suh sur-feur . . . okay, so for im is noh a matter ef success eur failure, food eur hungeur as it was feur ze firmeur fifty year ago. But ask these people' – he waves at the beach below where men and women in wetsuits are dismantling their equipment – 'feur the direction uf wind, tide, phase of moon, en say will tell you, und' – he holds up a long forefinger like he is testing the direction of the wind him-self – 'say will give you good prediction. Den you av the individ-ual. I ev read zis so tell me uf I am right – the ancien Celt, he believe in suh triomph of suh individual un in suh tribe. Wif no unity of tribes, the Romans smash them up. Right?'

He is right. The paradox in promoting individuality whilst encouraging strong communities is one that the Celts have always been familiar with.

'Well, zees people ear, zey survive alone in ze surf, zey ate ze state. Zey daunt pay taxes. Zey all strong individuelles, but noh so ambitious. Zey av spiritual freedom. Yet, ze community we av is veh, veh strong. And zen you av what ze Breton peoples sink. If you respec Bretagne, ze people, ze culture, ze beach, den ze Breton people accept you. Respect is everysing . . . *pardon*.'

He darts inside again. It is an interesting idea and one that has not occurred to me before: that the surfers and their like are the natural inheritors of the Celtic Fringe, that they are the real modern Celts, not by blood, origin or language, but by deed and action and belief. Does living on the Fringe, and on the Atlantic, require certain human characteristics which the surfers have? I think he is right about the attitudinal individuality of surfers and their attachment to the 'surf tribe', to the exclusion of any wider or national identity. Community was and is crucial to all the Celts. But I am still not convinced. It is a dangerously alluring argument: bronzed, renegade surfers hiding out in their Atlantic redoubts sharing weather predictions, cheap wine and jokes about the tax assessor with wizened old fishermen and gnarly farmers. My instincts tell me that it may not be the perfect marriage of two heroic counter-cultures, one time-honoured and one modern, that Alex suggests. I tell him when he returns.

'Whey,' he says, throwing up his arms in a grand exclamatory gesture, 'ah daunt care what you sink . . . un, hey, seah is anuver Celtic fing us surfeurs share. We daunt care!' He smiles and slaps my shoulder. Then he walks into the road whistling loudly through his teeth to get the attention of someone down by the sea and the still booming surf.

The campsite – it is more like a field actually – just outside Paimpol is run by an extraordinary-looking old man. The index and middle fingers on his left hand are missing, he has a grey drooping moustache and great thistles of hair poking out of his nostrils. I take a stab that he was once a fisherman, not a bad punt for Paimpol, and I am right. He holds up his mutilated hand and laughs, setting those nose-thistles shimmering. I say I am from the Isle of Man and he seems to like that. I want to ask him what he thinks about the surfing community but I can scarcely understand anything he says, including the basics that my French usually covers. When I ask him directions to the village I am heading for this evening, I only get the half of it. So I am surprised when I set off on foot, to find him gunning his old charabanc down the road behind me.

He was offering me a lift, I now gather, which I am grateful for because the village of Pommerit le Vicomte is further than I thought. I am heading there for a *fest noz*, the Breton equivalent of a ceilidh (or a *nos lawen* as the Welsh call it). Many aspects of Breton culture have benefited from a huge resurgence of interest in the last thirty years. At the heart of this resurgence is the *fest noz*.

A *fest noz* (literally 'night party') has its origins in rural and traditional community get-togethers, just as the ceilidh does in Ireland and Scotland. A *fest noz* was basically a barn dance – an occasion for music and dance and making merry with the family and neighbours, though there was often some ritual significance. In the late 1950s, when the peasant culture of Brittany was eroding fast, folklorists and Breton cultural enthusiasts appropriated the name and the idea to re-popularise Breton dance and music. It has worked to an astonishing extent – creating a whole new Celtic-folk music scene along the way – and nowadays there are hundreds of *fest noz* all over Brittany all summer long. I did not have to look hard to find one. Though it does not please everyone, *festou-noz* have done much to shape the modern Breton identity.

I am not a *fest noz* virgin. The Breton band at Yn Chruinnaght festival in the Isle of Man back in July took centre stage one night and engaged us in the basics of a Breton hoedown. At Lorient, there was a traditional *fest noz* every night. I have to say – and I risk being pitchforked by the next Breton I meet so I do not express this opinion lightly – I am not a big fan. I guess it is a Breton thing. You know how it is: English people like being trussed up and spanked, the Scots think McEwan's Export is a classy beer, the Spanish like their women to grow compost under their armpits. We all have our national foibles. For the Bretons, it is a love of *fest noz*. Anyway, I decide to give it one more go.

On the way into the village, I notice that it is twinned with a place in Ireland where I have just been. Almost every Breton town and village I pass through seems to be twinned with somewhere in Ireland or Wales. The hall is a grandiose affair, no doubt built with EU cash. There are only about thirty people when I arrive at 9 p.m., but it quickly fills up. The list of bands taped to the stage indicates that we have nine to get through, the last band finishing up at 3 a.m.

I spend half an hour cruising the edge of the dance floor and popping to the bar. The first band is a traditional *bombarde* and *biniou* duet. The *bombarde* is a curious instrument. It looks like a small oboe and it has a penetrating, reedy sound which makes me think of snake charmers. It is a sound that would be a more appropriate soundtrack to a walk in the souks of Marrakech rather than an evening in Brittany. The *biniou* is a diminutive set of bagpipes, ventilated with the mouth.

The dancing is under way too. I met a Breton folklorist at Lorient who told me about a number of the dances. Many were once regional, like the step dances of Ireland and the Isle of Man, though that has changed with the fluidity of culture around the region in the last thirty years. One of the most popular is Le Plinn and this is what they are dancing now.

The dancers form a chain, connected by their little fingers, and in time to the music, and with a little show of steps, the chain circulates to the left, round and round the room. Compared with – and this is not easy to do – even the simplest Irish or Scottish traditional dances, Le Plinn is remarkably easy and, er, boring. There are a few other beginners and I watch them pick up the steps quickly. Even I, with my two toeless left feet, can do it, but, rather like Groucho Marx, who would never join a club that would have him as a member, I will participate in no dance that I can learn in the time it takes to drink a bottle of cider.

But looking aloof and isolated is a mistake at a *fest noz*, as I find out. A lady who must be a clean foot taller than me, dressed in egregious purple culottes and a rather racy 1960s neck scarf, is standing before me, pointing her pinkie in my general direction.

'*Voulez-vous danser, monsieur?*' she says in an 'I am a woman of experience, don't be shy with me, dear boy' kind of way.

'*Vous êtes gentille, mais je connais pas des dances, madame.*'

'*Moi non plus,*' she says, giggling and wiggling her pinkie again. There is nothing for it. I knot my little finger in hers and we join the chain. Perhaps the most striking aspect of the hopping and skipping step of Le Plinn is what it does to the female mammary glands. No sooner have I joined the dancing train than I am toe to toe, or rather nose to nipple, with a lady who has the ferret fight of all ferret fights going on underneath her blouse. This mammary mayhem takes my mind off my own feet for a moment and I tread on the toes of the lady in purple culottes twice, to the beat of the *bombarde*. And round we go. Clearly I am going to have to apply myself or I will be bounced out of here. But it is not easy. There are knockers of every imaginable size and shape passing before me, trying to free themselves of apparel. My dancing does not improve. When the tune finishes, the culottes lady gives me a thin smile and disappears.

I had planned to chat the organiser of the *fest noz* up and blag a moment to recite a poem. Now I am here, I cannot imagine anything more inappropriate. Remembering how the indomitable Gauls in Asterix books either fled screaming or attacked Cacophonix, the illustrious village bard, when he broke into song, I see sense and bury the idea. I manage a few more turns on the dance floor, but things scarcely improve. My footwork continues to be marred by the random activity of others' bodily parts. It is midnight and there are still kids frolicking about when I call it a night and leave the Bretons to it.

As with all the Celtic Fringe countries, Brittany gets more obviously Breton and Celtic the further west you go. The far southwest corner is hardcore. I arrive in the town of Douarnenez at dusk and the streets are quiet. There are no holidaymakers or artists or second home-owners in Douarnenez. It is a hard-working town and few have the time to break a smile for a stranger. As befits its reputation, there is a tense feeling about the place, which I like.

On my way here today, I have noticed more place names and road signs in Breton as well as in French. Walking through Douarnenez, I pick up on another subliminal code that indicates the level of pro-Celtic vigilance: car stickers. There are Breton flag stickers in their hundreds and, in their tens, a sticker that says: '*Après L'Ecosse et Le Pays de Galles, un statut particulier pour La Bretagne*'. The bottom line is that the Bretons are as unlikely to get independence as the Cornish are. But some degree of autonomy through a regional assembly may not be beyond their reach and the creation of the National Assembly in Wales and the restitution of the Scottish Parliament will certainly have encouraged the Bretons who demand it.

From time to time, it strikes me as odd that there is not a greater level of political exchange between the Celtic countries. The ties that do exist at an organisational level scarcely go beyond culture and language. De Valera, I read, dabbled with the idea of throwing Irish weight behind home rule for Scotland and Wales between the World Wars, but he gave up before he got started. The notion of some sort of political integration in a federation of Celtic states has been floated from time to time, usually by people who have been hitting the potcheen. There is an organisation called the Celtic League, a stated aim of which is 'campaigning for a formal association of Celtic nations to take place once two or more of them have achieved self-government' but the organisation seems to have little weight or support.

For all the hot air spoken about some form of Celtic political unity, it has amounted to nothing. Each Celtic country has been left to its own devices, to advance its own cause for recognition and political autonomy. Each country has had its own wild bearded gang of cottage-torchers and bomb-throwers, all with their own methods to gain nationalism. In fact – and this is a real Celtic trait at work here – each country commonly starts with one bearded gang, which splits and splits until there are dozens of similarly named, tiny and powerless groups all propounding one nationalist cause, but by different means.

I ask the *patron* of the first bar I step into near the port in Douarnenez if he speaks Breton and he launches himself straight into the language, with its profusion of Ks, Ws and Zs. It is very like Cornish, which I have only heard spoken once, bizarrely by a girl who also spoke Breton – she had a parent from each. When the *patron* has finished his speech, I tell him that I am from the Isle of Man. He is chuffed and he shouts me a beer. We talk for a bit and he shouts me another drink. He seems delighted that I have come all the way from the Isle of Man just to frequent his seedy bar. With his heavy brogue and my terrible French, we struggle to understand each other, but his enthusiasm flows over any problems this creates.

There is only one other customer in the bar. He is content sipping *vin de pays* and watching horse racing on the TV. I have another drink, a beer called Pelforth Brune which I have not drunk since I was rolling round the streets of Chamonix with Pascal over a decade ago. It was his favourite and it is the closest thing to stout that the French make. I only have to smell it to be reminded that it packs a cracking punch. Pascal! How happy to be reminded of him. The *patron* has the same dark hair and moustache. I tell him as much about Pascal as I am able.

'Kkwazzzuwwwwww zwurk kernawazer waka waka waka,' he says, or something like that. It is a Breton toast. We have another Pelforth. I suggest a whiskey, an Irish one. The idea is so good that he comes round the bar and embraces me. Doubles appear.

At some point – I think we are on our fourth Pelforth and our third large Bushmills – I let slip that I am a poet. He pounds his hand on the zinc bar top. Then he is round the front of the bar arranging tables and chairs and breaking an ashtray. The pale-faced man watching the horses doesn't flinch. My stage is ready. We have another Pelforth. And another big whiskey. Putting my kilt on in the bog – it is hardly necessary for an audience of two, but I am so whammoed now that it seems to be a matter of life and death – I lose a shoe down the bowl of the squat toilet. We have a Pelforth for the poem. The *patron* insists on turning the horse racing off for my recital, but I notice that the old boy does not once avert his gaze from the grey TV screen until it is switched on again.

I give him '*Aigh Vie* Tommy Collister'. He cannot understand a word of it, but he goes mad, banging on the bar and shouting things in Breton up at me. When I am through, we have a final

Pelforth and another Bushmills, followed by a vocal row over the bill, which he insists on standing in its entirety. We embrace again and, at 8.45 p.m., I walk out into the street and straight into a parked car.

Just as May is the best time of year to be in the north-west of Scotland, so September is the optimum month to be in south-west Brittany. The days are still long and the temperature – hot sunshine and a refreshing sea breeze – is perfect for walking as well as lazing. Most of the tourists and all of the children have gone home. The bars and restaurants and campsites are empty. The owners are at their ease: exhausted, but happy because their pockets are full. Winter is still a long way off. It is a good time to be roaming around Brittany, yet I cannot seem to shake off a dark and unidentified cloud that lours over me.

I think this is my reaction to the sense of decay that autumn brings. Walking along the lanes and the coastal footpaths, this decomposition of nature is impossible to ignore. The heather – the brilliant flash of high Celtic summer – is now pallid, dry and fading fast. The gorse is still yellow, but the pungent aroma that has followed me for the last few months has gone. The hortensias and agapanthus sag wearily with the weight of dead heads. The fuchsia bushes and the montbretia are dying back too.

It is not all about decay. The blackthorn thickets are sprouting their blue-black berries – the sloes that flavour gin. At the other end of the Celtic Fringe, along the watercourses that carve their way between the mountains of the Highlands, the rowan tree will be bearing scarlet berries – the ambrosial food of the fairies, they say. But this last, late gasp of summer only highlights what the decay is saying: come in, Ned Clague, your time is up, the 'lighted half' is nearly over.

I still have two festivals to attend – one in Scotland and one in Cornwall – but the sense of the end being in sight is impossible to ignore. The festival of Samhain is only five weeks away. I am already preparing myself for the return to my normal life in south London. Just like the heather, the life of Ned is slowly fading away. This makes me even more conscious of the fact that my poetic output is looking a little thin. I asked the Irish poet I bumped into at the railway station as we were leaving Lorient how many poems he writes a year: 'Poems that I like?' he replied. 'Maybe a hundred or more.' I have written four. I like two of them.

I tell a lie. There are, in fact, five poems in the collected works of Ned Clague. I have written a poem entirely in Manx, but it is atrocious and risible, so I am not boasting about it. A poet can only realistically expect to write well in one language – the language of a lifetime's experiences, memories and dreams – and as my harvest of verses suggests, I have struggled hard enough in that one language.

I am not then, nor am I ever likely to be, a prolific bard. However, I have learnt that you need only one good poem to be a wandering bard and to hold the silence of a smoke-choked bar room. To my surprise, I have grown to enjoy reciting poetry enormously. I would never have guessed that it could be as much fun and as exhilarating as it has been.

I think it is the sense that the opportunity to recite poems may come to an end at Samhain (it certainly will if my wife has anything to do with it) and it is this which drags a dark cloud above me as I head south along the Brittany coast. This stretch of the Celtic Fringe does not have the drama of Pembrokeshire or Kerry, but it is beautiful after its own fashion. The cliffs are no more than 300 feet high, but at the intermittent points that protrude into the ocean they are untamed. At the end of these points, in a timeless battle with the sea, the land tapers to a vertiginous cliff. Encircled by white water and only a hellish leap from the mainland is a towering stack. Beyond that are lower stacks that fade to coarse-cut boulders, like a set of tinker's teeth. Beyond is the ocean, ribbed with rows of swelling combers.

Even on this, a bright clear day, the coast feels raw. The footpath, marked with dabs of red and white paint on stones, hugs the cliffs and occasionally meanders across the hinterland where the low stone walls mark out the small fields of the last generation of farmers, now abandoned and reclaimed by heather and clumps of gorse.

It is the third or fourth headland that I rise up on which affords a view beyond Cap de la Chèvre, my destination today, and I can see as far south as Pointe du Van. Immediately below me is a long stretch of golden sand. There are glistening dots at the far end of it, which I initially take to be beached seals, not that you ever see seals on a beach. They prefer rocks. Halfway down the headland, I realise they are people. Halfway down the beach, I realise they are naked people.

The Celts are congenitally modest when it comes to the matter of their own bodies. I once had an Irish girlfriend who got undressed and dressed again under the sheets. Even the Scots, with their reputation for leaping into combat in their birthday suits and for going 'guerrilla' underneath their kilts, rarely holiday in naturist resorts. They are a shy lot, as am I. For all the high-festival buttock flashing I have done this summer, I remain coy about running around in the buff. Years ago, I crewed on a yacht across the Bay of Bengal with an Australian couple old enough to be my parents. We had only known each other twelve hours, but we were a mile off Phuket and their togs came off. I clung to my shorts and they laughed at me all the way to Sri Lanka.

So these naturists I am approaching are, and I can be absolutely certain about this, not Breton. No, they will be tourists – French, Dutch and Germans – who like the sun to shine all over. In my torn safari shorts and walking boots, I look like a shipwrecked man and I feel a little odd mingling among them. Yet my presence does not seem to disturb the man who is walking towards me through the surf. I fear that he is going to come and talk to me. Perhaps he will suggest I join in, or even ask to see my 'beautiful zizi'. Thankfully, he veers off at the last moment, back up the beach, sunlight glancing off his penis and reddening his ripe sloes.

I see the end of the beach in a gap between the swimmers and the sunbathers and I quicken my pace, difficult as it is to walk fast on sand. But the faster I walk, the more people move to cross my path. A lady swoops down out of the banked sand dunes on my left, trotting and brushing sand off her mons pubis. It is all too much really, on this hot day. I am not sure if I want to dive into the surf to cool off or bend her over in the dunes and spank her with cashmere gloves on.

When I get back up on to the next headland, I find the remains of an Iron Age hill fort. The squat vestiges of the walls are a reminder of tens of similar ancient Celtic sites that I have seen along the Atlantic coast this summer. There are more untamed beaches but no more untamed mons pubises before I reach a large patch of bare heath and the headland of Cap de la Chèvre.

This is as far south as I go today. Pointe de Penmarch, the very south-western extremity of Brittany, and the opposite end of the Celtic Fringe from Ness on the Isle of Lewis, is yet further south but I am not going to make it there on this trip. I have lingered too long in the green Breton hinterland and I now have to dash back up to Scotland for the Mod, the big Scottish Gaelic cultural hoo-hah and tartan fest in the seaside town of Largs. Again, this is a journey that could be easily made by sea but I am looking at buses, boats, coaches and whatever else comes my way to get me there. I have one last, long look at the bay of Douarnenez. Then I turn north.

14

For a Mod Song

I love Scotrail. Thousands don't. I love the fact that trains get cancelled for proper reasons. Not for leaves on the track or doggy-doo on the conductor's shoes, but for industrial action. Strikes. Train drivers' strikes, guards' strikes, everyone's bloody strikes. It reminds me of my youth – the good old days of industrial action, before Thatcher ruined it.

The other thing I love about Scotrail, and in particular the London to Glasgow service, is that you arrive before you get there, if you see what I mean. It is like going to get a visa at the Indian Embassy in London, where you get a glimpse of the smell and the chaos that is going to roast you when you walk out of Delhi International Airport. So, you get just a taste of Glasgow on the train: there are always lads swigging cans of McEwan's Export in the passages between trains, even when there are free seats; every fourth person is wearing a Celtic or a Rangers football shirt; at least one of the staff in the buffet car has an accent so strong that you might as well be outside Delhi International Airport.

Today, that one member of staff is pushing the buffet trolley and I have just woken up when it arrives beside my seat.

'What sandwiches do you have, please?' I ask.

'Egg on Beckham . . . Beckham lays a tomato . . . D'ya noo Mays on her knees . . . Rod Stewart as a pickled salami . . .'

'Right. And what is that one on the poster?'

'Beckham lays a tomato.'

'I'll have one of them, please, and a Mars Bar. How much is that?'

'Graeme Souness is a greatest.'

'Uh? Here's five pounds.'

'Drugs, sir?'

'Drugs?'

'Aye, Coke . . . Fanta . . .'

'Oh, no, no, no. Thank you.'

'Kenny Dalgliesh,' he says, half smiling, and with that he is gone, leaving me to wrestle with the plastic container and consider my lot as the hills of Cumbria roll by. Leaving my wife, who is now eight months pregnant, is getting increasingly difficult. To make matters worse, while I was in Brittany, Vicky fell over and sprained her ankle badly. I made a show of parading my lower joints, still swollen with the first signs of gout, but this did not humour her. The baby is due four days before Samhain, on 27 October. After six months of almost continuous absence, it now looks reasonably likely that I will not be there for the birth. I was there when Lucas was born – an experience I liken to being in a field hospital in Nha Trang during the Tet Offensive – and for reasons I cannot explain, I would like to be there again. More importantly, Vicky would like me to be there and the prospect that I may not be adds worry to an already stressed Penn household. I tried the 'Ned Clague dies, a baby is born, the wheel of the year turns, life gives way to life . . . so let's call the baby Ned, or Nedina if it's a girl' line, but to be perfectly honest, at this stage my best gags are going down about as well as the poll tax did in Scotland.

The one positive development on the home front is that Lucas is now able to say 'Cheers' in all six Celtic languages. For some reason, he chooses to put them together in a medley with a little dance which takes the form of a sort of Celtic 'haka'. He finishes the routine by galloping across the kitchen brandishing my blackthorn stick and lancing the cooker. I am a proud dad.

Largs is a strange little town, full of tearooms and trinket shops. It feels as if time stood still here in the early 1970s. The Isle of Man

was like this until the mid-1990s when it hit the money. The reason
for the time warp in Largs (as formerly in the Isle of Man) is the
number of retirees. It is the Hibernian answer to Updike's Florida.
All the old people are in flight from the high rises and the smack-
heads and the modern art of Glasgow. It is not the sort of earthy,
rugged and remote place where you would expect to witness the
largest annual celebration of Scottish Gaelic culture. But the
Mod, as the festival is called, learnt much from the Welsh
Eisteddfod in its early years, and, in the same fashion, it cruises
through venues the length of the west coast in the hope of being
inclusive.

With competitors and merry-makers and earnest supporters of
the Mod in town, I knew there would be a rush on beds, so I
booked a B & B in advance. When I arrive outside the establish-
ment on Charles Street, it is everything I anticipated: a smart,
granite-built terraced house. The front lawn is groomed like a general's haircut. The door is freshly painted. The house could be
called Dunroamin or Dunravin or Dunsexualintercourse, but a
house name would probably be too common on a nobby street like
this. It just has a number.

Mrs Mclean opens the door before I even ring. She has been cur-
tain twitching. 'Muster Clig, is ut? Ah cheeked the treen times. Ah
thought yud be hier just noo. Doo cum un, please.' She speaks like
one of the Krankies, arguably the worst comedy act of all time. It
is a middle-class Morningside accent, full of air and self-conscious
status. I know why the Scottish toffs speak with an English accent
now: the Scottish accent just doesn't do 'posh'. It does Glaswegian
street fighter and dry Highland stalker beautifully, and with gravi-
tas. But in the mouth of a retiree who is trying to hold up her 'tuts'
and her social status in the face of having to run a B & B, the
Scottish accent reeks. I know instantly that we are not going to get
along.

I am glad that I feel this. This is the way a good Celt should feel.
The Celtic peoples have always been intolerant of anyone seeking

to better themselves. Arrogance is a trait they despise, which manifests itself in an abhorrence of class structure. Deference to toffs may be a virtue to the English, but it has never meant much to the Celts, whose natural social order has always been a horizontal one. The Welsh have never abided a large and obvious aristocracy in the way that their cap-doffing neighbours have and anyone who has aped the ways of the gentry across the border has been vigorously derided. The Manx have never imitated anyone and even today in the Isle of Man, if you try and pull yourself head and shoulders above the Manx people, someone will chop you off at the knees. In Australia and Canada, they call this 'tall poppy syndrome'. It is only a hunch of mine, but I would like to think that the relatively classless society of the New World countries is, at least in part, a legacy of the influence of the Celts who emigrated to them early in their histories. The Celts demand parity in society. The heroes of the Celts through the ages have not been lords and generals, rulers and colonialists. They have been outlaws, squatters, guerrillas, poachers, wreckers and smugglers – common people whose raison d'être has been defiance of foreign landlords and institutions.

Mrs Mclean's drawing room is a treasure of trinkets. There is barely a square inch of flat surface unencumbered with silver salvers or china pots. I have a sense that if I were to pick something up, the outline of its base would be chalked on the wood like the tool board in a mechanic's workshop.

'Doo hev air seat, Muster Clig.' I have not farted or even thought about farting all day, yet in what must be a psychosomatic reaction to my surroundings, I sit down in front of a muffin tray and immediately feel a rumbling in my lower stomach.

'Wart is it yoo doo fur a living, Muster Clig?' Mrs Mclean asks, hauling a brown leather book out of the desk drawer. I feel like I am being interviewed for the job of PE teacher at a private academy for girls, though Mrs Mclean, I have to say, makes Miss Jean Brodie look positively frivolous and fruity.

'I'm a poet.' Her face crumples. The pocket of air presses harder on my colon. Something told me that she was not the type to have a soft spot for a foolish, long-haired, bibulous poet. She hands me the leathery tome – a guesthouse registration book masquerading as the sort of visitors' book that you find in gentrified homes. There are four columns: date, name, address and remarks. I briefly fantasise about filling in the latter before I leave: 'Have had a super stay. Great weather. Why is there a cat turd in the muffin tray?'

I follow Mrs Mclean's overripened bottom up the stairs to the attic and my room, where, to my horror, I learn that we are to share a bathroom.

'Noo, a few hoos rules, Muster Clig. Normally, I lock the doors ut tin furty five p.m. But as thus week us the Mod und aye noo peepel will be oot injoying themselves, I am happy to give yoo a key. But mind' – she raises a finger at me like she is reprimanding a dog – 'thur us ta bee noo cumming hoom hinebriated.'

'Hinebriated?'

'Drrrrunk, Muster Clig. I do nooht tulerate drrrrunkenness in ma geests.'

'Quite right too, Mrs Mclean. Now tell me, you don't have any granddaughters that need a good seeing to while I am here, do you?' No, I don't say that. The thought dances through my head but I know for a fact that every bed in Largs is booked so it will be the park bench if I blow this one. I clench my buttocks, bow my head and nod.

'Un thees,' she continues after a testing moment of silence, pointing to a tray on the bedside table with a dram and a biscuit on it, 'us a Heylind welcome, Muster Clig.'

When I hear the latch close on the door at the bottom of the stairs, I slam the whisky, fling the shortbread out of the window at the seagulls, fart very loudly and dance around the room slapping my bottom, shouting, 'Get yer ya yas out for the Mod.'

*

The Mod is also known as the 'Whisky Olympics'. I am sitting at a table with four Scots and it feels more like an AA meeting. I have just bought a round of drinks for these lads – four Diet Cokes and a pint of Belhaven best for myself. We are at a ceilidh, but it is as cheery as a Presbyterian congress. The music is dreadful and the conversation isn't much better. I only know one of these men. He is a strange fish called Ian. I met him when I was hitching across South Uist in May. This afternoon, when I went up to the Mod office to get a programme for the next few days, I bumped into him and he immediately recognised me.

'Hugh neh-ver keem to see me,' he blasted accusatorially. I had hoped to, but my time in the Western Isles ran out.

'I did telephone,' I blurted anxiously. He rubbed his chin in the palm of his hand as if this finally was the moment when he would decide whether to forgive me or not. The embarrassing thing was that he remembered my name, Rob Penn, and that I was working on a book about the Celts. We were standing outside the Mod office where there were a number of people who now knew me as Ned Clague, the poet. My double life was always going to catch up with me somewhere.

Ian chose to forgive me for not paying him a visit, but things took a turn for the worse when he insisted I call the Convenor of the Mod; an invaluable contact, he said, and a gentleman who knew all about the history of the Gaels. Ian said I must arrange an interview and he stood over me while I called him on my mobile. I nearly dropped the phone when the Convenor said, 'Wheel see you tahmorrow theen, at mud-day, Rob. Nor tell me, d'ya noo a poo-ht from the Eela Man bah the nim ah Ned Clague?'

'Um . . . sort of . . .'

'Wheel, he phoned me sum weeks agooh abut reading poo-htry a tha Mod un ah believe he's here noo.'

'Very good. I'll look out for him.'

To humour Ian, I have come to hear him sing this evening. He appears to be well known among the Mod enthusiasts and he has won many competitions over the years. He was, he tells me, an operatic singer for a while and he knows personally a few of the accomplished musicians that have come out of the Isle of Man in recent years. When the ceilidh band interrupts their awful noise to let him sing, the evening does improve. He has a remarkable voice.

When we first met, I was an ingenuous journalist interested in all the things dear to him – the Gaelic language, the oral tradition and singing. Now I am sitting around in my kilt, clutching my blackthorn stick, and he is not quite sure what to make of me, and I can hardly blame him. A few months ago I would have panicked if I thought people were suspicious of me. Now, I really don't care. I have discovered a degree of confidence in being Ned Clague. I suppose this is partly because I am more accustomed to the role and partly because I enjoy reciting the poetry. But, perhaps most crucially, I have come to realise that I do share a number of what I perceive to be the characteristics of the Celts. And of this, I am proud. To begin with, I felt like a devious and incompetent spy in a sort of Celtic 'Great Game' that I had invented. As it turns out, I now feel right at home.

'Thaht wus something tear-ribble,' Ian says, marching across the car park and on to the Largs esplanade. We have abandoned the ceilidh and we are off to find out what other entertainments the town has to offer. Going on a pub-crawl with a man who drinks Diet Coke is hardly my idea of a rip-snorting night on the tear but he does at least know where he is going.

In each pub there are people who know him and he returns their greetings with the brusque manner of someone whose success and fame are behind him. In one pub, there is a man with the physique of Obelix singing Gaelic ballads. He is singing through a tinny PA system and accompanied by an electric piano, and the whole thing sounds like some hellish Scottish karaoke. It is a long way from the emotive, unaccompanied singing I heard in the pub in Listowel. Ian takes his turn at the gentle insistence of Obelix. Even his bold voice cannot dispel the sinking sensation I feel when the melody kicks off on the piano. I decide to cut my losses and get home before Mrs Mclean's curfew.

Sitting towards the back of the Inverclyde Sports Centre, waiting for the men's traditional solo singing competition to start, I do a quick white hair count. My survey says: two out of three people in this room today are entitled to a bus pass. I read in the programme that next year will be the hundredth Mod and I wonder how many of this lot were at the first one. And therein lies the rub of the Mod – nearly everyone here collects a pension.

This is only a heat for the Men's Solo Singing prize, one of the most prestigious competitions of the Mod, yet the singing is wonderful. The competitors, in full kilt and rig with cropped, black jackets and bow ties, take the stage one at a time. They all sing the same song, in Gaelic. I cannot understand a word of it, but I never tire of it. Once on stage, the pianist strikes one note for the singer to find his key and then he is off. Hands are clasped before the rigid body and the head barely stirs. In contrast, the voice is loaded with astonishing emotion. One of the singers returns to his seat in front of me and I overhear him say, 'Ah nearly sturted craying in the last verse.' This is, I romantically reflect, the music I would like to shuffle off this mortal coil to and if that cannot be, because I get flattened by a bus, then I would like the voice of one of these singers to ring out over my grave as I am lowered into the earth on a promontory overlooking the Atlantic, in a gale. And if that cannot be arranged, no matter, because this must surely be the sound that plays in the Elysian Fields.

Storytelling remains an important part of the bardic tradition for the Highlanders and Islanders and I am delighted to see that there are competitions in this discipline, for all ages. I sneak into the classroom at the secondary school where a storytelling competition for under-twelves is going on. A girl, who cannot be older than ten, bravely gets to her feet, straightens her red cardie and launches into a tale in Gaelic. Again, I cannot understand the story, but merely listening to the language with its crisp intonation and musical lilts sends me off into a reverie. The competitions have to be conducted in Gaelic – that is the whole point of the Mod, it is the festival of Scottish Gaelic – but a familiar problem occurs during the adjudication which is delivered in Gaelic by a storyteller from the Western Isles. As he finishes, someone in the audience says, 'Am terribly saw-ry, but am the feather a wun a tha winners. Ah noh hev tha Gaelic un cud yoo pawsably see tha agin ah English?'

English dominates the Mod, a fact that must grate with everyone who does speak Gaelic. Of course, I have heard it spoken often on the streets and in the pubs in the last two days, but the very fact that all the competitions – storytelling, poetry reading, folk tales, precenting psalms and (no kidding) Bible readings – are in Gaelic whilst English is used all around them ring-fences the language. It gives the whole event an odd flavour.

In the early evening, I bump into Ian again. He suggests that I attend a harp concert later on. He is, of course, singing in it himself. If someone had suggested to me six months ago that I attend a harp concert of my own free will, not to impress a girl or ingratiate myself with my mother-in-law or to win a bet, then I would have laughed like a hyena. Back then, a 'harp concert' meant something your tonsils play when you swallow your first slug of lager on a sunny day. I might have even guessed it was a smutty euphemism for a bout of awful flatulence. But this journey has been an education in the Celtic arts if nothing else, and there are few things the Celts do as well as play the harp.

Once again, I bring the average age of the audience down by ten years. The evening is organised by Ceolraidh Clarsaich, the national body that promotes harp playing in Scotland. There are a dozen ladies of all ages on the stage. They play as a group and then individually and the whole thing is compèred by a man who has a delightful accent. He speaks in English and occasionally in Gaelic.

The harp is a curious instrument and it takes me a few minutes to get over the notion that I might be at a medieval banquet. When I do, I am transported. Not only is the music delightful, but watching the performers is enthralling. Plucking the harp entails an extraordinary grace and ease of movement in the arms while the rest of the body remains motionless. A young girl plays something called a Cascade, a magical piece of music that pours out of her hands like a mountain stream. It would not be out of place on an Ibiza 'chill-out' CD.

I arrived early and chose to sit at the end of an aisle so I could slip out halfway through, but I am glued for the full two and a half hours including the triumphant finale and the laborious round of thank-yous that suggest no one is getting paid for this. On the way out, I surprise myself and buy the CD even though I know it will sound dreadful when I play it at home. Somehow, CDs you buy at gigs always do.

This is about my limit for culture. I head now for the Largs seafront and a pub with a bit of action where I can read a poem. McAuley's is a good, honest locals' bar. There is a band from Glasgow playing well-chosen cover songs by Neil Young, Dylan and the Stray Cats. The lead singer, who might just be the first person of my age that I have seen in days, says, 'Hez a real mod song,' and sings 'Sunny Afternoon' by the Kinks.

The guy slumped on the bar next to me looks like he has been on the vodka and Cokes for at least as long as I have been listening to harp recitals. When he looks up at me, his eyes speak but no words come out of his mouth. Then his eyes wander off around the bar and he mutters something like, 'Aminoch highun Ben Nevis un Andy Irvine'. He waves a hand at me that clearly weighs too much because he falls off his stool. I go back to listening to the band.

A few minutes later he is back. He has been out for a breath of fresh air, thrown some water on his face and he is standing at the bar with cash in his hand. 'Ding ding' for what must be this fellow's fifteenth and final round.

'Ka buya drink, big mun? Whaz tha tartan?'

'Manx. I am from the Isle of Man.'

'Ee, verhy good. Whuz uu here?'

'For the Mod.' He looks confounded. 'The Gaelic festival.'

'Our rite. Any gut? Ah wuz jus heyina a quiet pint bi maself. Wizzit, than?'

'Pint of heavy. Thanks.'

'Am Jim.'

Jim is from Paisley, halfway between here and Glasgow. He is on the piss because his 'bud' left him last week. He must be over forty and he is a big man. I quiz him about the Mod but it is as alien to him as the 'Kumbh Mela' is to me. He knows nothing about the event and next to nothing about Gaelic culture. It is a timely reminder that Scotland is a country divided along ethnic lines. Partly because the most obvious symbols of Scotland – tartan, bagpipes, clans, kilts and caber-tossing – all come from the Highlands and partly because of the nationalist cause, the divisions that exist between Highlanders and Lowlanders have often been confused. And I am not sure this serves the modern Scottish Celts well. It strikes me now that the Mod should be held in the Highlands, in Gaelic, and it should be organised by the Gaels themselves rather than the semi-gentrified, white-haired old men in tweed jackets who I keep bumping into.

'Fancy a bit of late night Mod action, Jim?'

'Luv it, big mun.'

In the first pub we go to, Jim is in a fight before I have bought drinks. I have picked a really wild card for company this evening, but something about the staidness of the Mod has pressed this upon me. In the next pub, Jimmy Smith's Bar, there is a ceilidh band playing. The bar is packed and the Whisky Olympics is beginning to get going now. Thankfully, Jim's antics are camouflaged by the general affray, albeit a late middle-aged affray. For all my concerns about the death knell ringing for Scottish Gaelic culture, it is pretty lively in here. Jim disappears and I presume he has passed out in the gents. I fall in with a group from Sutherland, way up on the west coast. Angus (actually Aonghas, he spells it out for me) reminds me of Fergie MacDonald. He is a bear of a Highland man and full of high spirits. He takes my stick and wields it around his head and prods a few ladies' backsides with it.

'Tha poo-ht's stick, Ned? Blackthorn?' he says, returning it before he gets into trouble, with a wink.

'It is. I am a poet.'

'Well let's hear ya. We muss. We muss,' he enthuses. When the band finish the song, Angus levers his way through the crowd to talk to the ceilidh bandleader, who then leans towards the microphone.

'Thiz er poo-ht bah nim-ah Need, free Aisla Mun. Wee aye yah, Need? Wull hee yah noo.'

When I am beside the microphone, I have a good look around the pub. It is like playtime at the asylum. It is way past midnight and everyone is loaded. Because this is the way I have always done it, I refuse the microphone offered to me. I bang my stick hard on a table and kick off, with a roar, into '*Aigh Vie* Tommy Collister'. No one is listening. No one can hear me. Angus is waving at me and cupping his ear but we might as well be talking across a busy runway at Heathrow. The people at the nearest table look up. A lady wolf-whistles but the commotion continues. I try harder and louder. I am really belting it out now and I am only eight lines in. My back is arched and I can feel the heat on my larynx. I am giving it all I have got and then . . . BOOM . . . I am travelling like a rocket-propelled grenade, over one stool, past several feet, above the swirling carpet and into a crowd of people and drinks. Then I am down, kissing the cigarette burns with beer pouring through my hair.

'Jim, you fucking idiot! What are you doing!' I shout this at the shins of the person in front of me, though it is actually addressed to Jim, who is still wrapped round my legs.

'Try-savin tackle, big mun,' he says, picking himself up. 'Saved the game.'

I try to apologise to the people I have crashed into but they are too off their trots to care. By the time things are as straight as they can be, there is a dame in tartan leisure coordinates with peroxide blonde hair crooning some other monstrous Scottish folk song into the microphone. My moment has passed.

Angus thinks my being flattened is the funniest thing he has seen since his wife fell out of a rowing boat on Loch Shiel when they were courting and he shouts me a couple of drams. When I get back to Mrs Mclean's, I am dribbling. I moony outside her door three times and fall on my bed fully clothed.

The morning is a mad rush. Eleven minutes from wake-up time to train departure, to include packing, necessary ablutions, paying my bill and a four-minute walk to the station. I smell like the carpet in Jimmy Smith's but there is no time to do anything about that. At the bottom of the stairs, Mrs Mclean is waiting for me like a Victorian nanny.

'Ad see you noo hev the team fur ya breakfast, Muster Clig. Av checked the train times.'

'Urrrrrgghh.'

'Un yoo wer in erful late lerst night so all be a rush fur ya thus murning.' She can't quite check the beatific smile that spreads across her face. She has saved £2.74 by not having to provide me with bacon and eggs and my mad rush is, she feels certain, some small retribution for allowing the devil and the drink to get the better of me.

I hit the pavement at a fast walk. I am probably going to miss the train but I am smiling now, and wondering just how long it will be before Mrs Mclean discovers that I have peed in her toilet brush holder.

15

One Last Poem at Lowender Peran

Crossing the River Tamar again, I have a sense that the event I am heading west to might just be one festival too far. As far as research is concerned, I have probably seen as much as I need to see. 'What can one more heavy drinking session with a bunch of bearded dwarfs possibly reveal to you?' is how my wife phrased it: nothing that I haven't already experienced is the answer. Though I had always planned for the Lowender Peran, Cornwall's small but deadly inter-Celtic festival, to be Ned Clague's last roar, I don't really need to be here. The only reason I am here is . . . well, I want to be and in the present domestic circumstances, this is not enough.

Vicky is eight and a half months pregnant now, and moving with the alacrity and precision of a tranquillised moose. Lucas, on the other hand, or rather in the blue corner, is two. He is elusive like a Welsh scrum half. Bath time at my house is a mismatch of Gulf War proportions. You could say I am the UN in this situation and, sitting on a train trundling through Cornwall, I am about as ineffectual.

So I am heavy with guilt as I bicycle up a steep hill away from Truro station, on to the spine of Cornwall where the stunted trees, bent and aged by the wind, seem to mock my gloom. Crossing the A30, the cloud begins to break up and patches of countryside are illuminated by golden sunlight out of the west. This cheers me a little, but it is the first taste of salt on my lips, carried on the breeze, that lifts my spirit fully as I freewheel down into Perranporth.

It is not a beautiful town – few in Cornwall are any more – and

314

it is obvious that it thrives on the emmet industry. But it is late October, the tourists have all gone and the locals look happy to have reclaimed Perranporth again. Another siege has been withstood; it is time to relax. The tide is out and the beach is lovely – a long, tapering stretch of rinsed sand. A hundred and fifty feet offshore, there is a rim of white water where the surf is folding and sounding its rough chorus. Great pink clouds are hurrying overhead, underlit by the late sun which is kissing the horizon. The moon is out. The early nights are closing in. The last surfers are doubling up the beach.

On the headland at the southern end of the beach there is a plaque that says 'St Piran, Cornwall's foremost saint, landed on this beach in the sixth century and established an oratory in the dunes.' The mention of the saint's name makes me think again of the lady I met on the train the first time I crossed the River Tamar back in June. I know rather a lot about St Piran now and the old duck might just be impressed.

Next to the plaque is a huge sundial embedded in the grass. It is calculated, another sign says, 'to Cornish time, showing a difference of 20 minutes to GMT'. Twenty minutes behind, that is. This makes me laugh. I can't be sure precisely why, but it strikes me that this is a good metaphor. Cornwall and indeed the Cornish are just that little bit – about twenty minutes I would say if you asked me to put my finger on it – out of sync with the rest of England, and proud of it.

The town is now lit up by a bluish, gloaming light from the sky, and by the orange of the street lamps. The footpaths and car parks are busy with kids on skateboards, paying homage to the unknown man who invented paving. There are no grown-ups about and Perranporth feels briefly like a town after the Armageddon that destroyed only adults.

The Ponsmere Hotel takes the prize for being the most hideous building in Perranporth. Sadly, it is also the largest and the most prominent, on top of the dunes overlooking the beach, before all to behold. It is square and plain and without any sort of architectural embellishment whatsoever – the perfect venue then for a Celtic festival.

The reception is carpeted with the sort of utilitarian flooring that you could parade a cavalry regiment over and still buff up in a jiffy. There is no one around. There are a few stalls peddling the usual stuff: jewellery lavished with Celtic motifs, stained glass, tie-dye, books about Cornwall including a couple of volumes of poetry, henna tattoos and a random collection of traditionally forged iron thingies that can have no household purpose whatsoever unless you like to disembowel your pets of a weekend.

There is one stall promoting 'The Cornish Revolution'. There are piles of information about the Stannary Parliament, the campaign for a Cornish Assembly and various other matters on Cornwall's political agenda. I am fingering a car sticker that reads 'I had a nightmare. I dreamt I was born an Englishman' printed over a map of Cornwall, when I feel the hot breath of a human on my neck.

'Kerni halp yu, thar?' the man says. He is wearing a Cornish tartan tie – it is not exactly tasteful but it has nothing on the Manx tartan – and a black blazer that fits his brick-like shoulders and is about three inches too long on the sleeves. It is a sartorial problem I know well, as do prop forwards everywhere and a large proportion of Celtic men. Off-the-peg jackets are like Elizabethan corsets if the arm length is right, or they fit comfortably across the shoulders and you forever carry evidence of your last meal in your cuffs.

'Er . . . yes . . . er,' I stutter. I have a plethora of questions to ask a politically motivated Cornish activist, but they all fly from my mind when I feel this fellow breathing on me.

'Um . . . Yes! What is the Stannary Parliament all about then?' Immediately I regret asking this. It is like asking a stamp collector to tell you about his favourite stamp. You hope he is going to say, 'Penny Black, of course,' and be done with it, but years of frustra-

tion at not having a captive audience, of not knowing anyone else
who is interested in the subject, come pouring out in an hour-long
eulogy to a rare late Victorian stamp from the Congo commemorating the castration of the fourth daughter of King
Effongozi the Great.

This man steadies himself on his feet, tugs his beard and begins:
'An 1201 tha Charter a King Jahn empurred tha Lord Warden o'
tha Stannaries a-try arl cases a-cept . . .' My ears are suddenly
filled with the sound of pounding surf. Only sporadically do his
words break through this wall of noise: '. . . savereign Parliament
. . . roits fur eight unred years . . . Palatine State . . . distinct frum
Englan . . . Duchy . . . irrevocable dacuments . . .' He taps my chest
at this point, breaking my daydream, and raises a fist to say, 'The
Cornish peepel air entitled ah enjoy ther inalienable roit tuh thar
own savereign government. Are ya wuth us?'

'Indeed, I am. Can you tell me where the gents is, please?'

When I eventually find a lady selling tickets to the Lowender
Peran festival, she tells me that they are sold out for both tonight
and Saturday night. I try my 'I'm a poet and I have come all the
way from the Isle of Man' line and then my 'I'm a journalist' line.
The latter looks like it is beginning to work with the rather sweet
woman who has her hand on the ticket box when a dragon sweeps
over and snaps it shut, barking something about 'breach of fire
regulations'. She is clearly the boss and that seems to be the end of
it. I want to say, 'Look, I am going to gatecrash anyway, so why
don't you just take my cash,' but I resist. Keeping numbers down
to comply with fire regulations hardly smacks of Celtic free spirit
and I can't imagine how much mirth such a suggestion would
cause an Irish publican, but there you go. This is Cornwall and the
long arm of the English reaches even up the backside of this Celtic
jamboree. I will have to devise a plan and wait for the full cover of
darkness before making my assault on the Ponsmere Hotel.

A hundred yards away on the beach is an airy, wooden shack
called the Watering Hole. It is a pub, a young friendly one full of

surfers and the like. It is a world away – and the opposite side of the Cornish cultural coin, I suppose – from the Ponsmere Hotel. You could hardly miss this fact, but it strikes me clean between the eyes when I order a drink. As it arrives on the bar, I realise that I have left my wallet in the B & B. After doing battle with the fork-tongued, anal-retentive lady at the Lowender Peran, I am in no mood for a debate with the barman. I apologise for the mistake and I am turning for the door when he says, 'Don't worry about it. Have the drink and run a slate. You look good for it. How long you around for? Pay me when you can.'

A blues band is doing a sound check for this evening's gig. They are raising money for a young person from Perranporth who is going abroad to work for an aid agency in Africa. There are more flat, bronzed and bare female midriffs in the Watering Hole than a man of a certain age is able to count. Pigtails seem to be in fashion, which is quite alarming, and most of the girls are wearing what one can only assume are their late grandfather's jeans. The lads have ponytails and fruity facial hair, tattoos and exclamatory T-shirts that, on analysis, mean nothing. Everyone is very friendly and relaxed. There is no Friday night clocking-off fever and I ask the barman about this. He has a good look around and announces without irony, 'No, no, thez a few people here who do have jobs.'

I think of Alex on the beach at Bréhec in Brittany. It strikes me now, though, that the inherent problem with what he was saying about the young surf crew being the natural inheritors of the way of life on the Celtic Fringe and its traditions is that the two communities – the surf tribe in the Watering Hole and the pan-Celtic enthusiasts in the Ponsmere Hotel – never meet. They exist in parallel universes, divided on this occasion by only a hundred yards of beach. I ask four young people who come to the bar if they will be going to the Lowender Peran this weekend: three girls ask me, 'What is it?' and the fourth, a young lad, says, 'What? And hang out with my parents? Are you mental?'

From the way he looks me up and down, I feel that he is actu-

ally saying: 'What? And hang out with my parents and people like
. . . you? Are you mental?' I want to catch hold of one of his gold
ear-loops and say, 'No, I'm not mental actually, but these days it
only takes a pint of whisky and a blast of fiddle music. I can be
there in half an hour, so don't push it, sweetie.'

I am on my third unpaid-for pint when a hand clamps on my
shoulder.

'Hey, Ned! Bloody hell, bay! Hiw ar ya?' It is a familiar face, a
friend from some late night whirl.

'Letz av a poohm then, Ned. Rite bay?'

Golowan? Listowel? Round the fire in a field in Pembrokeshire?
Quai des Indes? I haven't a clue where we met. A photocopy of his
face has been filed upstairs but all the other information relating
to where and when and who and how has been doused in ethanol
and torched. I am not embarrassed about it – this sort of thing
happens to Rob Penn all the time. No, the unease is Ned's: not
remembering this fellow redoubles my initial deceit. Not that he
minds. He blusters through the pleasantries without any of the
hesitation of an Englishman. He is Cornish and he has been
coming to the Lowender Peran festival for ten years. He tells me
that Friday night is a slow night. 'Sart-a-dee noit's differen all-
ogever. Suh rite belter. Save yourself ar that.'

Pedalling along the lane from Perranporth to St Agnes on a sunny
Saturday morning, I finally remember where I met the bloke I
bumped into last night. It was at Yn Chruinnaght on the Isle of
Man. He is a Cornishman, beloved of his Celtic ancestry, of his
pints and of the tremolo tunes that his arse can play upon request.
He is a friend of Dan, who was in the whitest buttock contest.
How could I forget him?

It is a textbook coastal Atlantic day: a firm south-westerly wind
– seemingly the same wind that I have been tussling with all
summer – is shaking the trees and buffeting the seagulls and flat-
tening the waves and scattering the sea spray across the granite

rocks. It is a wind that fills my head as I cycle into it. It is a wind that carries a timely warning: winter storms are coming.

There is a great view from the top of St Agnes beacon, over a long stretch of the gnarly north Cornish coast. Clouds have gathered in packs and they march overhead towards England like legions in an army from one of Tolkien's fantasies. I drop into the St Agnes Hotel where I had my wallet pinched back in June. I was hoping that it might have turned up, but it hasn't. I have a pint and read the Saturday *Guardian*.

I have been so engrossed in reading about, studying and being among the Celts for the past six months that I have failed to keep up with the way of the world. Newspapers are supposed to be my trade, but for six months I have only touched the serendipitous delights of local newspapers. It takes me three hours to read the *Guardian* from cover to cover and it is shocking to be brought up to date with the news in one blitz. The nub of events is this: the long arm of al-Qaeda remains strong and we can't find Bin Laden. The one place the intelligence services are sure al-Qaida don't operate from is Iraq, so President Bush is going to flatten Baghdad. And so the wheel of hatred gets spun again. Half of the countries that I love to travel in, that I visit for my work, are now off the map, made too dangerous by the spread of high-intensity hatred of the West amongst Muslims. Indonesia, peninsula Malaysia, Pakistan, Uzbekistan, Iran and Syria – they all carry a perceived risk now and I will get no page space writing about them. The traveller's map of the world has been redrawn. I wonder if my children will be able to visit half the places that I have? Probably not. It strikes me that between the dawning of the era of cheap intercontinental flights and 11 September 2001 there was a window on travel, a freedom to roam the planet, that is now being closed.

I mention all this because global events are, once again, changing what it means to be British, and thus what it means to be Celtic. The 'Alliance for Good', or whatever shallow, emetic title the US and British coalition takes, has begun to reshape, once again, how foreigners see the British. The last time Britain stood so prominently on the international stage was the Second World War, when Britain was one, when Cornish, Welsh and Scottish nationalism were subsumed into British nationalism. The resurgence of national identities and political shifts of the last fifty years have changed this. Is 'British' then an out-of-date term? Should Bush be talking about a coalition between the USA and England? Plenty of Celts think so.

When I travelled in Bosnia some years ago, not long after the Dayton Peace Agreement was signed, a man pulled a gun on me because he thought I was another meddling Englishman. I tried the Manx ticket, but he didn't know the Isle of Man so I settled for 'Me Ireland, me Ireland', at which news he put away the gun and bought me a beer. What I am trying to say is that, in a very short space of time, being English has come to mean that you carry a target round on your back. There are, of course, still Irish, Welsh, Cornish and Scottish soldiers in the British army, but the distinction between what and who is British (but not English) and what and who is English is increasingly understood abroad, just as it is at home.

So is it now both unfashionable and dangerous to be English? That might be putting it a little strongly. However, reading in the newspaper about Blair proselytising around the globe on the need to invade Iraq does make me think again about my identity and my allegiance. Bit by bit, I have grown more Manx.

The wind blows me all the way back to Perranporth where I nip into my B & B to get my stick and don my kilt. The old Manx hunting tartan has served me incredibly well. Usually, just to put it on fills me with a fresh flash of Celtomania. The blend of autumnal colours means that you can pour pretty much what you want down the front of the kilt and never feel the need to clean it. Half an hour on a radiator and a good whacking against a tree usually does the trick. That said, there are plenty of marks on it –

a Guinness stain from County Mayo, mutton gravy from Cloghane, the imprint of an oily prawn from Yn Chruinnaght, a dope burn from the Eisteddfod. These stains are a kind of alternative record of my Celtic journey.

When I first got the kilt, a friend suggested that I bury it in the garden for a week to make it look worn. As it has transpired, one Celtic festival was enough for it to earn its spurs. Today, it looks like an antique that could have hung around the girth of a Jacobite rebel as he charged the English field artillery.

The festival Lowender Peran is banging along at a fair tilt when I get back to the Ponsmere Hotel for the Saturday night 'belter'. It only occurs to me after I have taken the magic mushrooms that this is actually Ned Clague's last night of Celtic barding. Samhain is next week and I am heading back up to Edinburgh, but I don't imagine there being an opportunity to recite a poem then. This is the night then. This is it . . . which means one thing: no matter how high I get, I still have to read a poem. The mushrooms have been in my pocket for weeks. They grow and are consumed in abundance in the damp, green Celtic domains (an illuminating fact in itself and no doubt the answer to a thousand behavioural queries that autumnal visitors to the west of Britain have) and this handful were picked on a bosomy hillock of the Kerry hinterland and given to me, if I remember correctly, by Fergus at the Fleadh. I had completely forgotten I had them until ten minutes ago when I was rummaging in my bum bag for my crystal and my Celtic stones. The envelope practically sprang open in my lap. Hello. Now that's a good idea, I thought, and before I had really considered the matter I had wolfed the lot – two chews, the taste of compost, a grimace, a gag and they were gone.

Downstairs in the Sunset bar there is a young Cornish group called Naked Feet playing a gig. I have been hoping to catch them performing somewhere all summer. They are excellent. I am standing at the back of the bar, marking the rumblings in the pit of my stomach, and listening to the rocking Celtic folk tunes when a man comes hopping from foot to foot towards me.

'Whoiz new wan dancin?' he says, bobbing up and down beside me now.

'I don't know. The music is great.'

'Aye. Am Dave, boy the way.' He has the crazed eyes of someone who has just been interrupted in the middle of a fist fight. Perhaps he is loaded on mushrooms too.

'I'm Ned.' Dave hands some coins over the bar and hurls a shot of tequila back.

'I think url kick things awf,' he declares, breathing the fumes of his drink over me.

The room is dimly lit but most people are sitting down, so Dave finds his way to the front easily enough. Then he starts pogoing wildly, like a man caught on a barbed-wire fence being strafed by machine-gun fire. It is a hell of a performance but he has not been going long before a great commotion breaks out. People leap on to the dance floor from every side and Dave tumbles about between them.

When he gets back to the bar, I ask, 'What was all that about?'

'Theza baby a tha darts floor.'

'What?'

'Theza baby a tha darts floor.'

'There's a baby on the dance floor?'

'Ar, theza baby a tha darts floor.'

'What the fuck do you mean, "There's a baby on the dance floor"?'

'Theza a baby a tha darts floor un I trod un it. Go'n ava look fur youself.'

I do. He is right. There is a baby on the dance floor, fast asleep in a car seat.

'Sorry, Dave, I didn't get you for a moment there, but you're right,' I say when I am back at the bar. 'There is a baby on the dance floor. Tequila?'

'Un a combat kilt.'

'And a combat kilt?'

323

'Un a combat kilt. O'er there, on a fat bloke. I wuz in army fur ten year un I never saw no combat kilt.'

There is a rotund Cornishman – who I have met before – in a cowboy hat, a black T-shirt recalling some booze-frenzied festival of yesteryear, work boots and, astonishingly, a kilt made out of army regulation combat material. It is the right length and it has all the pleats in the back and the buckles in the right places. It is a gem.

'The Celts are mobilising,' I say. 'Either that or they are being dressed by Jean-Paul Gaultier.'

'Theza baby a tha darts floor un a combat kilt in the toime ut takes a drink two tequilas,' Dave enthuses. 'Unreal. I'm almost moved a pay fur me tickut . . . wha dya think? Could be er title fur a song? Be a Ramones song, eh?' He starts playing air guitar, doing the Chuck Berry duck walk backwards, singing 'Baby a tha darts floor in a combat kilt . . . nan-na nan-na nah-na nah nah nah . . . baby a tha darts floor in a combat kilt . . .' Tiny threads of pink and green light trace his outline as he goes cavorting across the room, spinning on his heels, and the back of my head starts to tingle. We have lift-off.

Upstairs, the festival is in full swing, and so am I. Two dance floors are full of reelers involved in *troyls* – the Cornish word for a ceilidh – and the bar is full of revellers. Richard is a friend of Dave's. He is younger and shorter than me and he has a sprig of ginger hair protruding from his scalp. He is passionately, self-consciously Celtic even though, or possibly because, he grew up and still lives only a hundred yards from the west bank of the River Tamar. Richard is a poet, and he knows from Dave that I am one too. He tells me about his latest work – a poem called 'Renaissance Pan-Keltica'. There is a verse about each Celtic country and he offers to jot down the one about the Isle of Man in my notebook.

I quite like the clubby idea of poets swapping poems, but when I read it, I am moved to think otherwise. It's a shocker. I think it is nearly as bad as 'Port of Ness', my first risible attempt at a poem on the Isle of Lewis way back in May. I have a disturbing feeling of being asphyxiated as I read what is scrawled in my notebook again. The mushrooms are not helping the situation. I have really lost the run of myself. Richard produces his own notebook, but I realise that I will struggle to write anything down now.

'How about I read it?' I suggest.

There must be eighty people in the bar. Some are dancing in groups, grappling with each other just to stay upright. The barmen and women are weaving a furious pattern to keep the increasingly rowdy drinkers armed and at bay. Conversations and arguments are raging. Someone is playing the fiddle and someone else is giving a tin whistle a blow. It is a rollicking scene of abandon and conviviality. Here, now, in this cacophonic, spinning session, I have a flash of intense clarity, a vision through the hallucinogenic haze. This, I realise, is the zenith of the evening: the high point of the night, and of the Lowender Peran festival and of Ned Clague's short, sweet life. It is the moment in time when the mythic tracts of all the Celtic ethnicities intersect, the point when the temperament and the sensibility of this community of disparate peoples fleetingly meet. It is the moment at which these festivals mean something. It is THE moment.

The night is about to descend into disorder. May the fighting begin! But before it does, I have to crown this moment, the beginning of the end for Ned Clague but the end of the beginning for Rob Penn, with a poem. Climbing up on to the pool table is fine, but when I stand up straight, I get a powerful rush that sends the whole room whirling. I am very high. I must press on.

'Will ya hear a poem, then?'

There are a few 'ayes' and a couple of whistles. Reciting my poems may be like riding a bike to me by now, but quietening a crowd of bearded dwarfs remains as difficult as ever. I wait for a moment and try louder.

'WILL YA HEAR A POEM, THEN?'

More cheers. The guy playing the fiddle stops. Dave is standing at the far end of the bar, squared up towards me, shoulders hunched as if we are about to begin a game of British bulldog. He is shouting. I try again, as loud as I can go now.

'WILL YA HEAR A POEM, THEN?'

Yet more jeers and cheers. A few people are on my side now, whistling and telling others to be quiet. A young Cornish lad walks past the pool table beneath me. He whips out a hand and flicks up the front of my kilt. There is a massive cheer. I have half a mind to drop down and stuff a fist in his pretty face. A fight? A poem? Right now, I don't care. Right now I am up for anything. Right now, I am a Celt.

When the cheers retreat there is quiet. Nearly everyone is silent. One snatched glance at my 'zizi' is clearly all that was needed. Before I know it, I am off, with my stick above my head, bouncing through the first few lines of '*Aigh Vie* Tommy Collister'. All the nerves that I once had about doing this – about standing up in front of a crowd of strangers, a crowd who are supposedly dis-cerning about poetry, and reading my own poems – are completely gone. I don't know if this is because I am more experienced or more courageous or merely because the intensity of this moment has let loose an undifferentiated energy that has gripped me. My mind is loose and on the run. I am on galloping autopilot, a night flight trip. I am in over the edge of what I know, free-falling in a wild, rude and airy mushroom and whisky whirl, but the lines of the poem keep coming.

In some sort of out-of-body experience, I feel completely de-tached from the voice speaking, shouting and quavering with the anxiety of a thousand years of yearning. I hear it like I am in the audi-ence. I don't really know what I am doing. I am just being. I could not say if this action, the time I am on the pool table, takes a second or an hour. I see my fists wheel in front of my face. A hand punches the air. I could walk straight off the pool table at any moment. I am powerless to control anything that I am doing. Sometimes, the poem stops. I can hear my own breathing then – short, heavy breaths. But

I am never frightened. I know it is all there, I know that the words will come pouring out again when they are ready.

I am looking up at the ceiling, bent over backwards, bellowing, longer and louder. When I reach the last lines, I feel the movement of my mouth as each syllable is defined on my lips, resting there for an instant before being hucked off over the heads and the slack-jawed faces that are glaring at me:

'*AIGH VIE* TOMMY COLLISTER!'

It is a primeval wail, like a cry to a man drowning at sea. I hear cheers and jeers come back from the room.

> Yessa, we had a night of it and yer lookin a mess.
> Treat . . . her . . . right . . . now . . . and . . . take . . .
> off . . . . that . . . . . fuckin . . . . . . dress.

I flop forward, bending over double, clasping the backs of my knees, watching the tartan checks turn into fluid circles and shift subtly across the fabric of my kilt.

There are cheers and whistles and taunts – the usual barracking from a bar full of Celtic ale-heads. Dave is signalling madly and Combat Kilt is waving his hat in the air. When I get down from the pool table, a hand falls heavily on my shoulder.

'Nice wan, bay.' A lean man in Doc Martens, tight white cords, a yellow singlet and a pork-pie hat is searching in my eyes. He looks feverish or half dead from thirst. 'Fawckin brilliant!' he goes on, shaking my shoulder. 'Am Baz.' He offers me a hand. Baz or Bap or Bad, I am not sure as he leads me off to the bar.

A Breton couple appear, firing questions at me in French, which I cannot cope with. I start laughing.

'They wuz a know wha tha por-hm zabout, Ned.'

'A stag night. It's about a stag night in the Isle of Man,' I gasp.

Baz takes up the task of translating.

'Vearey good,' the lady says.

Baz passes me a pint. We clunk glasses and he shouts, 'Free Kernow' down the bar.

327

The mushrooms are cooling down a bit and the beer tastes good. I am coming back to myself. 'What are you then,' I ask Baz, 'Mebyon Kernow?'

He spits a mouthful of beer across the backs of the Breton couple and beyond, for which there is a volley of apologies. 'No, no,' he says animatedly, 'nat Mebyon Kernow.' Cornish national-ism – in true Celtic fashion – has had more schisms than the Protestant Church. 'Ev you eard a tha People's Poplar Frunt fur tha Liberation a Curnall? Well, wez tha Frunt fur tha Poplar Liberation a tha People uv Curnall.' He swings round to face the crowd in the bar. 'That bloke thare, he's a Curnish Solidarity, un tha bloke thar's a Curnish Nationalist Party, nat a be confused wif a Curnish National Party, un oh thar, he's a Free Kernow party un someone a ere is frum An Gof, but I don't no hoo. Divoided we shul fall, eh, Ned?' he declares, chinking glasses again and pour-ing stout down my arm. 'How bout nuver por-hm then?'

The psilocybin is working in waves now. One minute I think I am straightening out and the next I feel like I am standing under-neath a helicopter as it comes in to land. I find a seat. Combat Kilt walks past and grunts at me, raising a clenched fist. 'Power to us, power to the Celts, Celts forever,' the gesticulation says, rather than 'I am going to ram this forearm so far down your throat that I will know what you had for breakfast.' This is a relief. A weak-ness has come over me. I could not fight a fairy cake right now.

It is 2 a.m. when I look at my watch for the first time tonight. I could have just blinked. The bar is still full, but it is full with the essential residue of the festival – the boozers and the debaters and musicians and poets that for me represent the essence of the Celtic Fringe. For all the overly romantic bullshit propounded at these festivals, their digest is true. There are people from all six Celtic countries here. Watching them now, as they surge through the night, urged on by the dynamism of each other's company, it is impossible not to feel that – despite their very great differences – they do have a unique affinity.

'These us ah people,' Baz says, waving an arm tangled with protruding veins across the room. 'So, huw about wun last poo-hm fur us, eh, Ned?'

One last, I am thinking, the last, the very last. Back up on the pool table, the room looks different. Enough of the faces are familiar. It feels like it could be my local pub. There are the usual guttural groans and moans. A stocky Breton man in a kilt and a dinner jacket leaps on to the table beside me. While I am thinking about a poem, he rants and garbles in a lunatic fashion – I think he is imitating me – then he jumps round and bares his arse. There are loud cheers and the all-in wrestling going on at the other end of the room briefly stops.

I go with '*Skeallaght ny Feayn-Skeallagh*'. It is a paean to the Celts and it has its place now. Some people are quiet. They look my way, but many don't bother – too eager for conversation. I don't stretch my voice to clutch their attention. I don't care who listens. This poem is for Ned Clague, for the Celtic part of my soul, for me. I travel slowly through the lines, at ease with the cadence of the poem. Before I know it, I have ghosted through the whole thing. The end. I jump down from the table. Baz claps. I can see Dave waving – he still looks like he took the brown acid at Woodstock and is waiting to come down. I swill the last of my whisky and drain it. Someone is shouting, 'Ga awn, Ned Clague, ga awn,' as I walk down the steps and out of the door and on to the moonlit beach.

16

Samhain

The Scots take their 'guising' seriously. You just have to get involved. Thus I find myself in the bog of an Edinburgh pub leering into a cracked mirror with a cork in one hand and a lighter in the other, all set up for a game of Ibble Dibble.

It is Samhain (pronounced 'sow-in' as in female pig), 31 October, New Year's Eve for the ancient Celts, the night of the dead, the festival of endings and transformations, the beginning of winter, the last night of the lighted half of the year, the end of my journey and the time for Ned Clague to take his leave for the Celestial City. The ancient Celts believed that on this night the veil which separates the two worlds of the living and the dead is at its thinnest point. The mischievous and malevolent spirits of the underworld are abroad. To protect against their pranks, we mortals must travel this night in disguise. At a more practical level, as a Scot I just met in the pub put it, 'Weirin a mask may also marginally umproov yeur chances a gettin laid.'

Figuratively, I suppose I have been guising for the last six months. 'So why bother with an extra layer of camouflage now?' I ask myself as I smear the charred cork about my cheeks. When in Rome, I suppose, or as the Gaelic adage has it: '*Beus na tuath, far am bithear se nithear*' or 'The manners of the folk where thou art, thou must adopt'. In the end, it is only one more layer of deception for me to scrub off in the morning. When I finally look something like Michael Jackson having a bad make-up day, I conclude that I am ready.

I pick up my blackthorn stick and check my shirt pocket –

tobacco, cash, crystal and my Celtic stones. The one thing I am paranoid about losing is my mobile phone, which I have tucked in to the waistband of my kilt. I desperately don't want it to ring, but I have to be there to answer it if it does. Vicky is now four days overdue with our second baby. She could easily give birth tonight. I really shouldn't be here at all, but my wife is a magnificent woman. In the end we struck a deal: she calls me after the first contraction and I drop everything, starting with the pint of stout I am likely to be holding, and race south by the fastest means possible. If my previous experiences traversing the Celtic Fringe are anything to go by, I should arrive home just as the baby is moving on to solids.

Apparently the debris we left on Calton Hill after the Beltane festival fetched the organisers a massive clean-up bill from the city council – a bill that the Beltane Fire Society has not yet been able to pay. So Samhain is a seriously scaled-down affair this year. There is a procession from the castle down the Royal Mile to the cobbled Parliament Square in front of the High Kirk of St Giles, which is where I catch up with the hellzapoppin.

A few of the figures and costumes are familiar to me from Beltane. The Green Man or Jack-in-the-Green is here in the form of a fifteen-foot puppet mounted on someone's shoulders. Samhain is symbolic of the demise of the power of the sun and it was the time when the ancient Celts brought their livestock off the hill again and finished preparations for winter, so the Green Man, the spirit of growth and vegetation, gets it tonight. The Queen of Winter's reign, on the other hand, begins here. The Cailleach Bheur, as she is also known in Scotland, has a mat of dark, tangled hair, a twisted hand and only one eye. She is a fearful creature, especially in the company of the Storm Hags – a dozen screeching women with white-painted faces and rotting hair. These crones are the same slim and strong White Warrior Women who led the May Queen round Calton Hill and protected her bower at Beltane.

The summer has not been good to them. I can't help wonder if they have been on the same festival circuit and diet as me.

The rest of the costumes are all random fancy dress: the Grim Reaper is here, as are Jack the Ripper, a pair of chemistry teachers, several witches, some pixies, a clown playing the bagpipes, a carnival butterfly and 'Swamp Monk' – a green-painted man in cappuccino-coloured Y-fronts. Lastly, there is the Winter King, whose time is near. He is a black puppet wrapped in animal skins, sprouting holly and great antlers. I can see him on the far side of the square, through the drizzle. He is giving the Green Man what for. His moon is rising as it were, which means one thing – it's curtains for Ned Clague.

I can't say I didn't know it was coming, of course. In the last couple of weeks, I have been trying to tie up the loose odds and ends of Ned's brief existence, in a rather trite imitation of a man who knows that he is about to pop his clogs, tying up his estate. I have returned several volumes of poetry that people lent me along the way. I have posted copies of my poems to those who asked for them. I have un-subscribed to a poetry e-mail group. I even, on a whim, jumped in a car and drove all the way from London to Machynlleth to find Seamus – who I had promised to bring a poem back to – in the Wynnstay Arms, where I got caned the night before I went up Cader Idris. He had left, the lady said, and gone off to work with horses in the hills, but he still dropped in from time to time to pick up his post. I added my poem to the pile.

So I am ready to consign Ned to his coffin, but I think all this fluffing around is illustrative of the fact that I don't really want to see him go. In a sense, though, he is going nowhere. I can't help reflecting that I set out to become a Celtic poet, but the Celtic poet became me. Or I already was one.

Despite some excruciating moments, Ned has been a good companion on this journey. He has turned out to be a tolerable poet too. Okay, so the poems may never have had 'the feeling for syllable and rhythm, penetrating far below the conscious levels of thought and feeling' that T.S. Eliot wrote of, nor will there be a motion put before the Welsh National Assembly to rename Cader Idris the Chair of Ned Clague. But, as pub poems go, they are all right. Well, put it like this: there are worse poets about. Not many, I grant you, but there are some . . . one or two . . . one, then – the rhyme-less poet I met at the Lowender Peran. And Ned's performances? Well, he may not have roused people into ecstatic fervour, then again he was never bottled off stage; people occasionally applauded and one Scottish girl was moved to bare her la las. I think that is a pretty triumphant record for a man who only six months ago thought a couplet was a small bra. But Lulla Corla, the gypsy who told my fortune at the Golowan festival, was right. I will carry on writing poems, but I can't ever see myself making a living as a prophetic bard, fun though that would be.

As the Samhain gathering begins to break up, I steal in next to a group of hooded musicians who are banging out some earthy, New Age beats on drums, bongos and a didgeridoo. There is a semicircle of clowns and freaks and painted faces before me, dancing wildly. They are leering and jeering at each other, like a gang of pikeys baiting an old badger. Others are scraping the wet cobbles with their boots, like fresh bulls into the ring. It is intense. For all the people who indulge in the guising and who feel the supernatural heat, Samhain is a powerful night. 'It is a time of non-time' as one dressed-up jester puts it to me, a night of transcendent revelry and exalted madness. It is a moment to let go.

Suddenly the flashing beacon on top of a truck looms immediately behind us. We have to scatter. Screams and yelps of delight and abandonment fill the square. It is almost empty, save for the rubbish truck. In that white-hot moment, we had not observed everyone leaving and the cleaners arriving.

I have a swig of whisky from the mickey on my hip, to wet my throat. A man in a cape with a bald head painted white swoops past me. He was in that frenzied moment. 'Nice wan, man,' he says in a south London accent. 'There za rave on at Ego. See you there. Yeeeh-aooow!'

Ego? It sounds dreadful. Do I have to surrender my Celtic soul in an Edinburgh nightclub? There must be a more appropriate and romantic venue. I have been to so many magical and beautiful places this summer: Harris, Barra, Great Blasket, Mount Brandon, Belmullet, Snaefell, Emain Macha, Madron Well, the Preseli Mountains, Brocéliande Forest, Cap de la Chèvre, St Agnes Beacon – the list goes on. Spending the last few hours of the 'lighted half' in a New Town dungeon is an anticlimax of wedding night proportions.

But do I really need to surrender my Celtic soul anyway? Sure, the roaming is over. Ned must hang up his stick; the kilt needs to go to the dry cleaners; I need to get a job. But everything else that I have learnt and felt this summer – do I need to give that up? I certainly don't want to and I wonder if I even can.

I started out with the premise that a 'true' Celt speaks a Celtic language. My Manx is about as fluent as George W. Bush's French. I still haven't even rediscovered what the Gaelic for the female reproductive organs is. Yet this classification is flawed. If you want to be pessimistic, these languages could all be dead in fifty years (save Welsh). Where will that leave the strict definition of a Celt? The net has to be wider than simply those who speak Celtic languages.

When I get to Princes Street, I stop in a bus shelter, out of the rain, to jot down in my notebook a few characteristics of the two ethnic groups that I am concerned with. The English love portrait painting, pragmatism, institutions, biography, bondage, gardens, shopkeeping, deference and irony. Englishness is an accumulative and dynamic notion that relies on the perpetual immigration of people and ideas to survive.

The Celts love poetry, music, fighting, the supernatural, empathy, provocative conversation, genealogy and community. Celticness is an exclusive notion: it has to stand still to survive. These are random lists. With a clear head and some thought, I could expand on them, but the point is made – the Celts are different.

The very nature of my journey suggests this. On numerous occasions I have tried to imagine undertaking a poet's tour of English pubs and festivals. Imagine standing up in a pub in Surrey and bawling, 'Will ya hear a poem, then?' A dozen people would be choking on saffron risotto as the barman telephones the emergency services. It is unimaginable.

What binds the diverse peoples of the Celtic nations into an ethnic group is more complex, not least because they have more differences than similarities. What they do have in common is an amalgam of things – character, culture, temperament, climate, history, language and geography. There are probably more.

So it is not language alone. Nor is it a continuous blood lineage linking us to the ancient Celts that makes us distinctive today. In fact, the ancient and modern Celts have little to do with each other. It would be straying into the realms of lunacy to aver that the ethnic Celtic identity as we know it today is a true historical construct. It is not. This identity bears more significantly on the myth and the metaphysical ideals of the Romantic Movement, which gave birth to pan-Celticism, than it does on the real history of the Celts. Before pan-Celticism, the people of these nations never identified themselves as a single ethnic group. Rather the Welsh were Welsh, the Manx were Manx and so on. (And as I discovered, the Irish are self-consciously Irish once again. Their Celtic wheel has turned full circle. The Irish have proved to be a role model for the other nations throughout the history of pan-Celticism. If this continues to be true, then perhaps the very notion of a Celtic identity will be dead and buried in fifty years.)

But the fact that the modern Celtic identity has only been around for 200 years does not mean that it is any more fraudulent than any other – French, German, or even British, for example.

Is my Celtic awakening, then, merely a matter of shifting

identities? Am I getting off a horse called British that (now the empire has gone) looks tired of making so much good running and mounting a fresher nag called Celtic which appears to have a bit more distance? Annoyingly, it is more complex than that.

For all that I have learnt about the mistreatment of the Celtic peoples at the hands of the English (and French) and for all the English bashing that I have witnessed or been a party to, I remain, at least in part, English. Ned may not, but I am. I support the English football and rugby teams, passionately. I even support the English cricket team, except when they are playing Australia when I display a nonchalant indifference to the whole game. My dad is English. I have lived in England for almost half of my life. I don't celebrate St George's Day, but I would if I knew when it is. I admire irony. I like bondage. No I don't. That was a joke, honestly. But I do like gardening, for fuck's sake. I can't give all this up just because I think 'If' is a dreadful poem and I fell for the whole romantic 'Celtic package'.

So where the hell have I got to then, once Ned has gone? Can I be both Celtic and English? (To a degree, everyone in England is Anglo-Celtic, or rather Anglo-Saxon-Celtic. We were all something else before the Romans and Angles and Saxons came barracking in.) I think I can be. I have to be. I am. What I have undergone then is simply a rejigging of priorities. Before I went seeking inspiration on the eyrie of Prince Idris, I was British, English, Manx, Celtic and a Londoner, in that order. Now I am Celtic, Manx, English, living in London and British. Not much has really changed then. It just feels like it has.

My nocturnal amblings have brought me to the door of Ego. There is a long queue of trendy undergraduates. My shirt is soaked from rain and my hair is clamped about my black-smeared face. I try the bouncer with 'I'm part of the Samhain festival crew' but he just sneers at me. Looking like a Scottish *Big Issue* seller down on his luck, I join the back of the line.

*

The club is monotonous. There are two rooms full of people, but no one wants to talk to me. I drink alone. I do run into Dave, who I met on top of Calton Hill before the Beltane festivities, but he barely recognises me and when he does work out who I am, he is even less inclined to make conversation. I try to tell him something about my journey. He carries on dancing. Only because I have nowhere to go, I stay. I mope around the corners of the club, drinking my whisky, moaning about how flawed an ending this is to it all.

At 2 a.m. we are pitched out on to the street. People prop each other up in pairs or groups and drift off under the neon street lamps that struggle to pierce the black night. Suddenly, I really want to be at home. I check my mobile again. I want it to ring now. I have a flight booked at 6.50 a.m. It is too late to go to sleep – I will never get up – and too early to go to the airport – I'll fall asleep. I ought to be celebrating the demise of Ned Clague – the Celts love a funeral like no one else – and here I am standing alone in the rain, drunk and trying to kill time.

Then the thought hits me. I need to go up a mountain. This trip began on top of Cader Idris. I need to end up . . . up something. It will give the entire journey symmetry. The ancient Celts loved symmetry – just look at their art. Okay, I am clutching at straws now, but it is still a good idea. I could go up Calton Hill, but that's no more than a pimple. No, it has to be Arthur's Seat – still not exactly K2 but I have been up it before and it is a fair stride to the top. With a purpose that I have been without since I blackened my face up, I start walking.

I know where Arthur's Seat is. You can't miss it, it looms over the city, but I have no idea how to get to it. I stop in an all-night kebab shop on North Bridge to ask directions. The Turkish owner points to a photo of a foaming chicken shaslyk on the wall behind his head. Obviously I have to play 'as the crow flies' and head directly for it. In the second garden I clamber through, I have to borrow a wheelbarrow to get over the back. Lights go on in the house as I am slapping around on top of the wooden fence. Then I am sprinting across an estate, down an alley and I am on the hill.

Despite the rain, which is slanting in now, it feels good to be out here. I head up and up. At times, it is so steep that I have to claw my way up on tufted clumps of grass with my stick in my teeth. The only worry I have is the Salisbury Crags – people do fall off, I have been told – and I stop every fifteen minutes to top up my courage with whisky. Eventually, I do arrive beneath the crags and I have to thread my way round them. It takes me a good hour of hard walking to get to the top.

It is a filthy night. The wind is swirling the rain about the summit. I must be in cloud because the lights of Edinburgh are dim. It is cold and wild and miserable. This is more like it. I should have composed a poem for this moment, the poet's passage into Tir na Nog, the otherworld, read with Ned Clague's terminal whisky-soaked breath. But I haven't and I would not be able to remember it or read it from a piece of paper anyway. I could recite another poem, but not even the wind is listening. There is nothing else for it. I have to get naked. A ceremonial de-robing, a meta-phorical shedding of Ned's skin. Rob Penn will re-emerge. This is the end, and the beginning.

When I am down to my boots, I start running around. Then I do some star jumps. I don't know why. It takes me ten minutes of cavorting before I calm down. It takes me another ten minutes to find my clothes again. I gather the crystal and my stones in my hand and I cock my arm to hurl them into the night, but some-thing stops me. I stuff them back into my shirt pocket. I check my phone. My kilt is sodden. To the droning of the wind, I get dressed. There is one last mouthful of whisky. Then I start walk-ing down.

'Jesus, mun,' the cabbie says. 'Ya look lak ya jees goh back frum the Battle a Culloden Muir. Y'ar reet, pal?'

'Never felt better. The airport, please.'

I pick up my rucksack at the train station and change on the way. Thankfully, things go smoothly at the Domestic Terminal. I check in. The flight is on time. I get some orange juice and a newspaper, have a wash, check my phone and sit down in the departure lounge. It is 6.20 a.m. Perfect.

A Filipina lady wakes me up trying to vacuum all the mud that has fallen off my boots. Ugh! I feel terrible. I scan the information screen. Huh! The 6.50 shuttle has gone. The 7.50 has gone, the 8.50 has . . . what the . . . the 12.50 has closed boarding. What happened? Where's my phone? My heart sinks at the sight of the little envelope. The anodyne voice comes through: 'Welcome to Orange answerphone. You have . . . nine messages . . .'

Oh shit!

Acknowledgements

Thanks a million to Mum and Dad, my brother James, Olly and Alison Olsen, Ant and Clare Griffith, Richard Williams, Mike Griffith, Anne-Marie Clegg, Dave Wyatt, Sabine Louet, Arnaud Rannou Ker, Dafydd Iwan, Ben Harbour, Raymond Scott, Al Hearn, Erica Pavord, Ben Weatherall, Sam Ware, Dympna O'Shea, Cath Urquhart, John Gibb, Sarah Spankie, Paulo and Ginny Baillie, my editors Helen Garnons-Williams and Katy Follain and my inspirational agent Camilla Hornby.

Author's Note

The Celts are well known as masters of artifice. An absolute respect for the truth – a highly prized virtue among the English – has never cut much with them. There were many times on my journey when I was pretending to be Ned Clague and the flicker of an eye, a change in intonation or the subtle shift of a stranger's smile indicated that I was fooling no one but myself. I was often left with a lingering doubt that I had only seen the shadow of a people who know well how to conceal their reality. That said, I must accept that some people will read this book and be surprised to learn that I am not, in fact, the Celtic bard that I claimed to be. To all of you, I apologise.

The Celtic brogues are, to my ear, the most delightful on the planet and it is largely for this reason that I have written the speech of the people I encountered in phonetics. Yet I am aware that there is just as great a difference between the accent of, say, a Donegal-man and a Kerry-man as there is between a Cockney and a Geordie. In the simple aim of being understood, I have ridden roughshod over these differences. I hope I will be forgiven for this.